IMAGES
of America

PIEDMONT

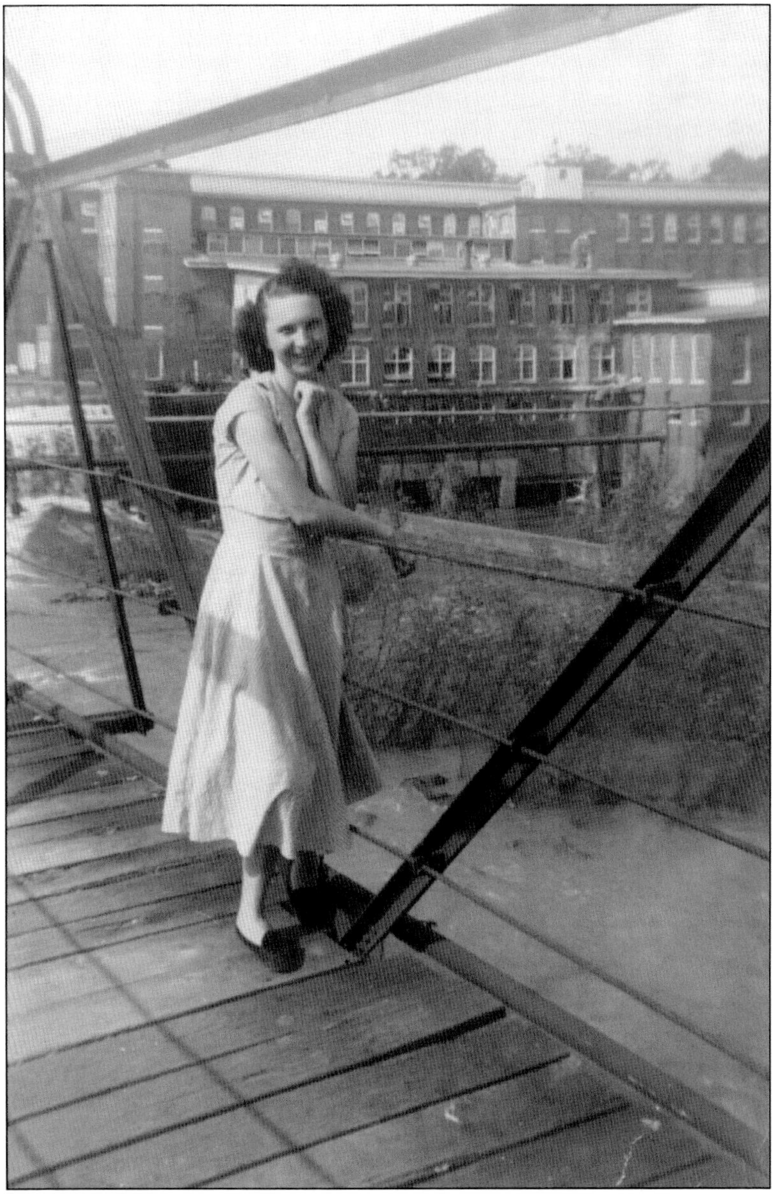

A young Ruby Allison Bryson poses on the footbridge spanning the Saluda River at the dam of Piedmont Manufacturing Company. (Courtesy of Mark and Jane McClain.)

On the Cover: In this late 1800s photograph, the Saluda River reflects Piedmont Manufacturing Company at the height of its glory. Once the largest textile mill in the South and one of the largest in the world, Piedmont Manufacturing ran four mills. Three stood on the Greenville side of the river and one on the Anderson side. Three bridges and a footbridge have crossed the river here, including a covered wooden bridge built about 1850, an iron and wood wagon bridge constructed just after the turn of the 20th century, and the current concrete bridge built in 1948. In order to expedite access from mill to mill, the footbridge across the Saluda was built after Mill No. 3 was constructed in Anderson County in 1888. The footbridge still stands as an important link to our past and future. (Courtesy of Piedmont Historical Collection.)

IMAGES
of America

PIEDMONT

Bonnes Amies Club

ARCADIA
PUBLISHING

ISBN 978-1-4671-1164-5

Published by Arcadia Publishing
Charleston, South Carolina

Printed in the United States of America

Library of Congress Control Number: 2013949633

For all general information, please contact Arcadia Publishing:
Telephone 843-853-2070
Fax 843-853-0044
E-mail sales@arcadiapublishing.com
For customer service and orders:
Toll-Free 1-888-313-2665

Visit us on the Internet at www.arcadiapublishing.com

For the historians on whose shoulders we stand, Frances Evans, Betty Davenport, and of course, Don Roper, our Saluda Sam.

We, the Bonnes Amies Club, dedicate this book to Dr. Anne Campbell Peden, who has been the guiding force throughout this project. With Anne's expertise, guidance, and unending patience, what could have been drudgery was instead a true labor of love. The long hours of scanning photos, meetings, and making tough decisions finally evolved into this important work. Anne's dedication honors her, the Bonnes Amies Club, and, most of all, honors and preserves the life memories of so many who have called Piedmont home.

Contents

ACKNOWLEDGMENTS

The Bonnes Amies book group wishes to acknowledge the work of the many folks who were willing to share their treasured photographs and stories with us. This type of work is limited always by the willingness of people to share. To those who have allowed us to scan their images for use herein, we thank you with a courtesy line under each photograph. Many hours went into selecting each piece to include, and we are saddened that we are unable to include every photograph we scanned. Please know that we oohed and aahed over them all. We are also grateful to Piedmont First Baptist Church for providing a space for the book group to work during the scanning process.

Several Piedmonters need special thanks for their work over many years in preserving the history of Piedmont. Betty Davenport wrote *A History of Piedmont*, and her sister Frances Evans and the late Glenn Shirley wrote *Mountain Memories* about the Piedmont Camp. Don Roper has written much about the history of the area under the pen name Saluda Sam, as well as other titles under his own name. Some of these include his historic timeline, articles for the *Piedmont Informer*'s Footbridge Festival issues, the *Saluda Valley Record*, the *Williamston Journal*, the *Piedmont Informer*, the *Powdersville Post*, and *Albert Smith Rowell, A Southern Yankee*. All of these works have been referenced for this publication. Pictured below, from left to right, are Betty Davenport, Frances Davenport Evans, and Don Roper.

Other references include the Greenville County Library, the Clemson University online photo archives, the Sanborn insurance maps on the State of South Carolina website, the Kizer map of Greenville County of 1882, the Strom Thurmond Institute, and the South Caroliniana Library of the University of South Carolina.

Finally, much thanks must be given to the Bonnes Amies book group, who spent a year collecting photographs. Not only did they search their own collections, but they also spread the word to find friends, family, acquaintances, and friends of friends who held coveted treasures. The club allowed the group to purchase the needed supplies to capture these photographs digitally, as well. The book group included Jane Carpenter, Paige Crawford, Maxie Freeman, Jane McClain, Gayle Payne, Anne Peden, Carolyn Reeves, Jessalene Watson, and Betty and Miranda White.

Without the support of all these Piedmont historians, this book would not have been feasible. Thank you all.

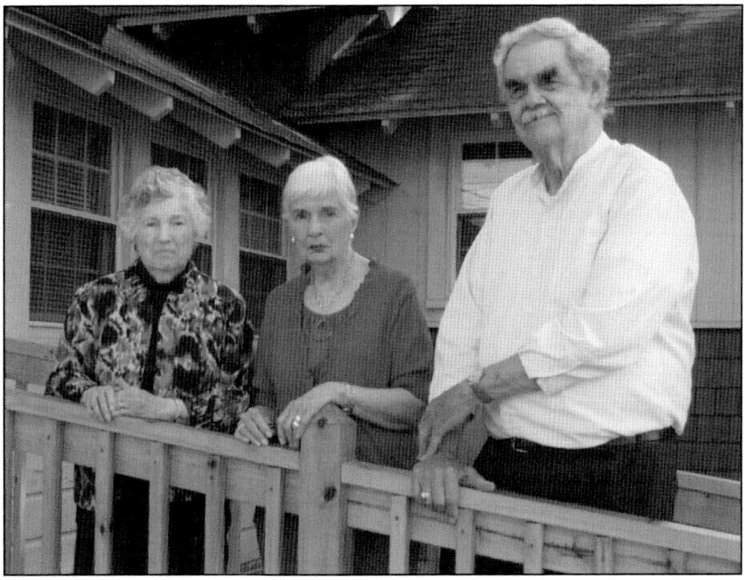

Introduction

Much of the history of Piedmont, South Carolina, situated in the rolling hills of the upstate along the Saluda River, is focused on the river itself. Tradition suggests that Saluda was the name of a Shawnee tribe that traveled through the foothills before the settlers arrived. According to Dora Lee Chappelear in a high school paper written in 1921 and titled "Piedmont, Her Past and Present," early arrow points, possibly Clovis points, were found around the Wesleyan church and on the Osteen Place. The fishing here was once famous, and the best ford for many miles was what the natives called the "Big Shoals of the Saluda." Chappelear also noted that two Indian trails could still be found leading from Osteen's to R.L. Simpson's home and then to Cherokee County.

One of the most interesting camps at the shoals was a small Tory fort during the Revolution. In 1780, this encampment was documented in an account by Maj. Samuel Hammond. Col. Elijah Clarke, a group of Georgia revolutionaries, and Hammond's force moved on a Loyalist fort at Colonel Hoil's (or Hoyle's) old establishment on the Saluda. Marching through the night, they reached the post at daylight, but the enemy had vacated and moved down the river to Rutledge's ford in Abbeville County. There, Clarke and others—including Hammond's men—skirmished over the river, with several men killed on both sides. Returning to Hoil's old place 17 or 18 miles north, part of the Georgia group led by Colonel Twiggs rested before heading back west. This story was shared recently by kayaker Ken Allen, who passed the battle marker in Abbeville County and, being a native Piedmonter, realized that the fort must have been at Garrison Shoals.

An infamous happening at the Big Shoals was the ambush of the sheriff of Washington District (Greenville, Anderson, Pickens, and Oconee) in November 1797. Robert Maxwell was appointed sheriff in 1795, and after an altercation over a slander that Captain Maxwell perceived by Dr. Joshua Kennedy, the captain was ambushed as he attempted to cross the Saluda on his way to court in Old Pickensville or, possibly, Old Pendleton. Although Dr. Kennedy was purported to be in Georgia at the time of the incident, he was tried for the assassination. This is discussed at length in *A History of the Upper Part of Greenville County South Carolina* by Mann Batson.

Settlers moved north into Indian Territory (Washington District) after the Treaty of DeWitt's Corner in the late 1700s, including David Garrison, who was attracted to the Big Shoals and moved to Greenville County in 1790. By 1843 he had established a log cabin and gristmill there, which was run by Zion Turner and, later, by a Mr. Langston, according to Chappelear.

Among many traditions, historian Judith Bainbridge suggests that Silas Trowbridge—who moved into the Grove Station area from Abbeville County with several members of his wife's family, the Nesbitts of Fairview—may have instigated the construction of a cotton mill at what was then called Garrison Shoals. He may have suggested the site to Henry Pinckney Hammett. Hammett had come from Laurens County, near the Nesbitts of Fairview and the area in Abbeville that was Trowbridge's home. They worked together with many others to make Hammett's dream of a large cotton mill come true. After purchasing most of the land from the Wigington family, Hammett found the money to start the building process, and when the Civil War and the Panic of 1873 threatened to drown his dream in the Saluda, he persevered. He found ways to overcome by firing his own brick, cutting the needed lumber, building an ironworks, and bringing craftsmen, engineers, architects, and workers into the dream.

By the time H.P. Hammett died in 1891, Piedmont Manufacturing Company was one of the largest textile mills in the world. By holding on to his dream, he helped establish the South, and Greenville especially, as the "Textile Center of the World."

For Don Roper's detailed historical timeline, go to: www.powdersvillecourier.com/2012/01/30/piedmont-sc-chronoligical-history/.

Piedmont has a history of which we ought to feel proud,
But let us cause the future to outshine the past.
Let us make Piedmont a better place because of having lived here.

—Dora Lee Chappelear
10th grade
1921

One

Early Times

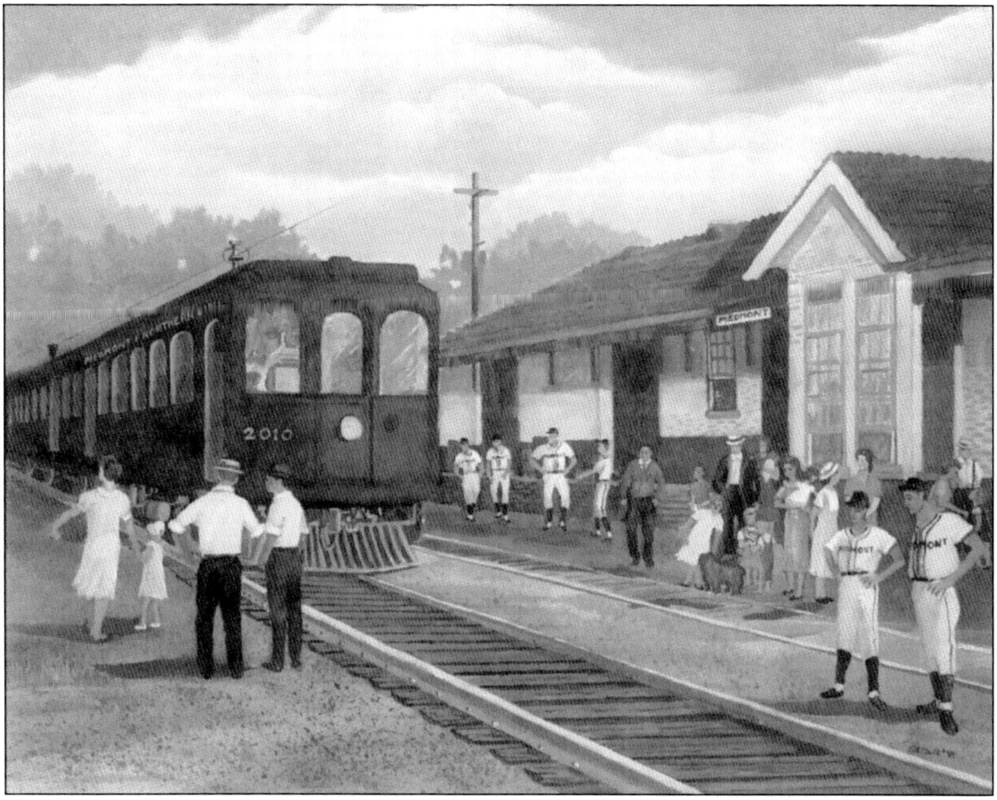

Although Piedmont's train station no longer serves the community, many remember riding up or down the line to shop in Greenville or visit family in Pelzer or Williamston. On The Line Road follows the tracks just east of where the station stood on Bessie Road. In Piedmont's heyday, this station was vital to the mill and the citizens. It is sorely missed. (Courtesy of the Bonnes Amies Club.)

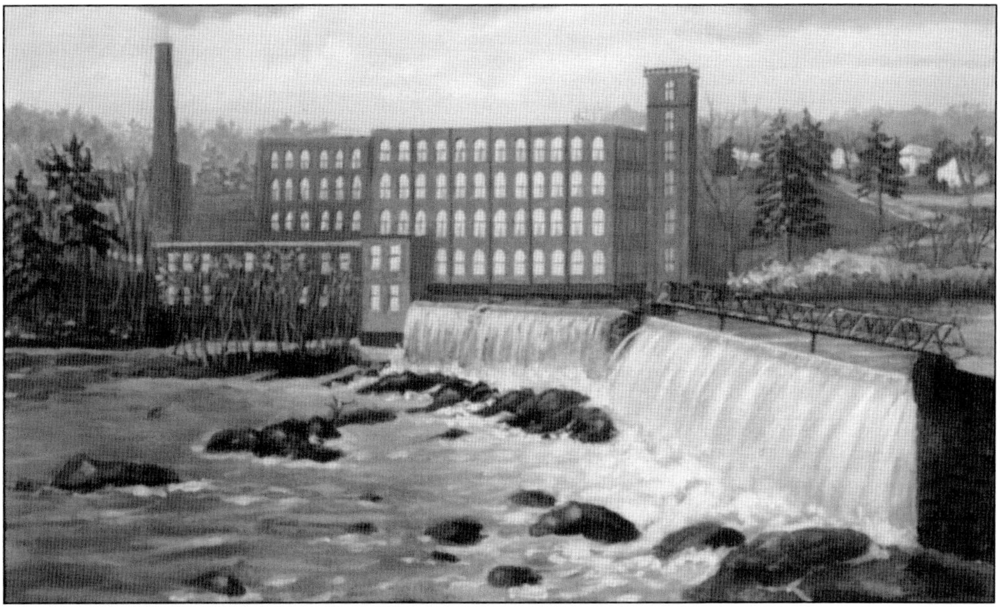

Native Americans crossed at "The Big Shoals of the Saluda," shown above from below the dam. According to Maj. Samuel Hammond's account of 1780, Tory soldiers supported a small fort here at Hoil's (Hoyle's) old place during the Revolution. Patriot forces approached the garrison, pursuing the Loyalists south to Rutledge's Ford in Abbeville County, where a skirmish took place. In November 1797, Sheriff Robert Maxwell of Washington County (Greenville, Anderson, Pickens and Oconee) came to the shoals for passage to court in Old Pickensville. Here, he was ambushed and killed, probably by his adversary Dr. Joshua Kennedy. Later, settlers called it "Garrison Shoals," possibly for David Garrison, who built a gristmill here about 1843. During this pre–Civil War period, the area was principally agrarian. As pictured below, a log cabin and small plantation house overlooked Garrison Shoals from atop a knoll east of the river now known as Hotel Hill. (Above, courtesy of the Bonnes Amies Club; below, courtesy of Margaret Payne.)

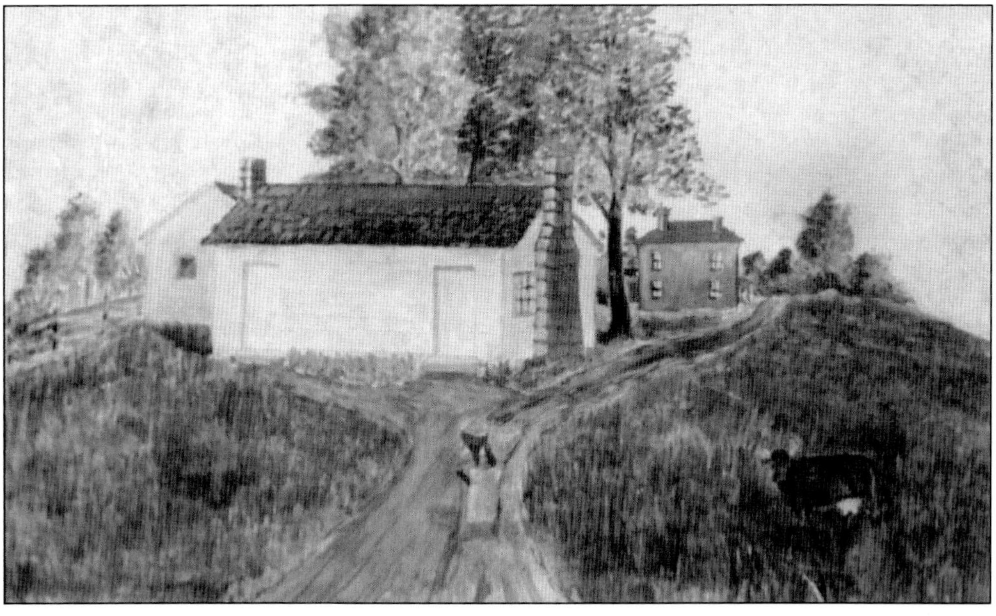

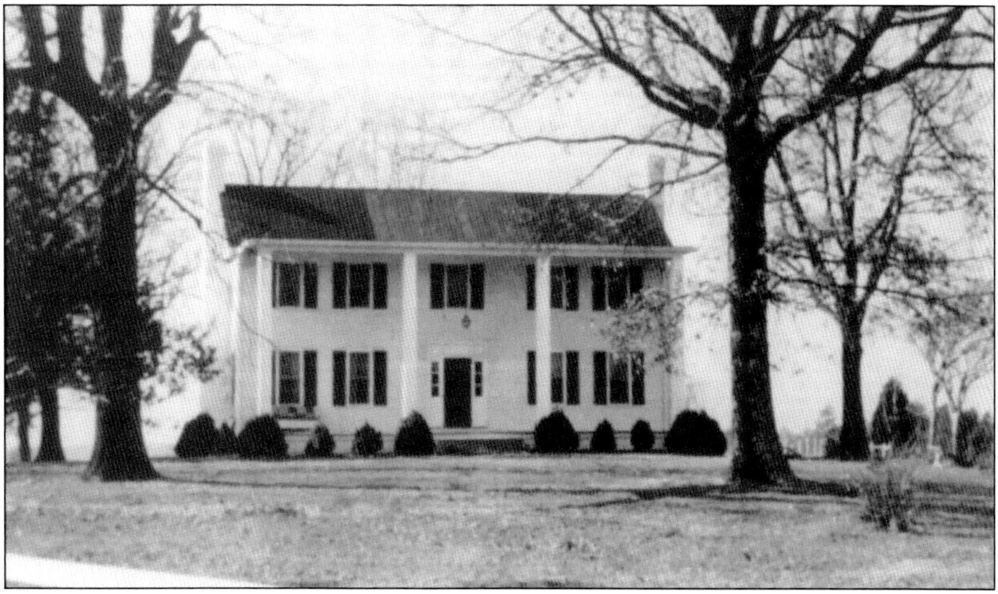

Still standing, this house was built by Ignatius Kattlet "Ike" Jenkins around 1880. He and his wife, Mary Elizabeth Few Jenkins, and 10 of their 13 children lived here (one child and a set of twins had died). He built the house with wooden pegs, evidence of which is present today. The house was in the area referred to as Grove Township during the time it was built. This area included territory between the Southern Railroad and Reedy River. (Courtesy of Virginia Agee Dean.)

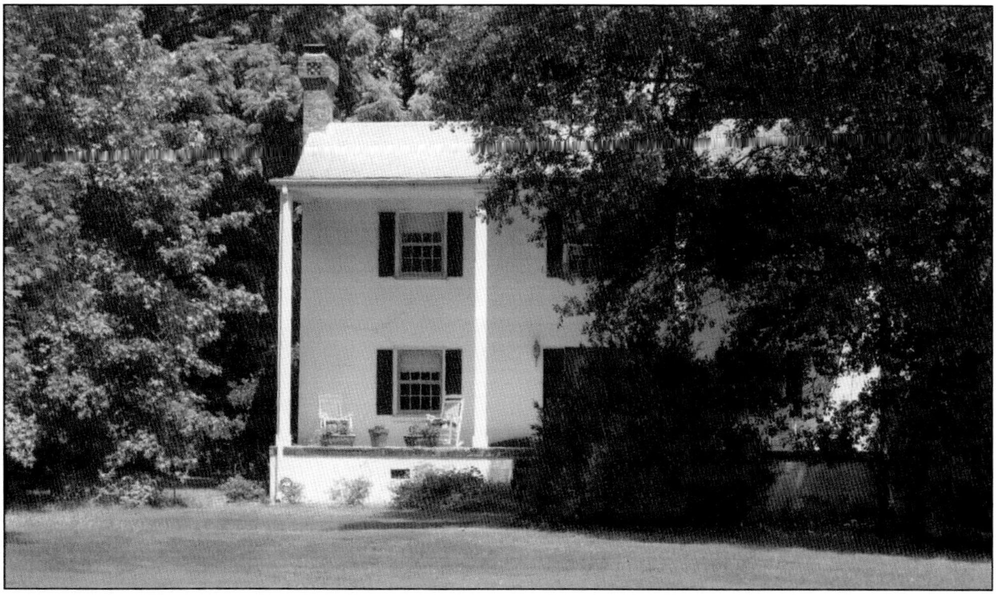

In 1848, Dr. Junius Smith from New England was an entrepreneur and lawyer who rented a large estate near Piedmont from the Garrison family. Planning Golden Grove Tea Plantation for years, Dr. Smith imported both tea plants and seeds and stated in 1851 that "his plants were doing finely and had withstood a snow 8 to 9 inches deep on January 3 of that year." Thus, he felt he had succeeded in establishing tea production in the United States. The venture collapsed in 1853 after his death from an attack by rivals upset by his political views. Pictured is the possible location of Dr. Smith's plantation near Grove Station. (Courtesy of Anne Peden.)

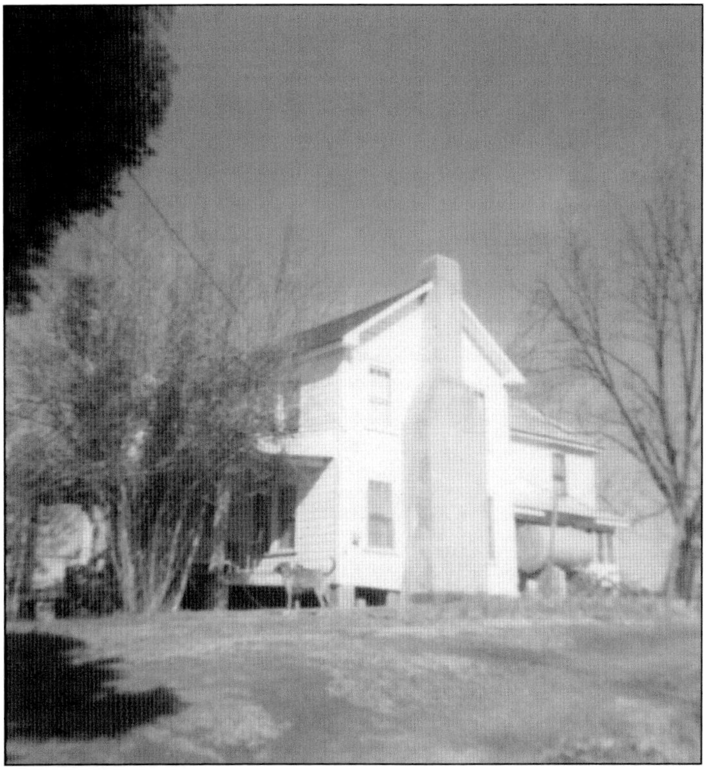

The Garrisons built the home now known as the Tarrant House in 1838. Of several Tarrant houses along Old Pelzer Road in 1882, this one was owned by Nancy Jane Tarrant, who later married John G. Payne and raised several children with him. Nancy was the daughter of Columbus B. Tarrant, who grew the famous cotton bale "Mr. Tarrant," which is displayed in the Community Building downtown. (Courtesy of Margaret Payne.)

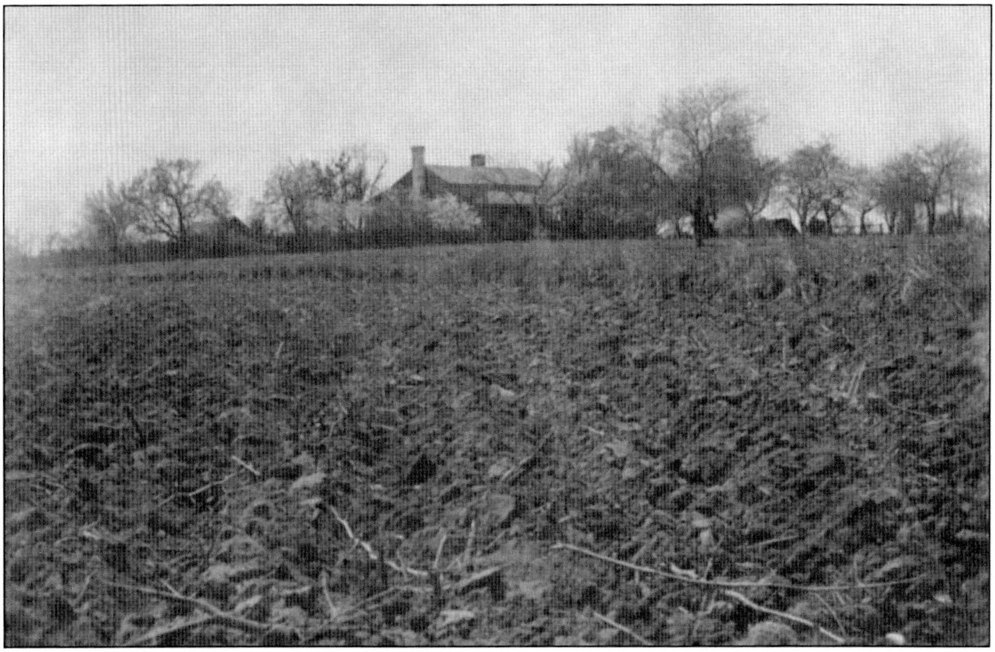

Capt. James Elliott Payne's original home along Payne Drive, just east of Piedmont off Highway 86, is pictured in the early 1900s. First built in 1771 by John Westfield, it overlooked plowed fields for over 100 years. As this idyllic scene rested to the east, change gripped the area along the river and moved the hills into a new society. (Courtesy of Margaret Payne.)

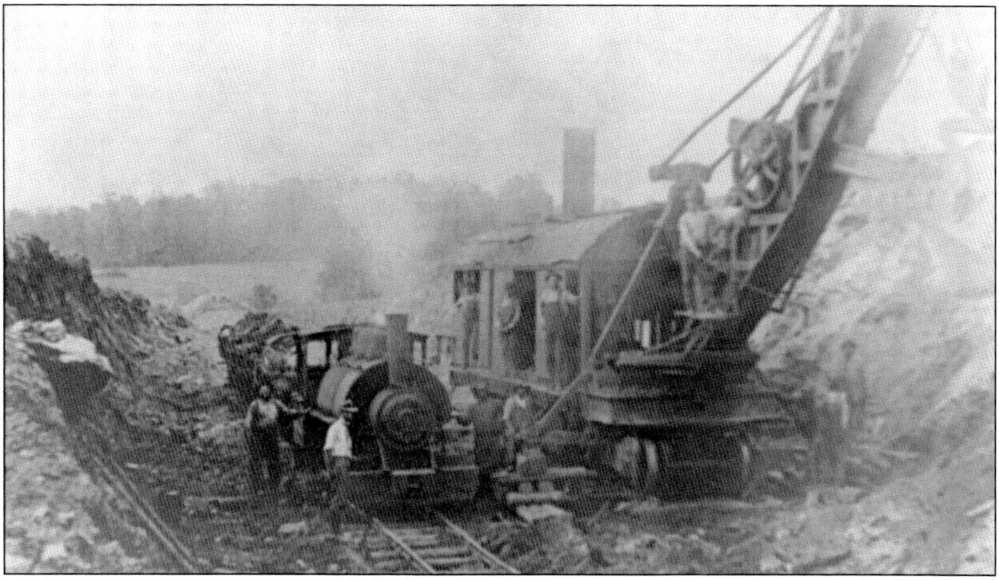

Henry Pinckney Hammett dreamed of a cotton mill at Garrison Shoals. When the Civil War ended, the board members decided to name their investment Piedmont Manufacturing Company and dubbed the town the same. As the mill began to rise along the Saluda, housing was needed, and artisans flowed into the area. One example was Silas Trowbridge, a carpenter who came to Grove Station from Abbeville County with his young wife, Nancy Nesbitt of Fairview. Later, Trowbridge sold the first bale of cotton to the mill and then bought and sold the first bale of 36-inch sheeting from his store, Trowbridge and Nesbitt. Merchants, architects, engineers, masons, contractors, and service people were all attracted to the rapid growth. Pictured in the pre-1900 photograph above are the dirt movers and trestle, track, and bridge builders that brought rapid transportation to this previously rural area. Engineers diverted the Saluda River to put in the iron bridge. Pictured below during construction are the pylons that can still be seen in the millpond. (Both, courtesy of Betty Davenport.)

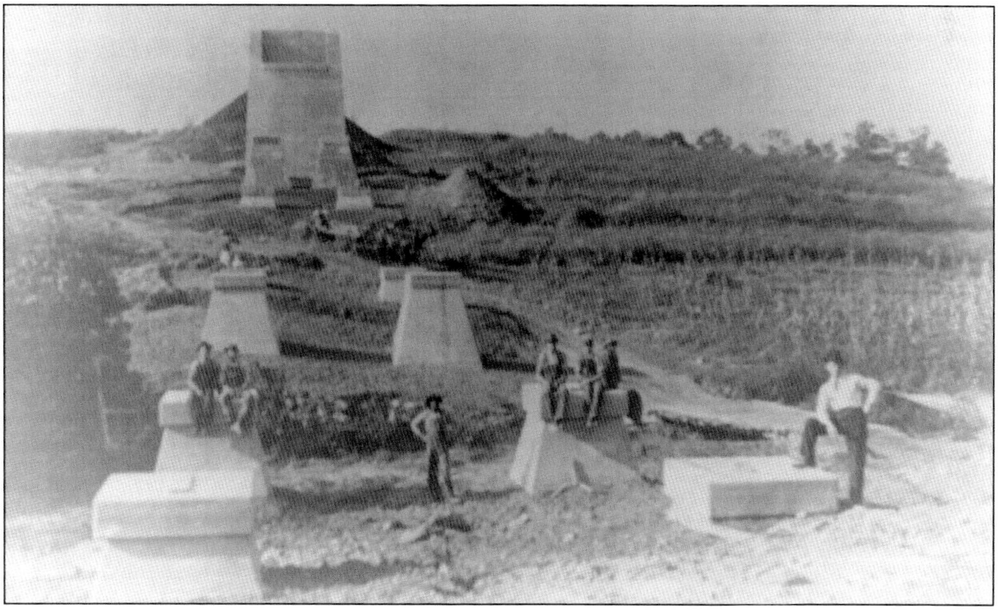

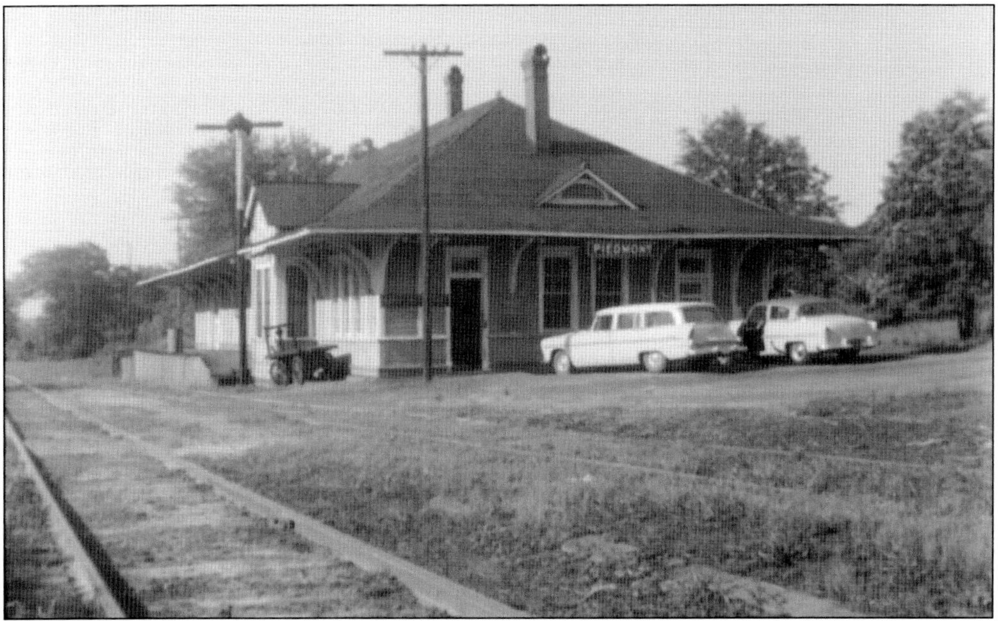

Businesses sprang up near the train depot east of town. One building just north of the depot was a cotton warehouse in 1902 and later became a guano warehouse. Another housed the Wigington Iron Works (later W.T. Beard Iron Works), which probably struck all the train tracks, cast iron columns, pilasters, thresholds, galvanized sheet metal cornices, and lintels for the new storefronts after the fire of 1903. Seen here is a view of the depot in the 1950s. (Courtesy of South Caroliniana Library, University of South Carolina.)

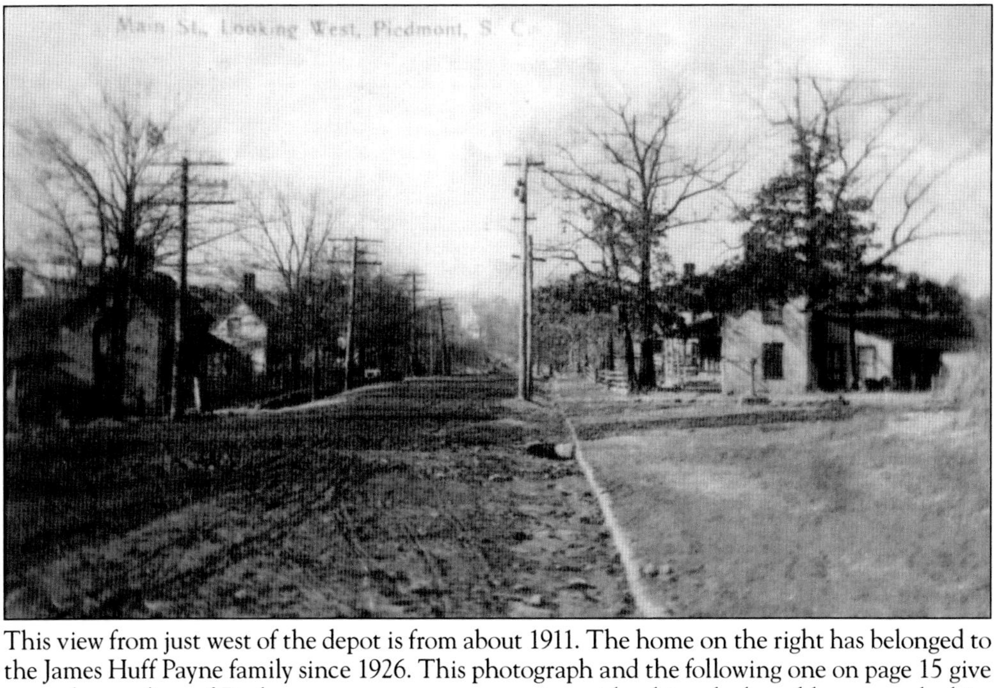

This view from just west of the depot is from about 1911. The home on the right has belonged to the James Huff Payne family since 1926. This photograph and the following one on page 15 give an understanding of Piedmont as a young community, with white clapboard homes and white fences lining a wide dirt avenue. (Courtesy of Margaret Payne.)

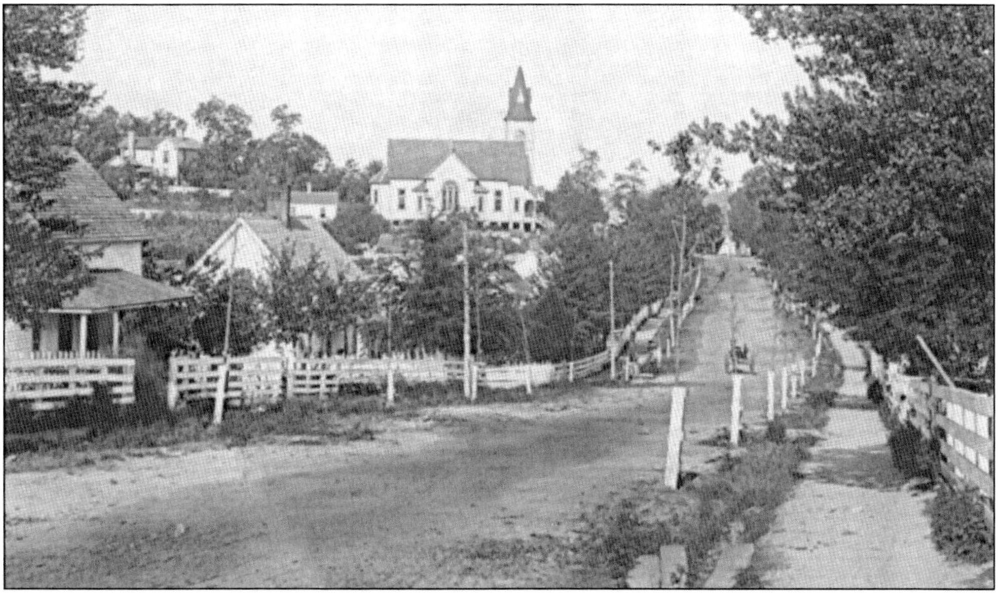

As the view moves just down the hill from the Payne house, the first Methodist church can be seen in the distance. Prior to the current bridge, Main Street wove through downtown and behind the shopping area to curve across the old iron Wagon Bridge. In 1902 there were two bridges, an iron one and a wooden covered bridge, which was below the warehouse that now houses the Saluda River Grill. (Courtesy of Piedmont Historical Collection.)

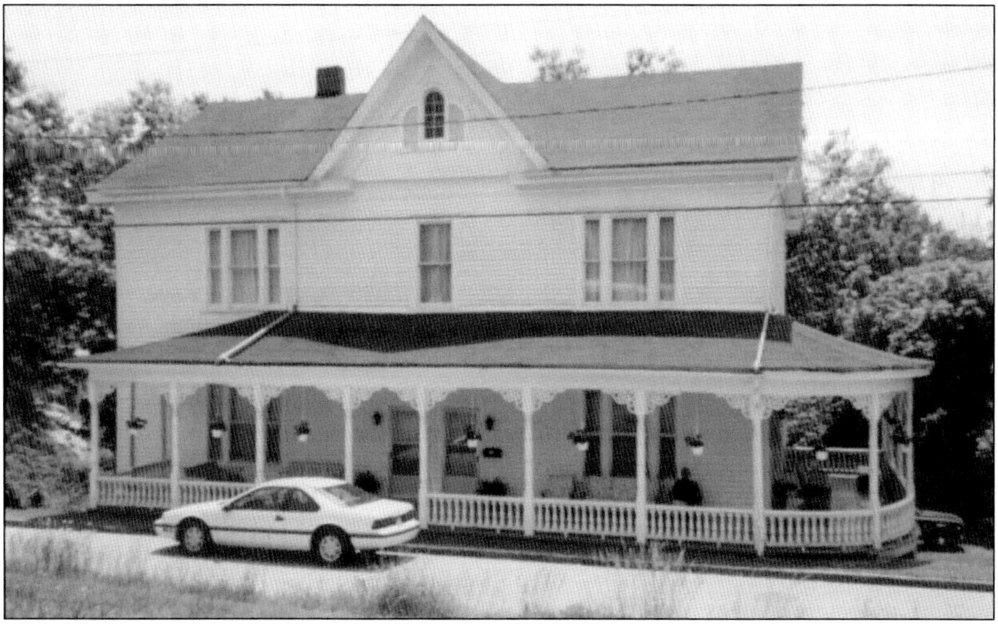

Located just across from the Methodist church in the middle of what is now Highway 86, the Women's Building was a YWCA. Built about 1908, this dwelling housed unmarried ladies who came to work in the mill and boarded six to eight in a room with one housemother. The upstairs was open and often used for large gatherings. During bridge construction in the 1940s, this historic structure was moved to Piedmont Avenue and has been the home of the James Oliver family for many decades. (Courtesy of the James Oliver family.)

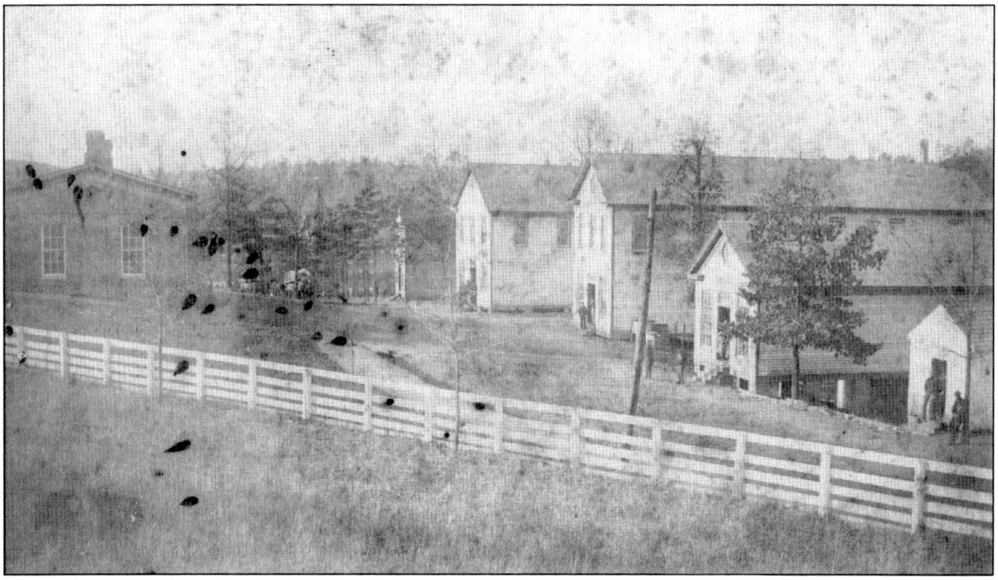

Around 1890, downtown Piedmont was lined by two-story white clapboard mercantile stores. Note the proprietors standing at the doors, anticipating this photographic record. Listed on the Sanborn fire map of November 1902 were buildings identified as mercantiles, dry goods, furniture, millinery, a building with drugs and notions, another divided into dentist and photos, barber, crockery, coffin maker and, of course, a post office. The white wooden fence separates the business section of town from Hotel Hill. Notice the Conestoga wagon moving up from the mill. (Courtesy of Piedmont Historical Collection.)

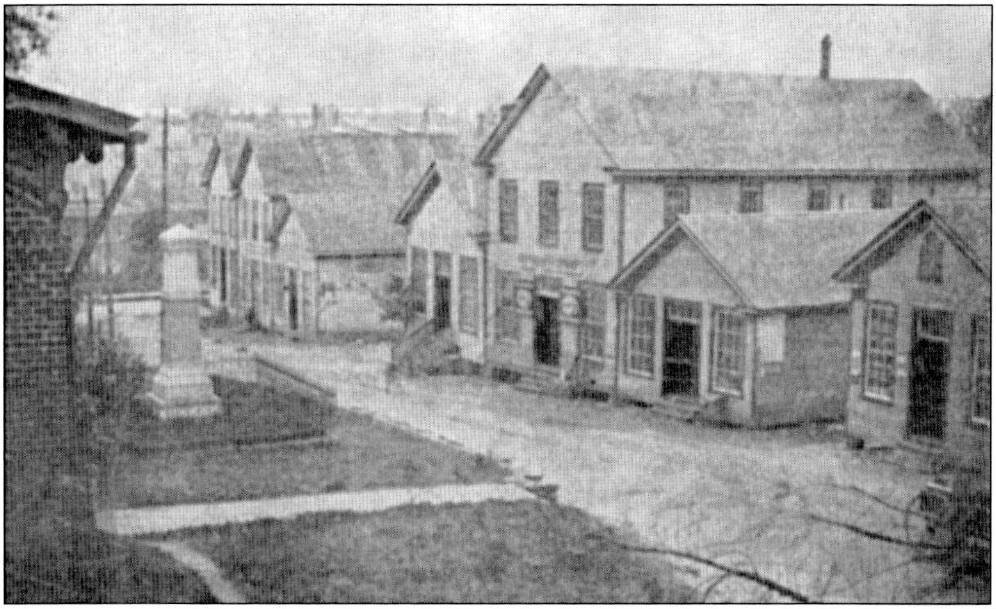

A few years later, several new stores had sprung up and a monument was placed in front of the mill office. Although the dirt road was still traveled mainly by wagons and buggies, Piedmont Manufacturing was growing rapidly and supporting progress in many ways. Other than merchants and businessmen, many highly educated doctors, lawyers, architects, and engineers were needed to support this growth. (Courtesy of Betty Davenport.)

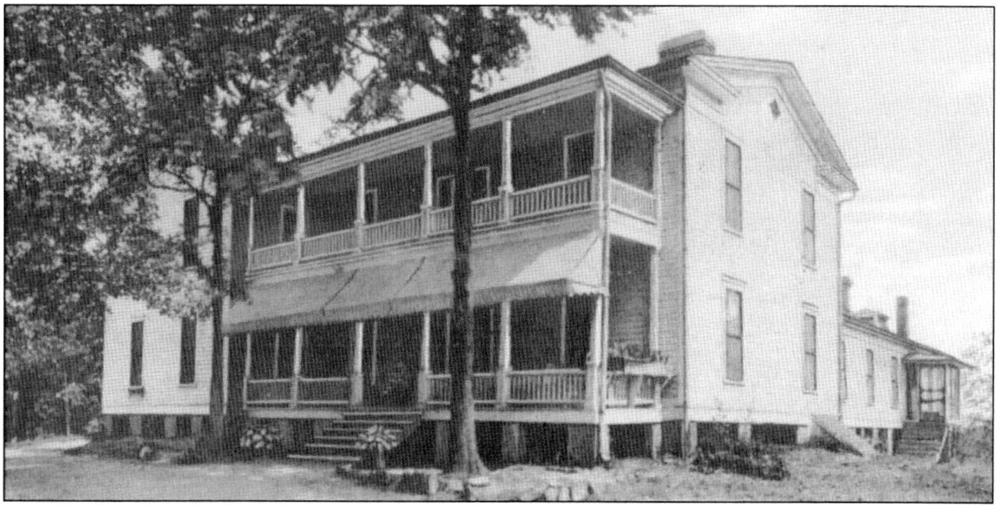

Hotel Hill rose above downtown, overlooking the stores, mills, river, and village to the west. Piedmont Hotel offered fine lodging for visitors to the mill town, and later became the local teacherage, where single female teachers were housed. Beside it stood the mill president's home, which is still a family residence today. Between this house and the Methodist church stood the early water tower. Today, three marble monuments are located at the base of the hill, honoring mill leaders Henry Pinkney Hammett, the originator, first president, and treasurer of the mill; James Lawrence Orr, mill president, treasurer, state legislator, solicitor, and lawyer; and William Edgeworth Beattie, mill president, treasurer, and director. These stones were moved to this location from the front of the mill office when it was demolished. (Above, courtesy of Pert Clifford; below, courtesy of Clemson University Archives at the Strom Thurmond Institute.)

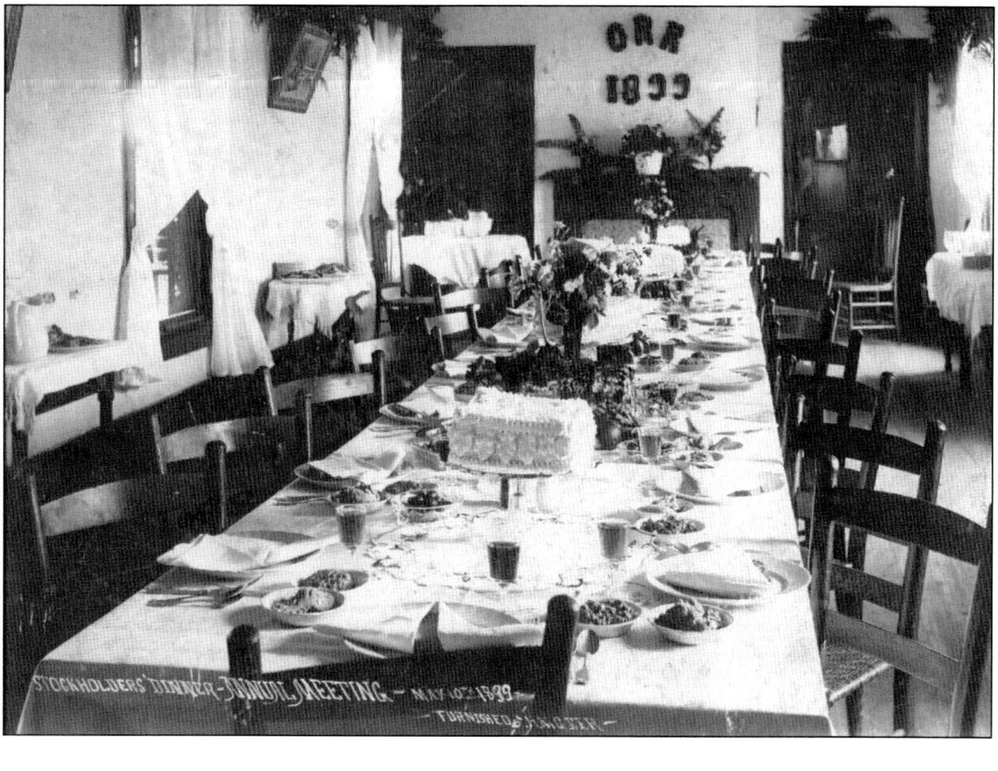

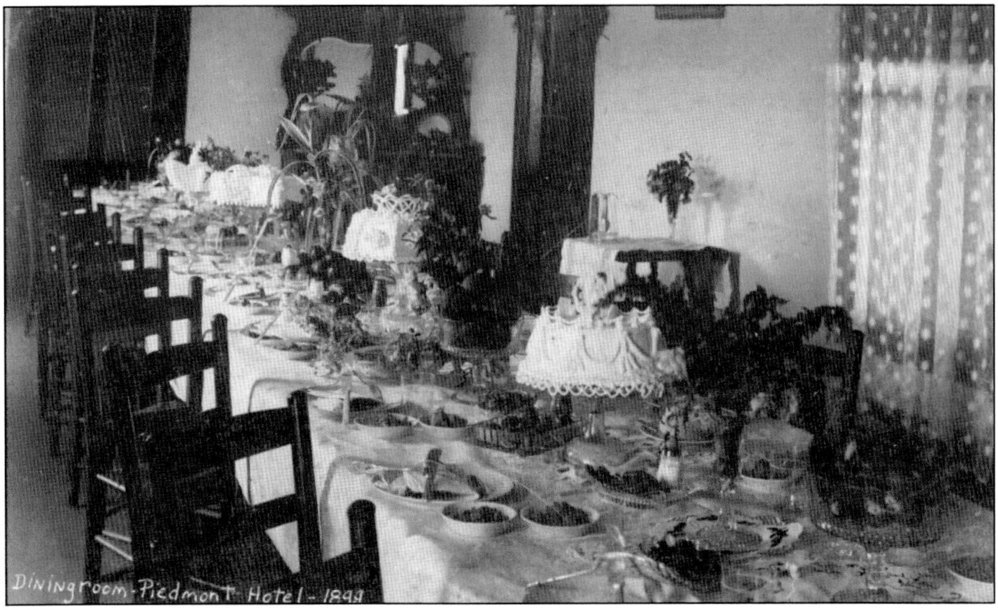

Inside the hotel was a fine dining room where Colonel Orr held the first meeting of the shareholders of his own newly established Orr Mill, built in Anderson. Both views of the hotel dining room were taken at the May 1899 meeting. The hotel proprietor, H.M. Greg, was proud of his beautifully decorated dining room and fine table setting. Just outside on the lawn, pastoral scenes like the one below were commonplace. In July 1900, J.H. Thompson's family posed for this portrait in front of the hotel, with a young thoroughbred grazing in the background. Notice the lovely fans and straw hats, which were probably purchased at the local haberdashery. In the Victorian era, ladies adorned themselves with frills and lace, and houses often displayed fretwork on expansive porches, as can be seen on the Men's and Women's Buildings near here. (Above, courtesy of Clemson University Archives at the Strom Thurmond Institute; below, courtesy of Betty Davenport.)

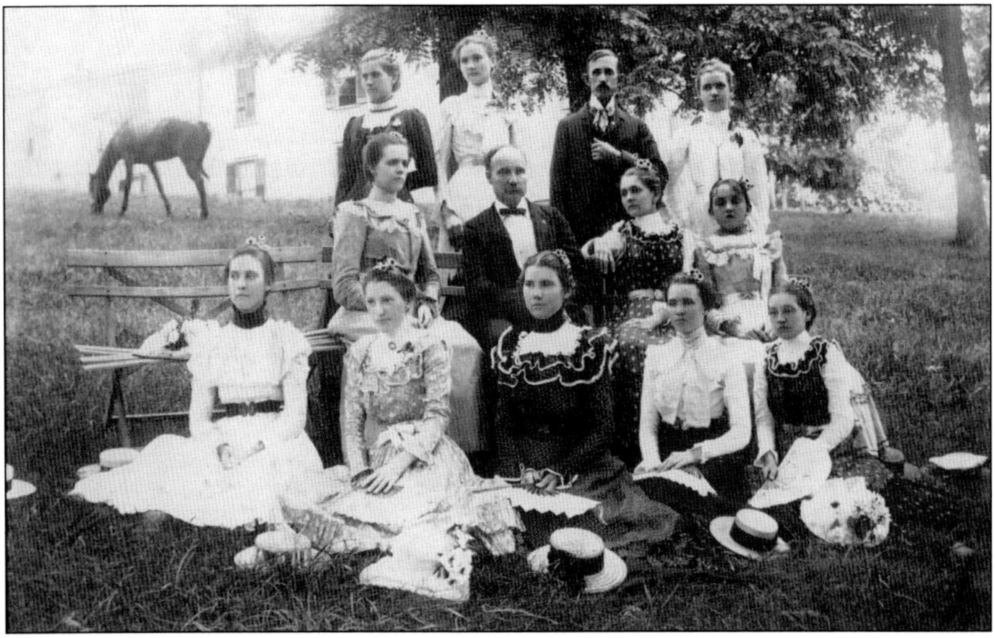

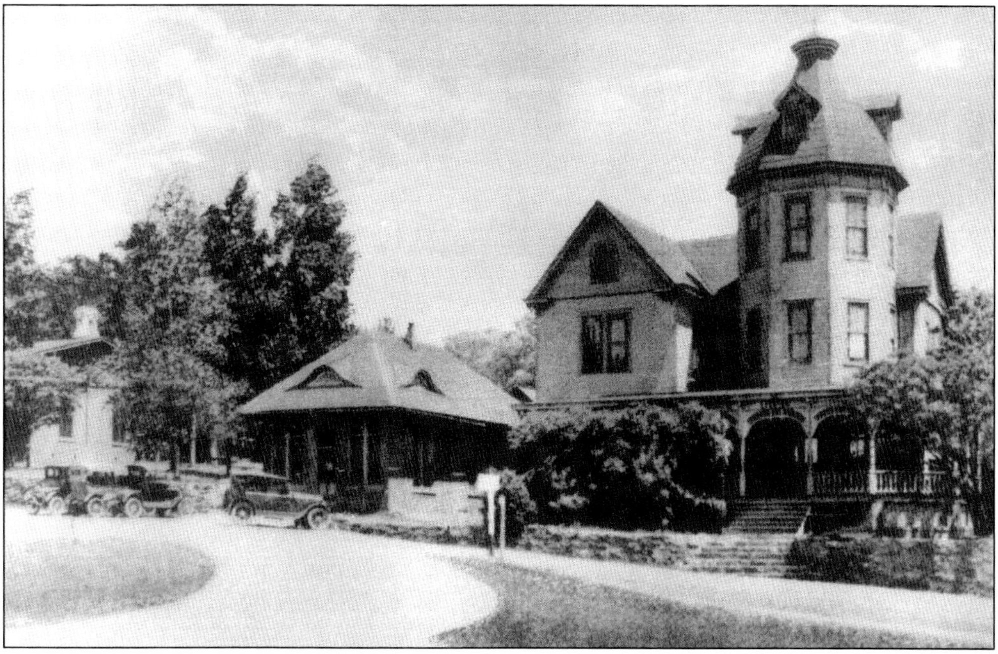

The c. 1916 image above shows the YMCA, which was located where the Community Building is today. The Men's Building, often called the "Lyceum," was a focal point of village life. The men would come to take baths and gather in the game room to play table games, such as cards, checkers, and backgammon. By 1908, a bowling alley was located behind the Lyceum. (Above, courtesy of Betty White; below, courtesy of Phil and Becky Buckheister.)

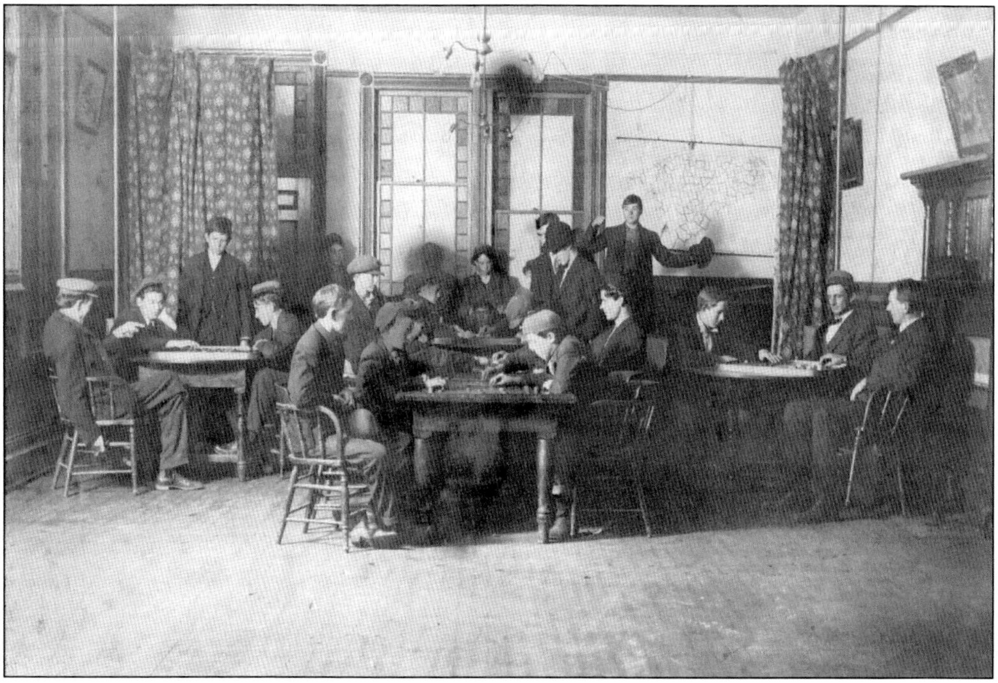

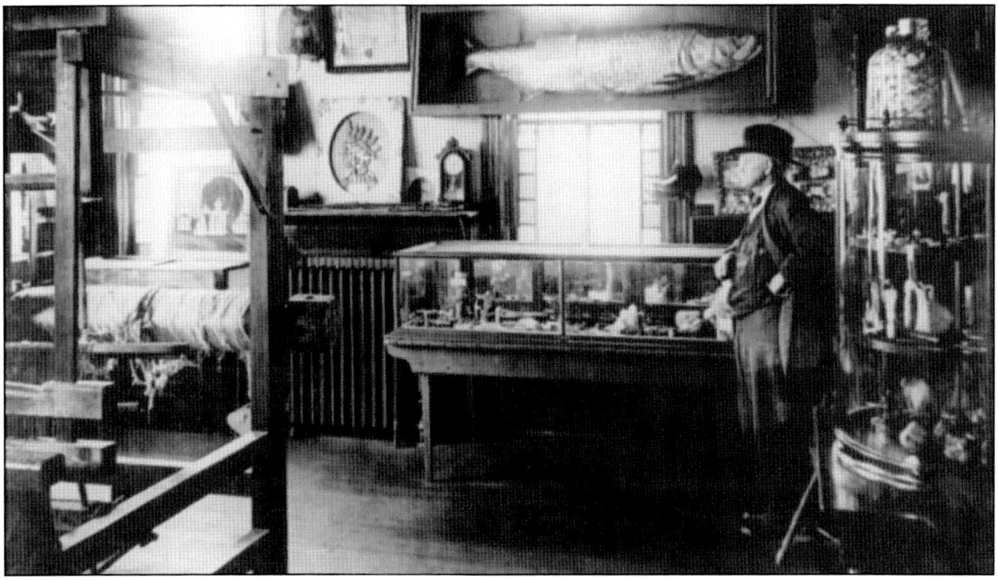

In 1877, H.P. Hammett hired a young man from Massachusetts to oversee the cloth room. Albert Smith Rowell was probably the best hire he made, because Rowell and his wife, Clara, led the community in many worthwhile endeavors over the years. Rowell was a prolific writer, reader, collector, and historian. He started many literary projects, including a library, the *Bridge* newspaper, the first Sunday school, and the Young Explorers (forerunner of the Boy Scouts), and wrote about the history of the area in his book *The Silver Bullet*. Interested in all things historical, especially Native American, his museum in the tower room in the YMCA included thousands of arrow points and even a totem pole. Rowell died on September 29, 1922, but his legacy and his museum lasted much longer. Although many of his artifacts were lost when the Men's Building burned in 1943, some were sent to the Charleston History Museum for storage and the family took others. A few remain in the Piedmont Historical Collection. The Rowell Club Room, a gathering room in the current Community Building, is named for him. The YMCA is pictured below after the fire. It was demolished and replaced by the Community Building. (Above, courtesy of Piedmont Historical Collection; below, courtesy of Betty White.)

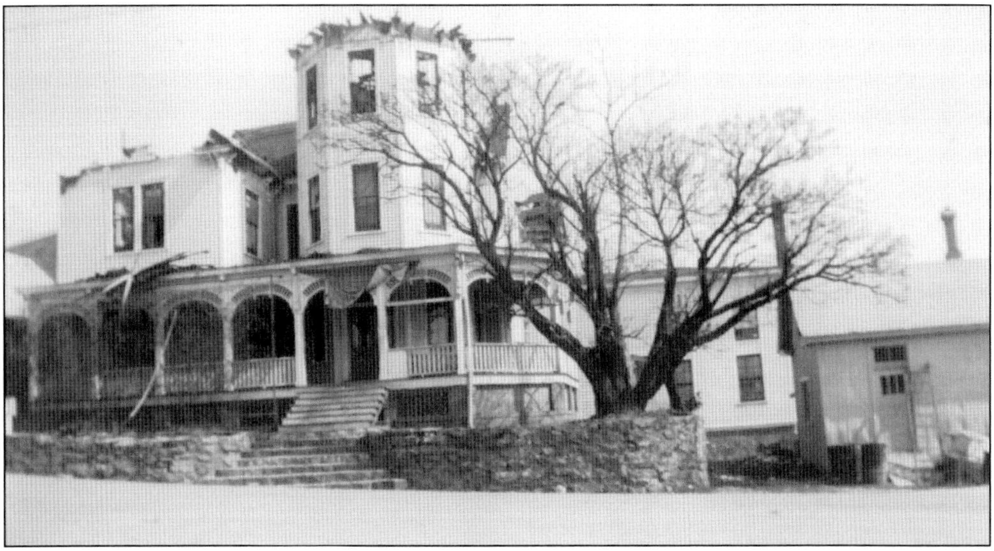

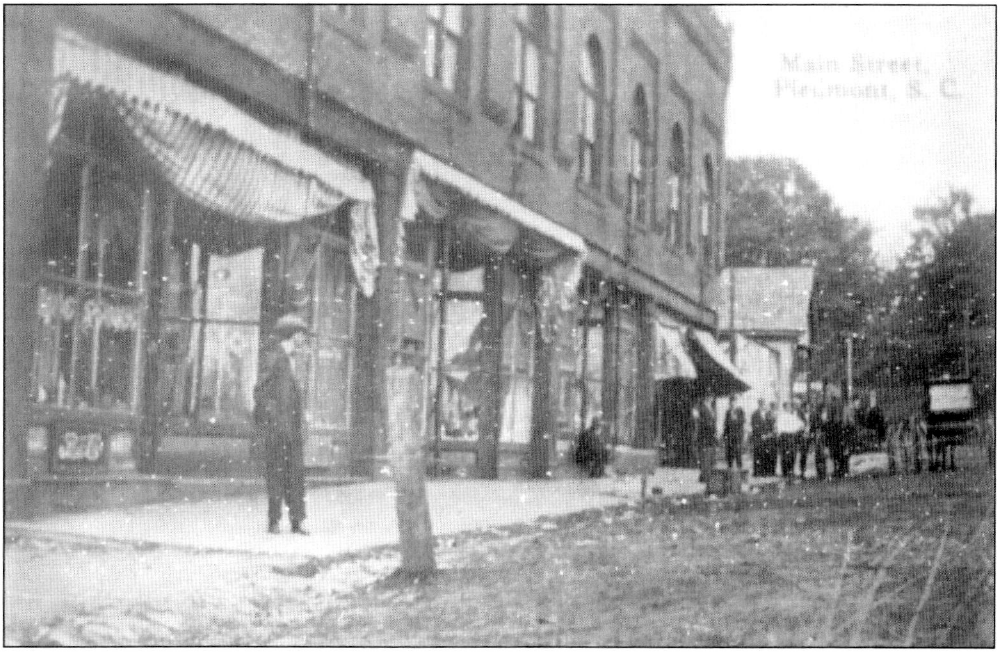

On December 3, 1903, a devastating fire ravaged downtown, demolishing 10 of the wooden store buildings. The town was immediately rebuilt in the style of the times, when brick storefronts included recessed entrance doors, prismatic glass transoms, cast-iron columns, and cloth awnings. The early image above includes a buggy on an unpaved street with a hitching post in the foreground. The new shop fronts included all the required architectural details, which were mostly crafted in Piedmont, as well as a concrete sidewalk. The establishment below was a haberdashery, millinery, and doll-maker shop. Every well-dressed man and woman around the turn of the 20th century needed a hat to complete his or her outfit. Ladies could purchase their patterns, cloth, and notions to make clothing. Standing in the center of the ladies is Clarence Smith's mother, Mollie Howard Smith. (Above, courtesy of Piedmont Historical Collection; below, courtesy of Betty White.)

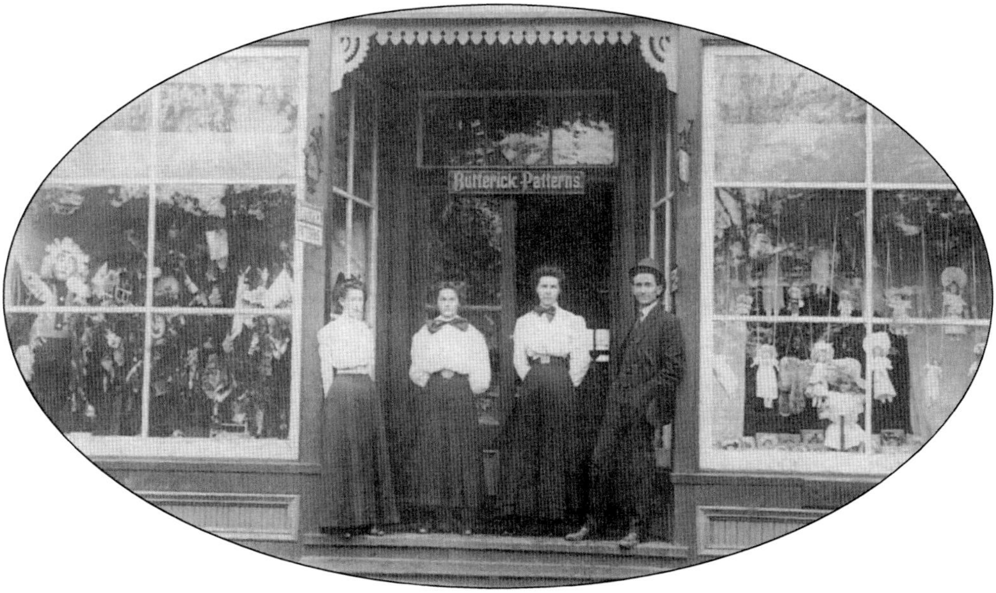

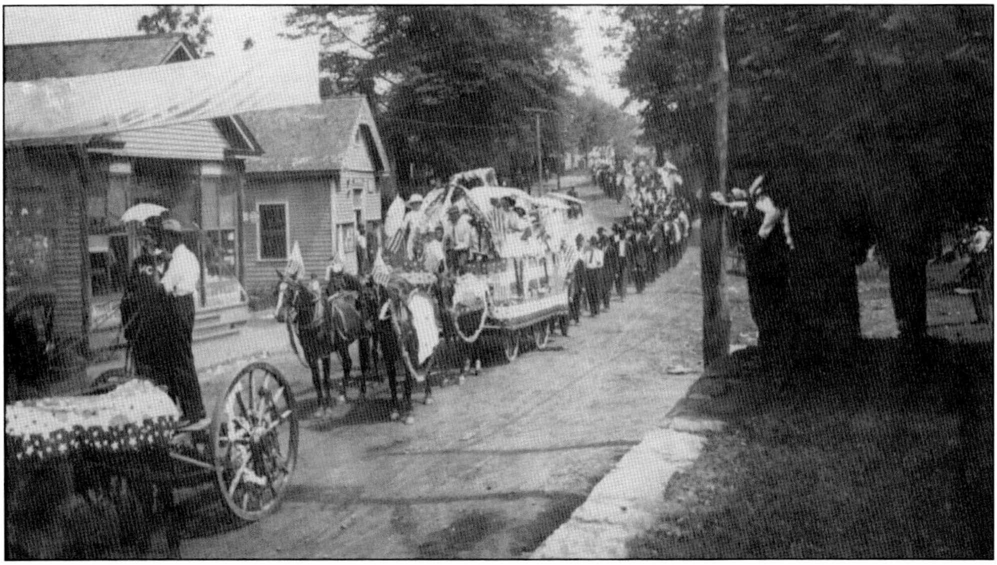

Piedmont joined the rest of the country in celebrating Armistice Day on November 11, 1919. President Wilson began the commemoration with these words, "To us in America, the reflections of Armistice Day will be filled with solemn pride in the heroism of those who died in the country's service and with gratitude for the victory, both because of the thing from which it has freed us and because of the opportunity it has given America to show her sympathy with peace and justice in the councils of the nations." (Courtesy of Linda Smith.)

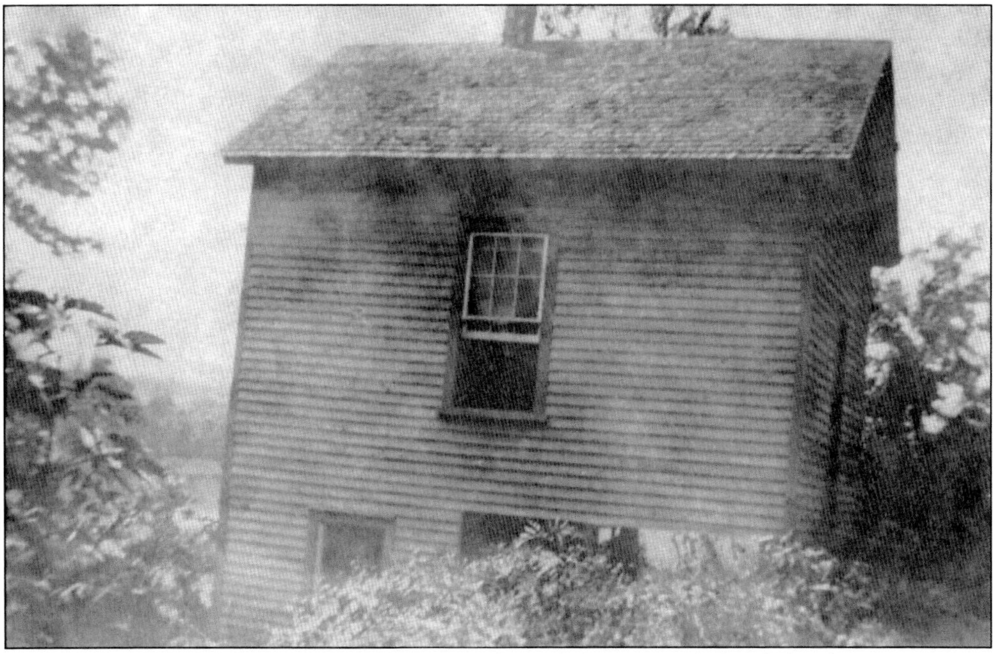

Prior to the current bridge, Main Street wove through downtown behind the shopping area to curve across the iron wagon bridge. In 1902, there was also a wooden covered bridge at this site. Sometime between 1902 and 1908, a wooden courthouse and jail were built at the river near the bridge. Pictured here is the original structure. Later, a concrete-block jail was built across the river. (Courtesy of Shirley Tice Elrod and the Bonnes Amies Club.)

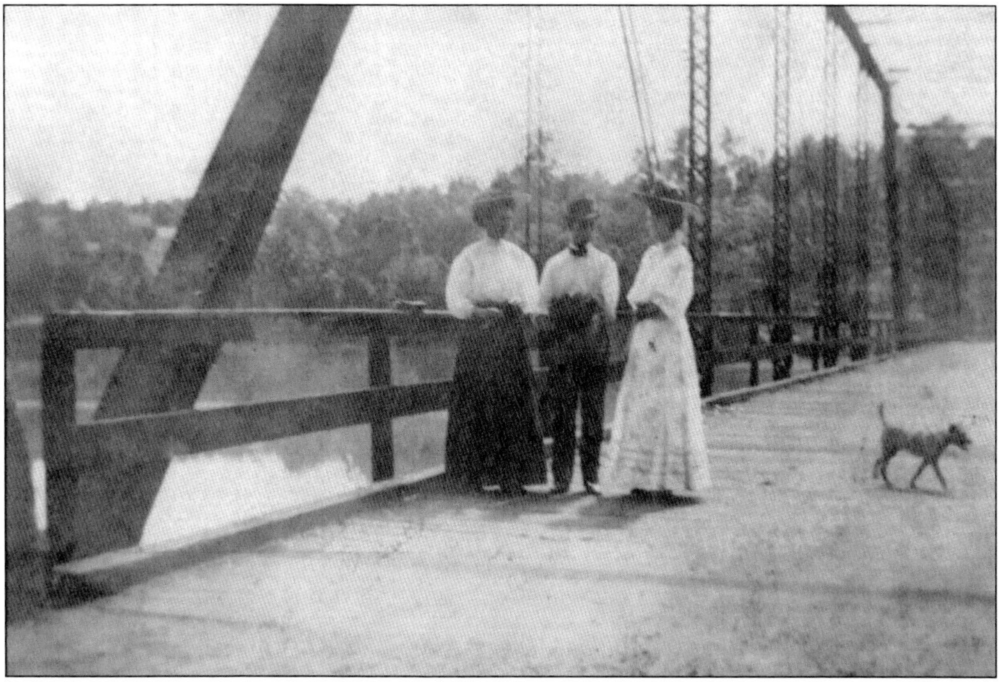

This c. 1895 photograph of the horse-and-buggy bridge was found in *Artworks Scenes in South Carolina*, a collection of postcard images. The buggy bridge crossed the river below the current site of the Saluda River Grill and gave access to the village on the Anderson side. It also allowed farmers from the western hills to bring their wares to town. Trading included cotton for the mill, skins, and flour from several gristmills, such as Moore's Mill on Hurricane Creek. (Courtesy of Shirley Tice Elrod.)

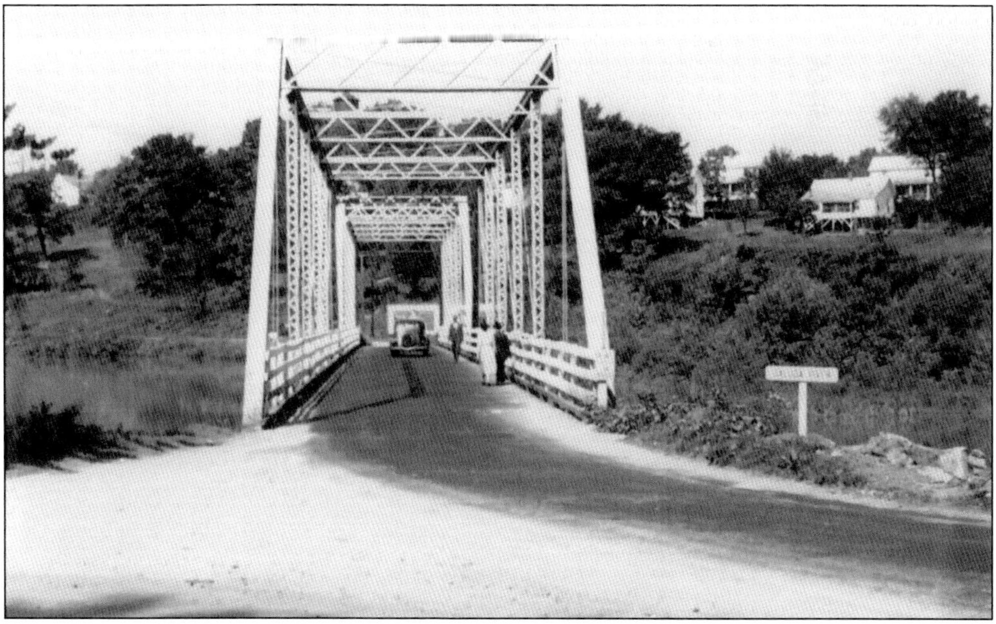

In the 1930s, buggies no longer crossed the iron bridge; however, it remained a walking bridge. (Courtesy of Jimmy Owens.)

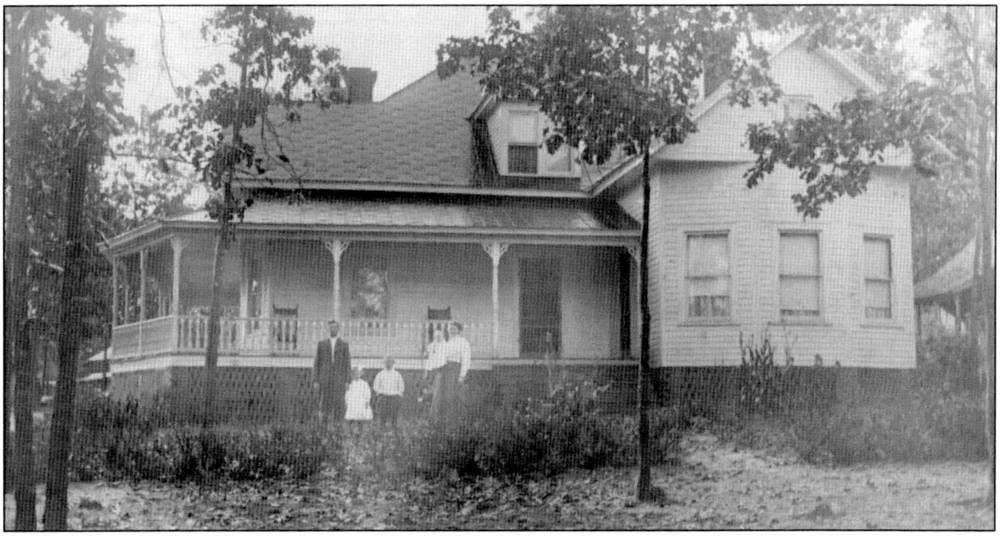

Named for the Simpson family, Simpsonville was an area of businesses west of Piedmont. In 1908, it included a barber, a blacksmith and paint shop, grocery and general stores, and at least one office. From Simpsonville, farms spread across the rolling hills. Many of these farms supplied cotton to the mill and were dependent on that commerce for part of their livelihood. The Edward King family is pictured as they prepared to attend church at Shiloh Methodist. Edward and his wife, Mourning Moore, married in 1902 and farmed for over 60 years. From left to right are Edward, Mae King Owen, Sam, baby Veldee, and Mourning. This home is located off Highway 17 west of Piedmont. (Courtesy of Jo King Hood.)

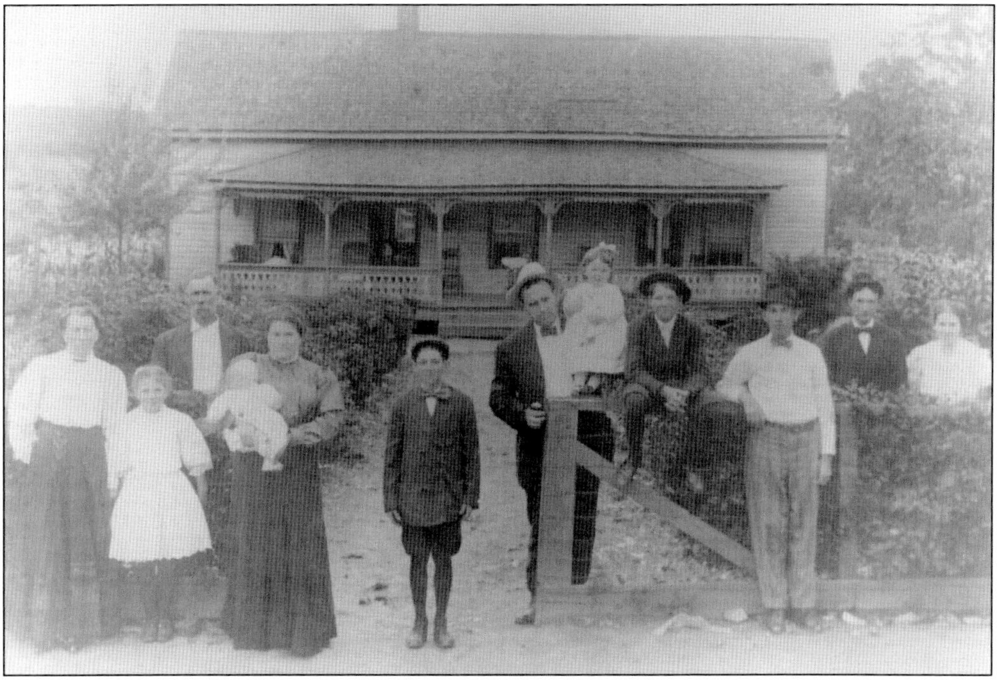

Fern Casey Durham's family lived near Mt. Springs Baptist Church and was active there for many years. This portrait captures Fern's parents, William and Pearl Moore Casey, just after their marriage in the early 1900s. They are the young couple on the right. (Courtesy of Fern Durham.)

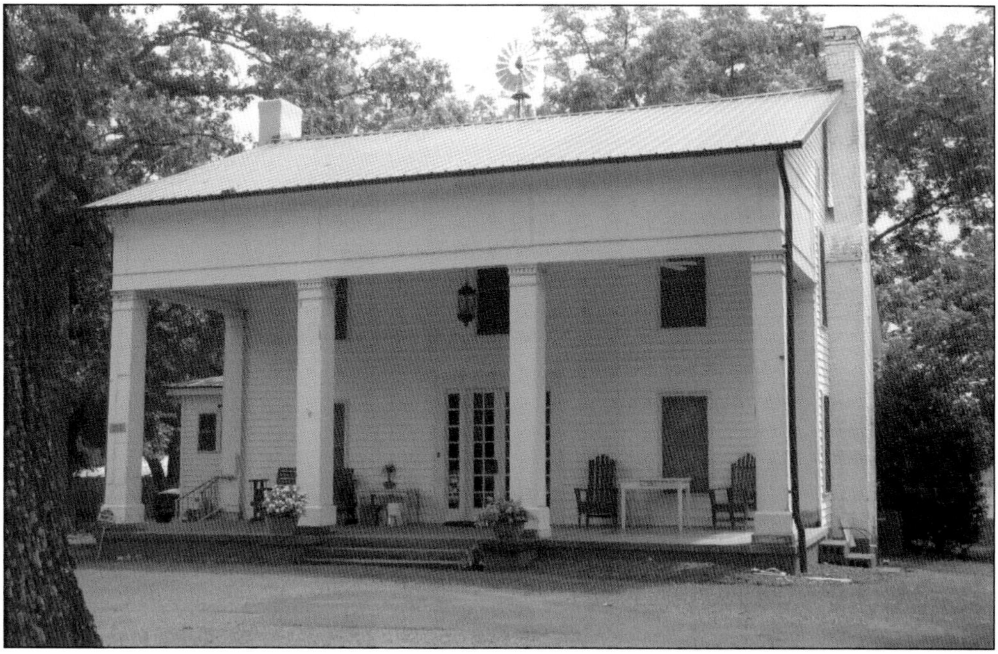

One of the oldest homes in the Piedmont area belongs to the Wigington family, leaders in farming and commerce for many years. Notice the windmill that is still located at the rear of the house—this innovation brought running water and indoor bathrooms to the house years before it was common. Across the road is the Newell post office and mercantile. (Courtesy of Anne Peden.)

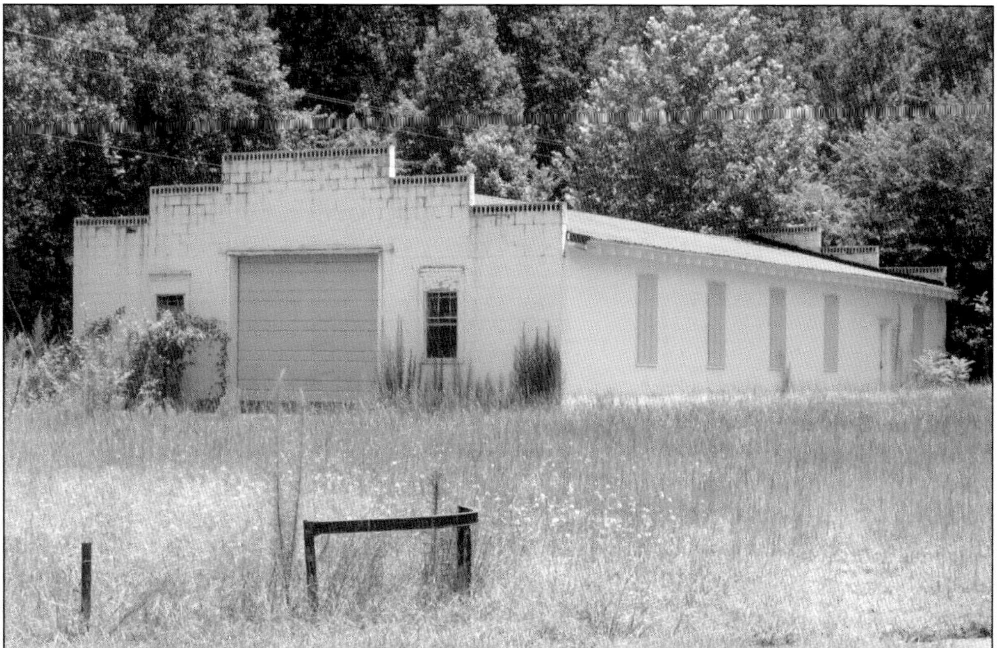

The old Singing Hall, which belongs to the Wigington family, is located near Mountain Springs Baptist Church. Built in the 1940s, it was a popular gathering place. (Courtesy of Anne Peden.)

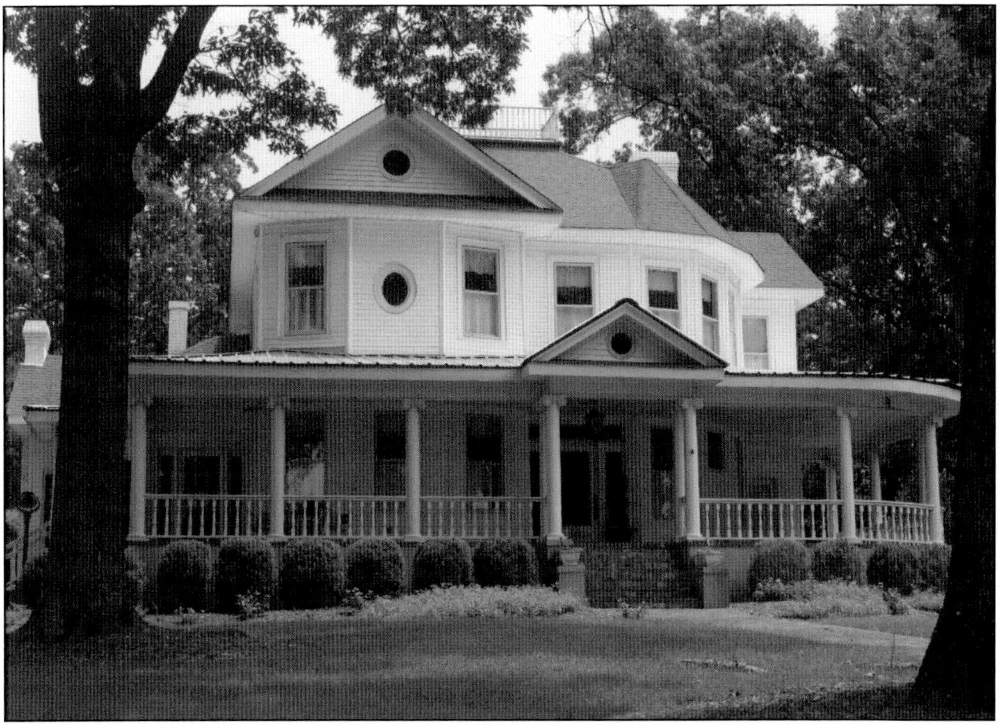

Near the Wren schools, two early homes still mark prominent farming families. Above, the Mauldin House, now owned by descendants of the Merritts, sits atop a hill. This Victorian-style home was probably built in the early 1900s, as evidenced by the wide porches and fretwork. Below is the restored store building that Mrs. Mauldin ran in the 1930s. (Both, courtesy of Anne Peden.)

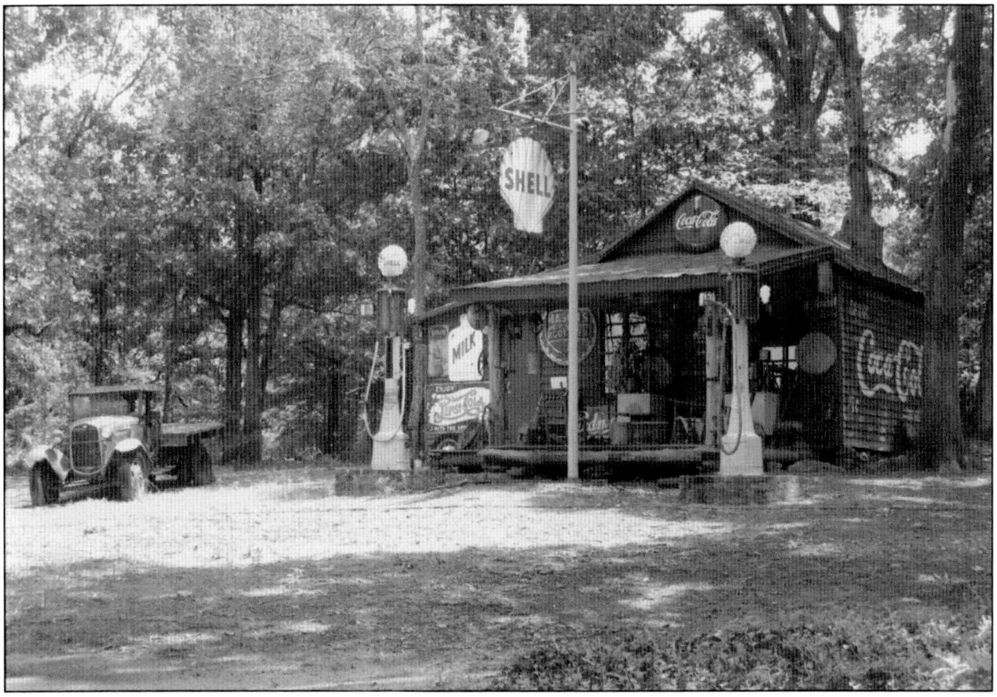

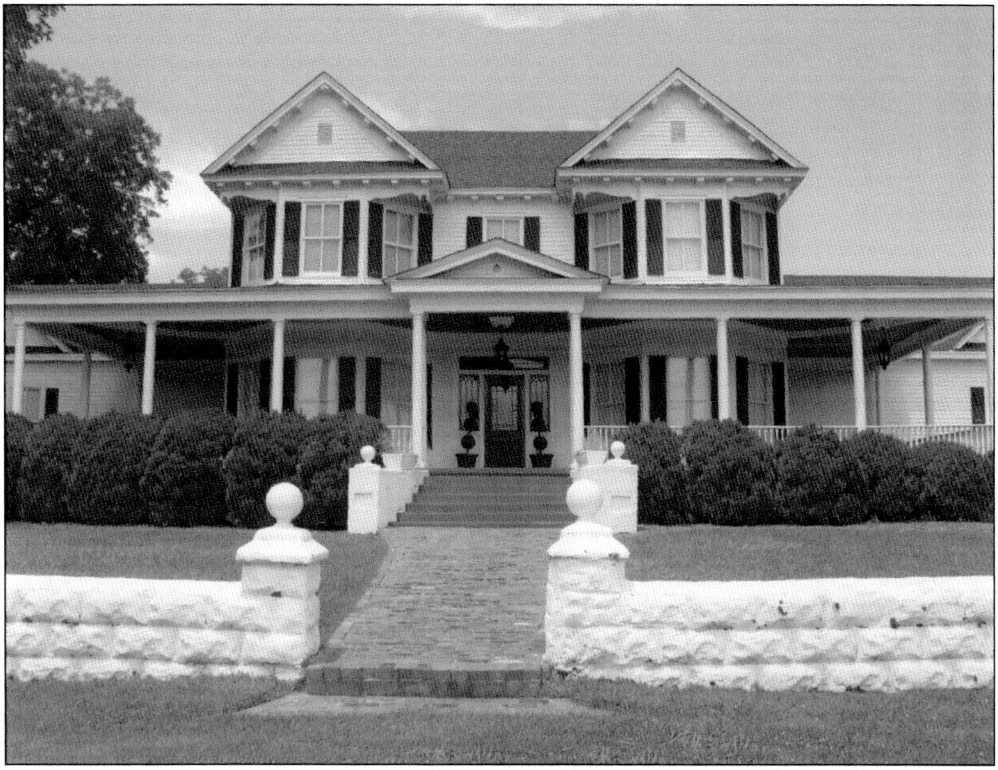

The original Merritt home place was built in the early 1800s and was added on to over the years. It is still in the family and is still a working farm. (Courtesy of Anne Peden.)

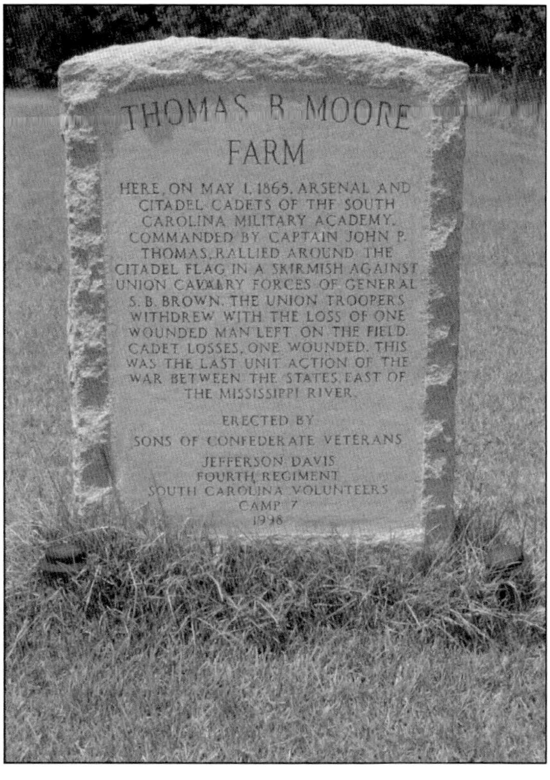

This stone marks the last unit action of the Civil War east of the Mississippi River, which occurred on May 1, 1865. Erected in 1998 by the Sons of Confederate Veterans, it can be seen behind Maynard's Furniture. (Courtesy of Anne Peden.)

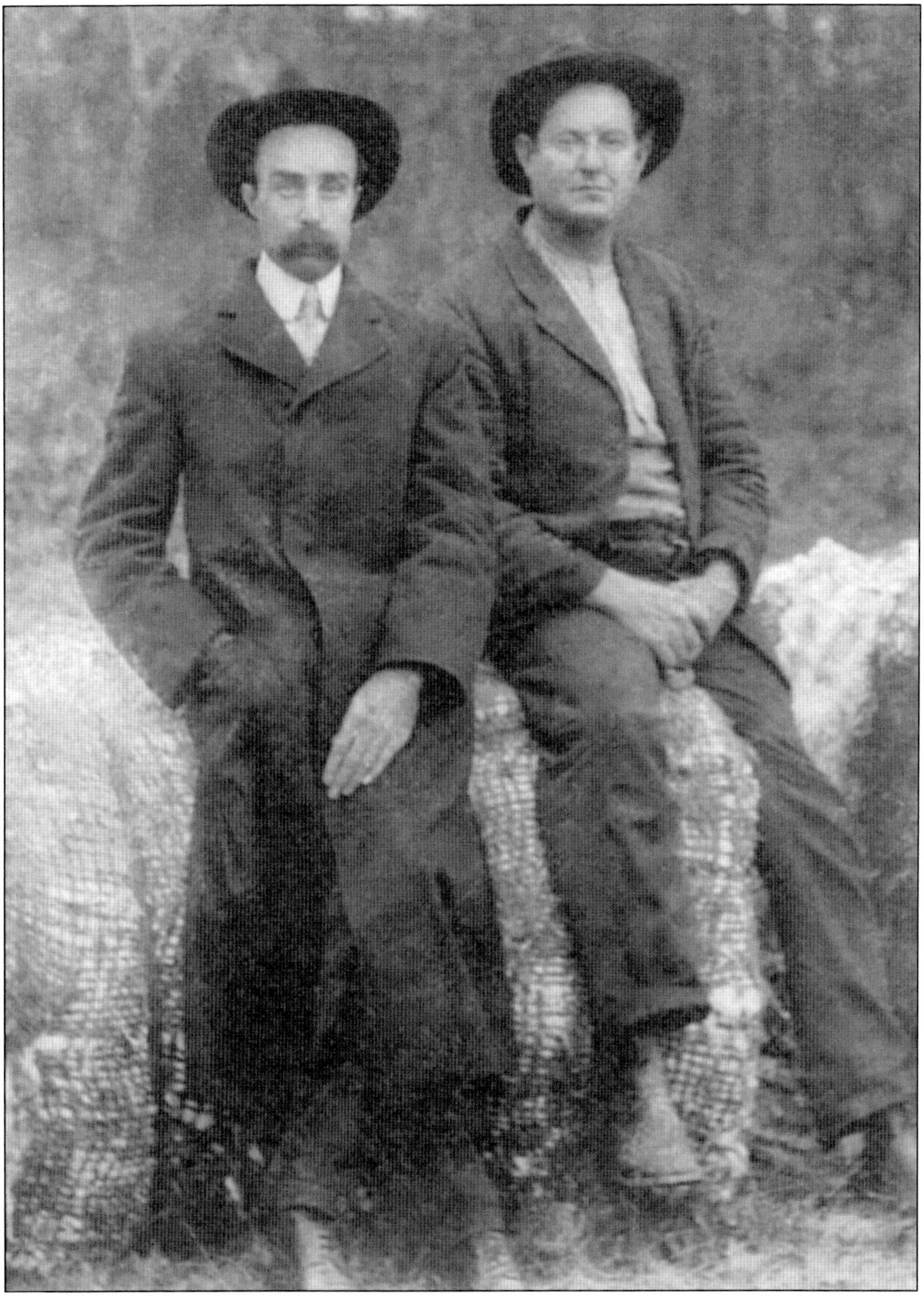

Cotton was king for the rural areas around Piedmont in the latter part of the 19th century. Here, Columbus Tarrant (left) and John Richardson, the brother of Mary Peden, rest on a bale of cotton. Tarrant's cotton was supposed to be of the highest quality. (Since Tarrant looks young in this photograph, could that be the famous bale known as "Mr. Tarrant" that is displayed in the Community Building?) (Courtesy of Margaret Payne.)

Two

Clubs and Organizations

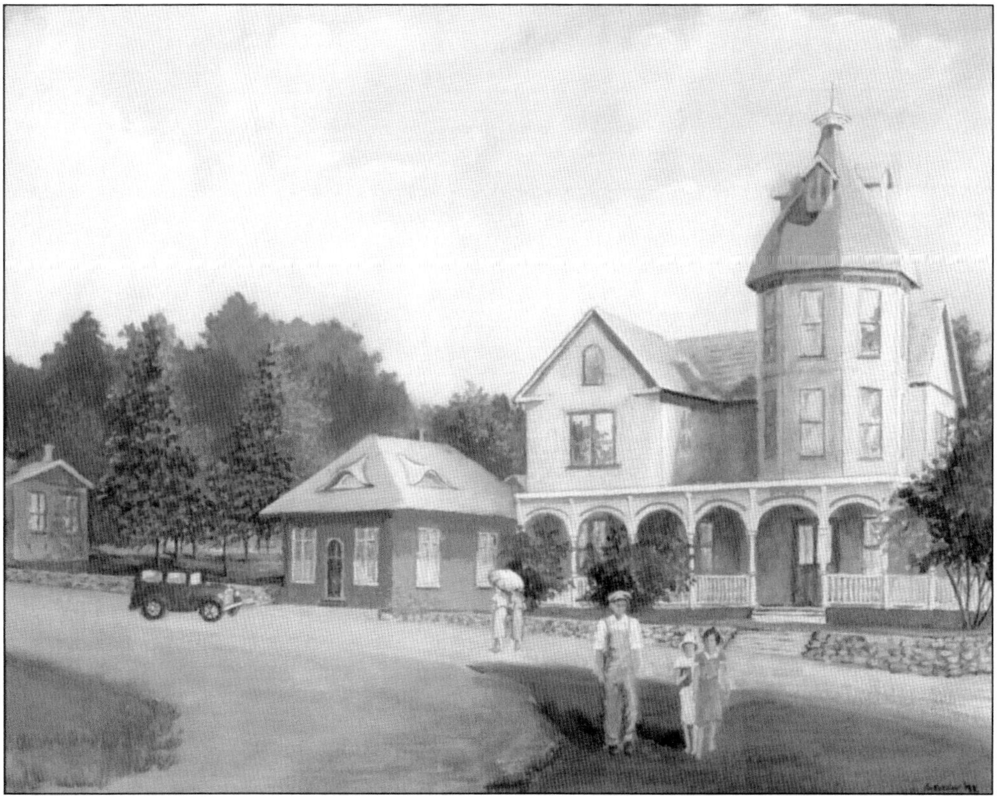

This painting of the Lyceum (also known as the Men's Building or YMCA) shows the building at the height of its use. It was built after 1902 but before 1908, when it appeared on the Sanborn fire insurance maps. Men came here for socialization until it burned down in 1943. (Courtesy of the Bonnes Amies Club.)

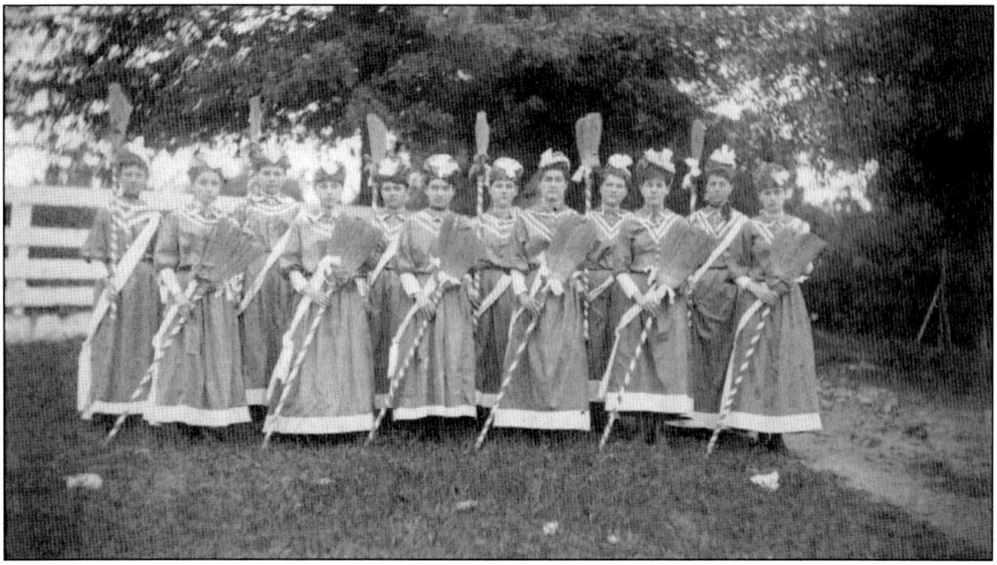

Popular in the late 19th century, broom brigades were a national auxiliary of Civil War veterans. Military-style women's drill teams wore matching uniforms and marched with brooms instead of rifles. Pictured from left to right are Rowena Chandler Tarrant, Corrie Snelgrobe Osteen, Jean Tinsley Till, Sue B. Stribling, possibly Laura Rogers, Hat Stepens, Maggie Chardley, Annie Timmons Hall, Minnie Rogers Norris, Andrella B. Yarborough, possibly Hattie or C. Rambo, and Lillie Poole Buchanan. Several of these ladies are also pictured on page 125 as members of Albert Smith Rowell's Sunday-school class. (Courtesy of the South Caroliniana Room, Greenville County Library.)

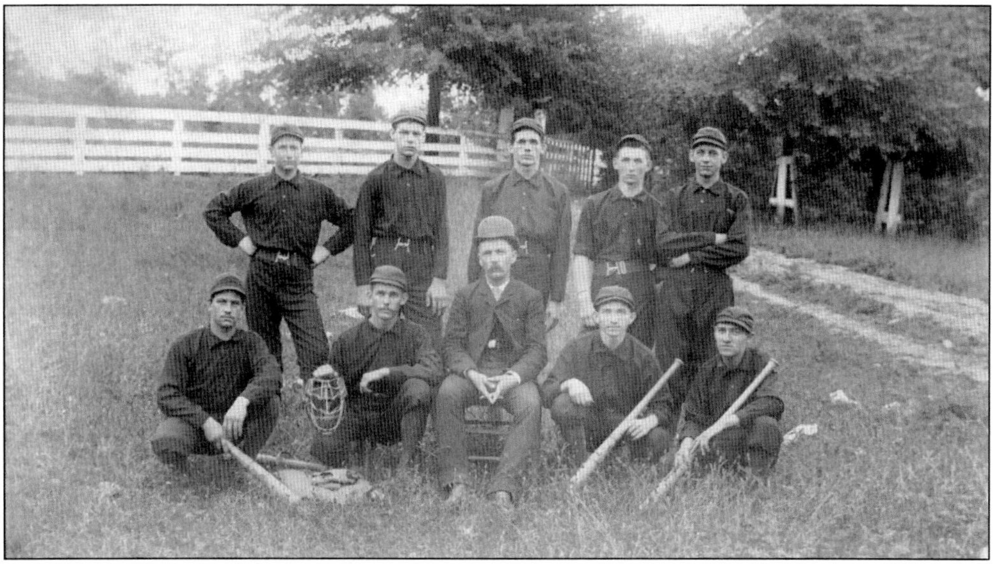

The men's baseball team is pictured here around 1890. From left to right are (first row) Jim McClellen, George Buchanan, Frank Walker, W.J. Clifford, and Ben Roswell; (second row) Jack Iler, George Young, S.T. Buchanan, ? Litem, and Charles Iler. In 1904, the textile mill baseball league had grown to importance with the success of players like James "Champ" Osteen, who was drafted to the New York Highlanders major-league team. Osteen is quoted as saying, "Piedmont's playing Pelzer and I'm needed." (Courtesy of the South Caroliniana Room, Greenville County Library.)

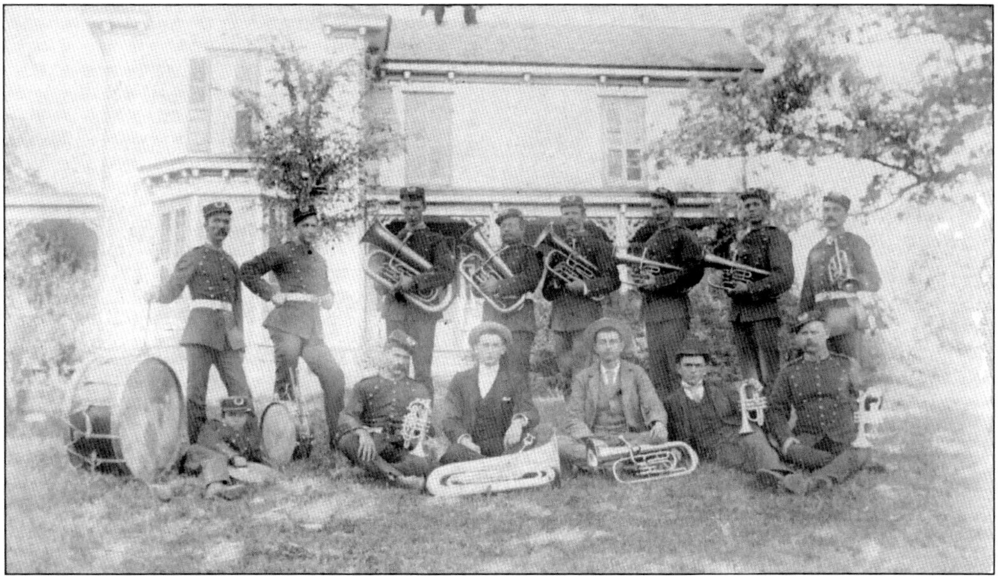

The Piedmont Cornet Band is shown here in June 1889. Pictured are J. Summey, J. Iler, A. Noblet, W. Iler, H. Cobb, F. Cox, S. Buchanan, B. Summey, W. McCall, S. Owens, A. Tiycan, A. Iler, W. Rector, and E. Hammett. Many streets in the village are named for these early Piedmonters. (Courtesy of the South Caroliniana Room, Greenville County Library.)

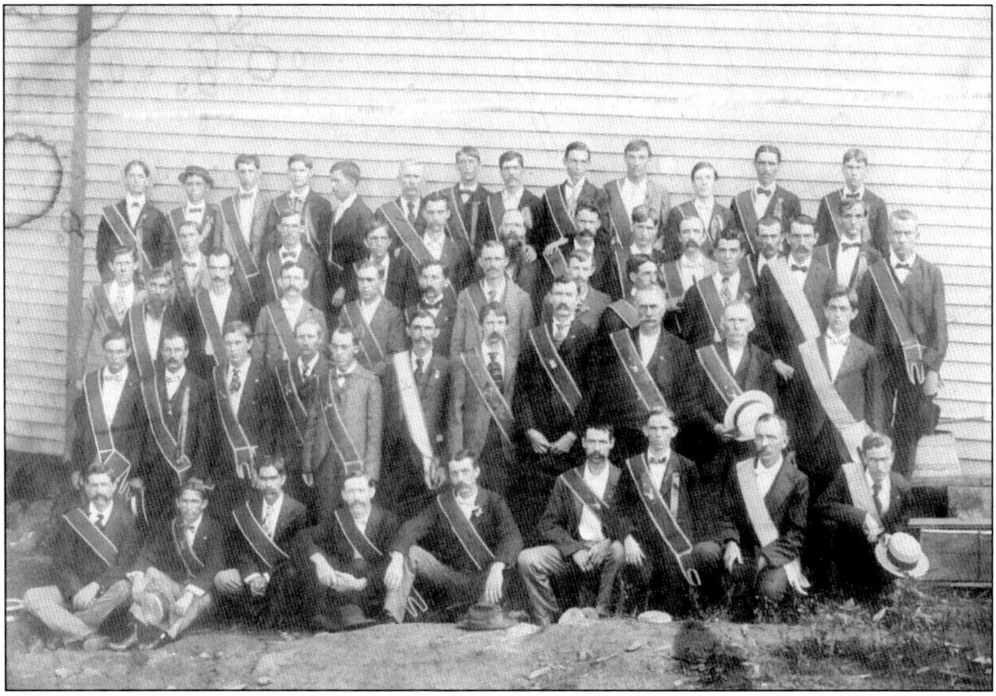

This men's organization is believed to be a branch of the Masonic temple. (Courtesy of Phil and Becky Buckhiester.)

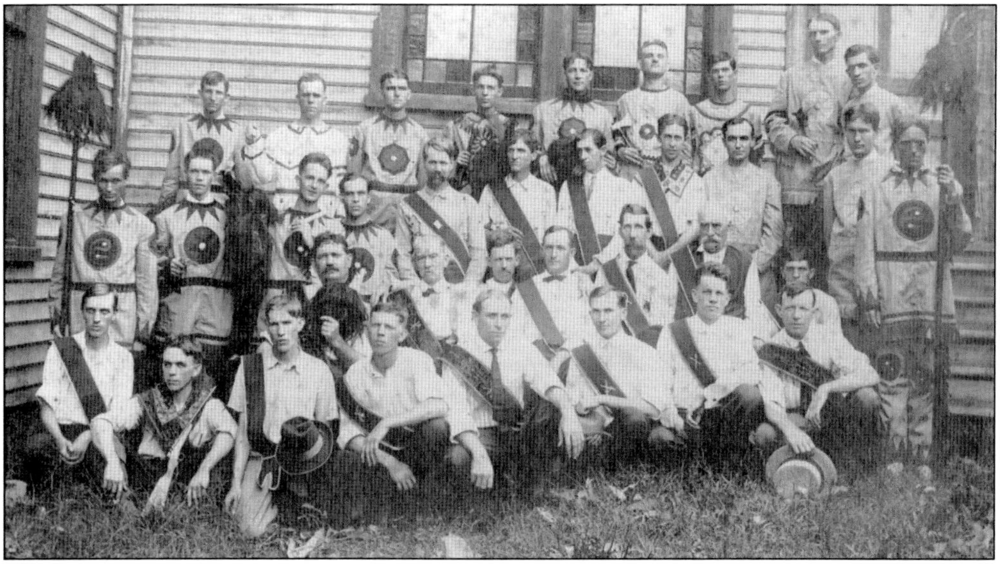

The Oklahoma Redmen, a national fraternity, is still in existence today. Pictured here around 1917 is Tribe No. 3, Piedmont's local unit of the Improved Order of Red Men. This group traces back to 1765 and is descended from the Sons of Liberty. They worked underground to help establish freedom and liberty. Patterned after the Iroquois Confederacy with elected representatives to govern tribal councils, it is a nonprofit organization devoted to inspiring a greater love for the United States and the principles of American liberty. (Courtesy of Frances Evans.)

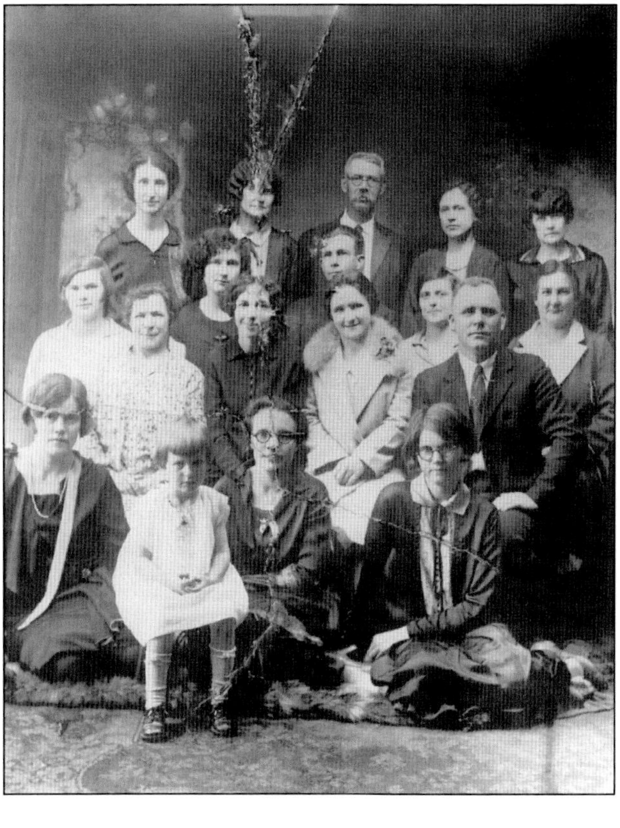

The Secret Order of Pocahontas is an auxiliary of the Red Men. Pictured in this 1926 image are, from left to right, (first row) Lillie Mae Clark, Laura Lindsey, Corrine Lindsey, and Rebecca Jenkins; (second row) Mrs. Shaw, Margie Lindsey, Irene Shaw, and Maurice Terry; (third row) Maiden Jenkins, Elvie Osteen, Elmer Wilson, Ruth Thompson, and Jean Brown; (fourth row) Lois Bishop, Cora Bishop, Will White, Vince Burdett, and Nettie Stone. (Courtesy of Gayle Payne.)

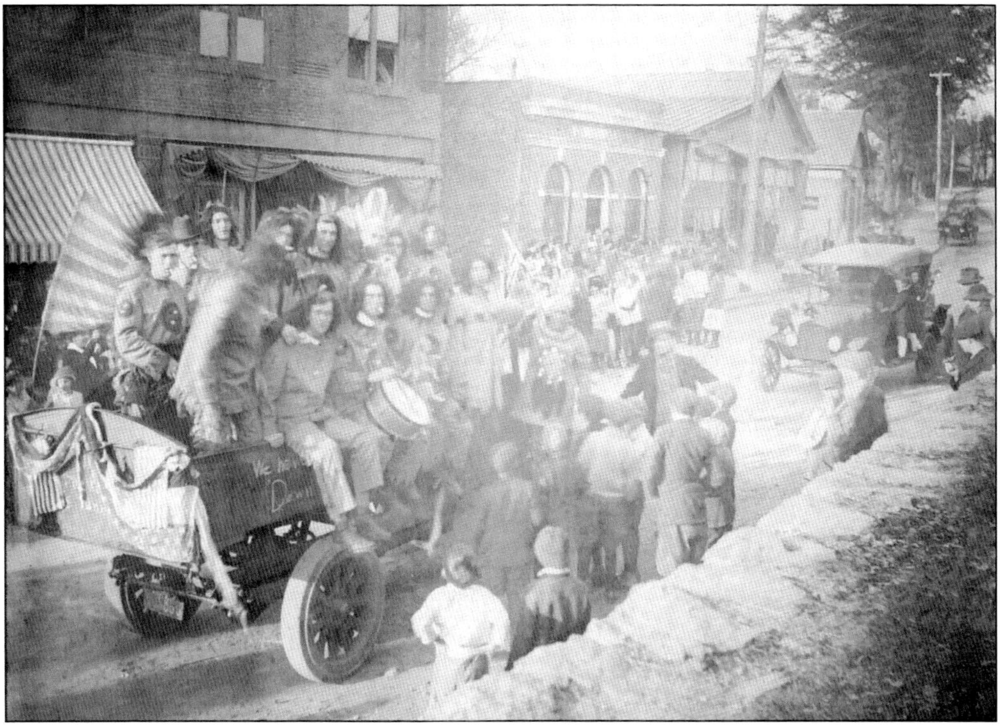

Red Men and Pocahontas groups worked together for this celebration parade on Main Street in the early 1900s. (Courtesy of Piedmont Historical Collection.)

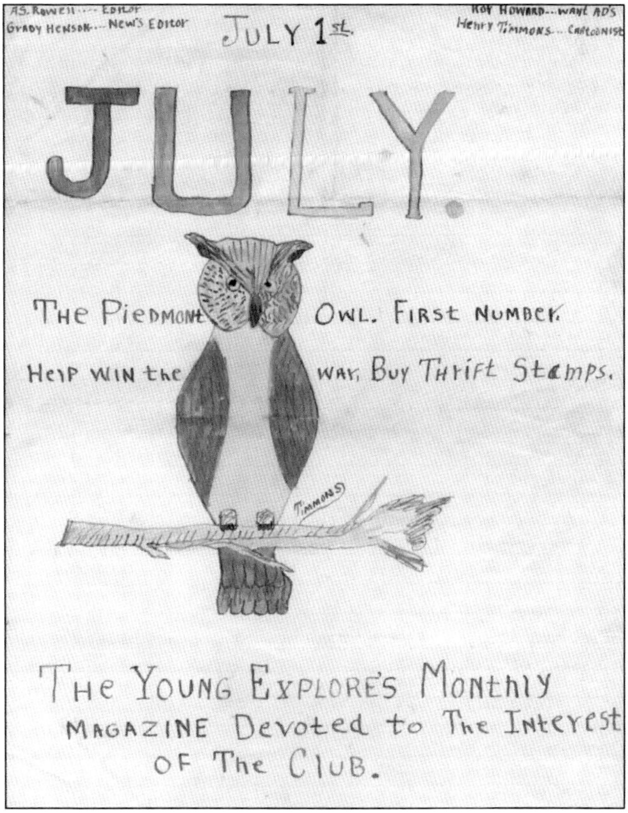

A.S. Rowell ---- Editor
Grady Henson --- News Editor

JULY 1st.

Roy Howard --- Want Ad's
Henry Timmons --- Cartoonist

JULY.

The Piedmont Owl. First Number.

Help win the war. Buy Thrift Stamps.

Timmons

The Young Explore's Monthly Magazine Devoted to The Interest of The Club.

Pictured here is the cover of a handmade newspaper, the *Piedmont Owl*. It was published by the Young Explorer's Club, which was a precursor of the Boy Scouts. A.S. Rowell started this group to help youth in Piedmont become productive citizens. (Courtesy of Piedmont Historical Collection.)

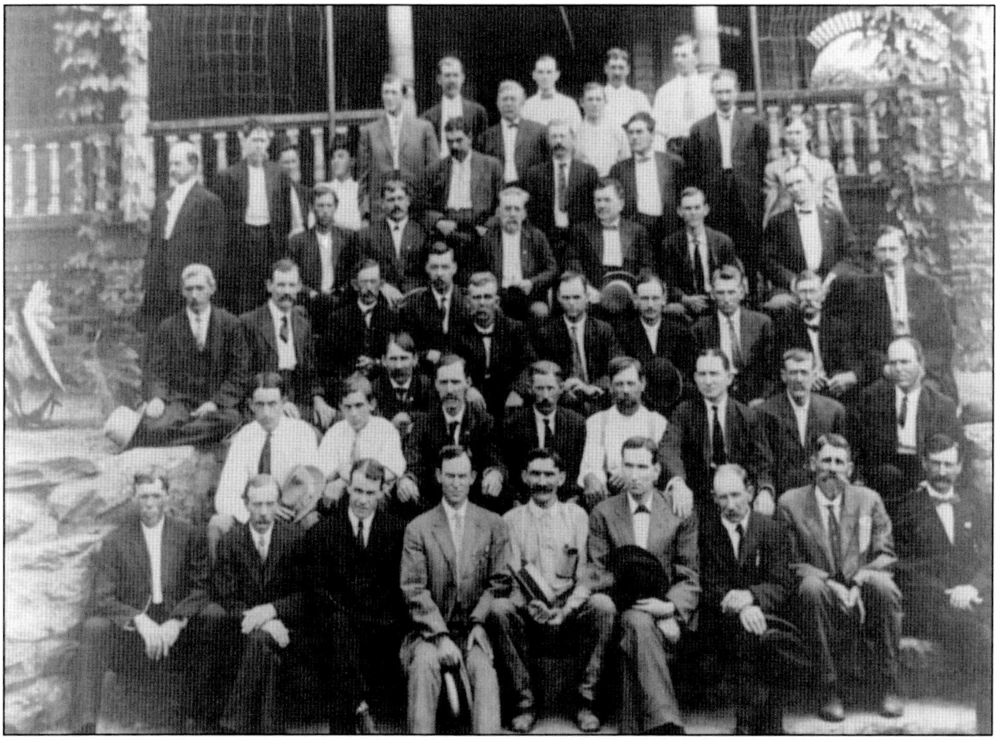

Woodmen of the World pose in front of the Men's Building in 1925. Included are members of the Buckheister family and, according to his granddaughter Brenda Pickelsimer Vinson, Butler Clardy. Notice the kudzu growing on the hog wire to shade the porch; it was a popular method of summer cooling in the area. (Courtesy of Piedmont Historical Collection.)

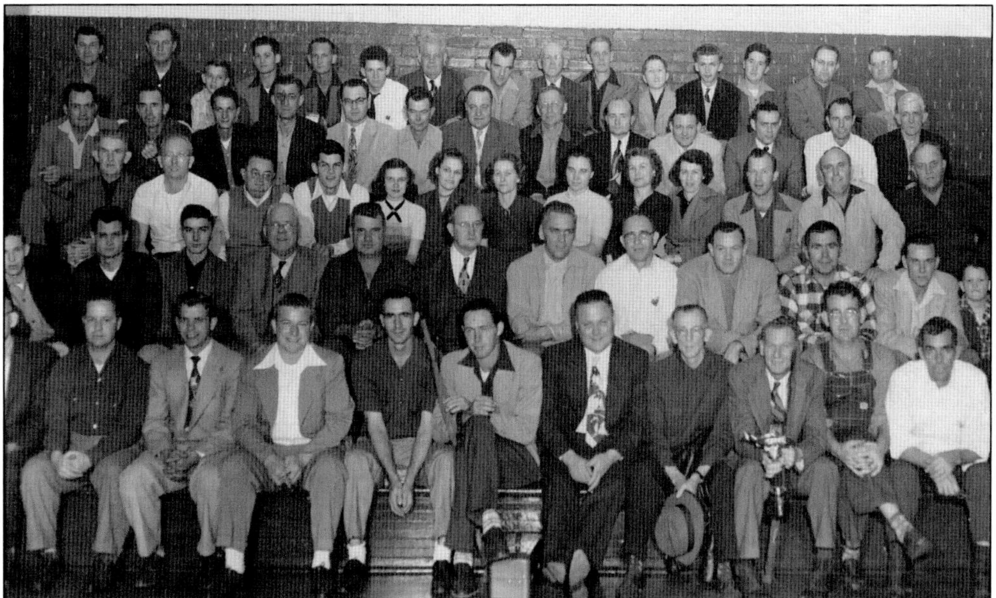

Piedmont Fishing Club was a large group, as evidenced by this 1952 photograph taken in the Community Building by J.E. Kirby of Pelzer. (Courtesy of Piedmont Historical Collection.)

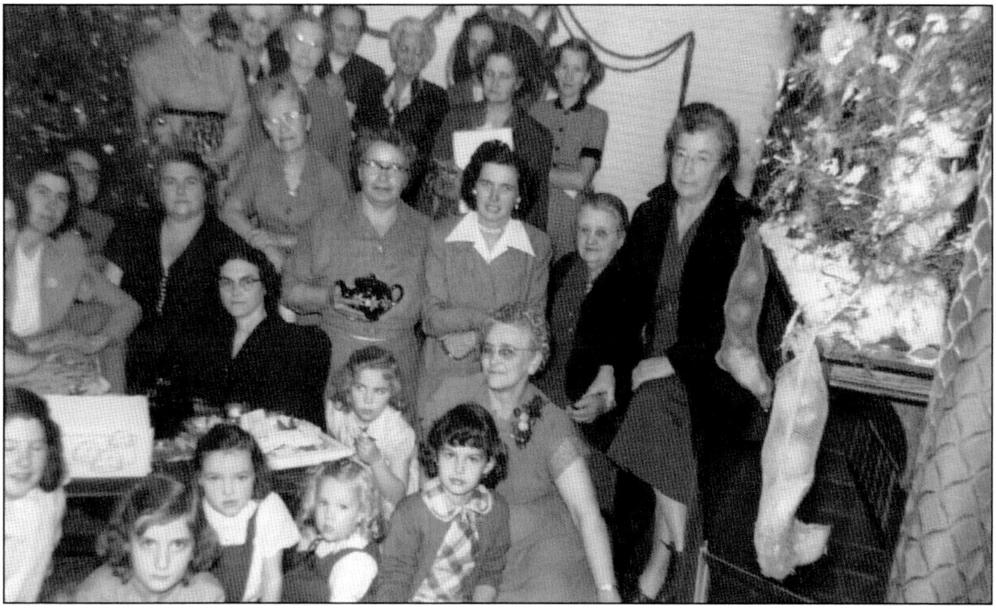

The Rock Hill Home Demonstration Club met at the home of Pearl C. Smith for this Christmas party in the early 1950s. From left to right are (first row) Betty Wilson, Carolyn Gillespie, Martha Weisner, Julia Hall, and Gayle Smith; (second row) Charlotte Reid and Pearl Smith; (third row) Ruby Wilson, Sallie Mae Foster, Bernice Jones, Effie Harris, Ossie Weisner, Mrs. Moore, and Mrs. Brissey; (fourth row) Montez Gillespie, Mrs. Moore, Ila McCoy, and Effie Hall. The fifth row is unidentified. (Courtesy of Gayle Payne.)

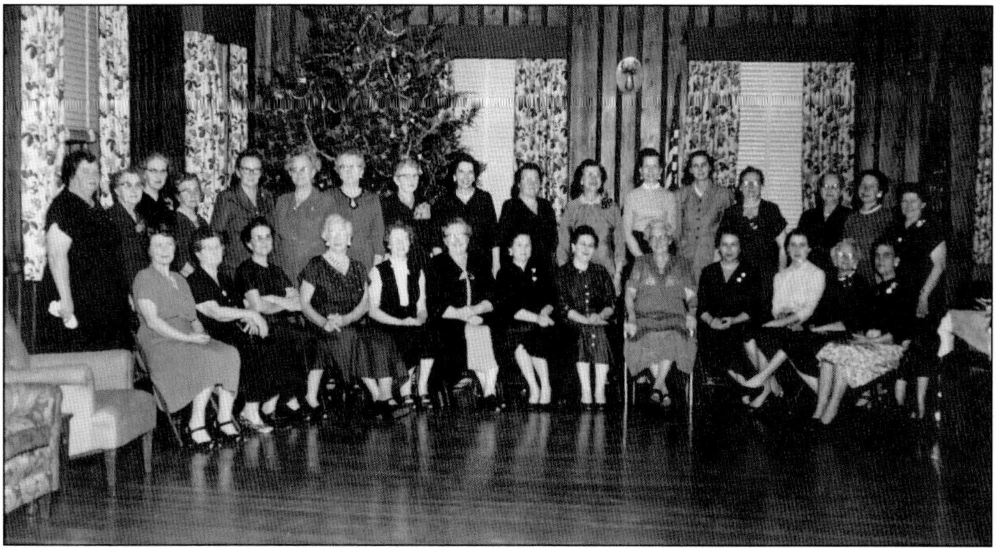

The Mother's Club was organized in 1936 at the home of Mamie Hollingsworth on Main Street in Piedmont. A group of ladies who met together to quilt decided to form a civic club that would benefit the community in various ways. Among the members pictured here are Mrs. Blant Parker, Bernice Parker, Mrs. Vernon Watts, Mrs. Jim McCall, and Ruth Thompson. Originally called the Quilting Club, its first meeting was on March 12, 1936. The club was later named the Daffodil Club and, finally, the Piedmont Mother's Club. The club is considered Piedmont's oldest civic club. They continue to undertake numerous charitable projects. (Courtesy of Linda Smith.)

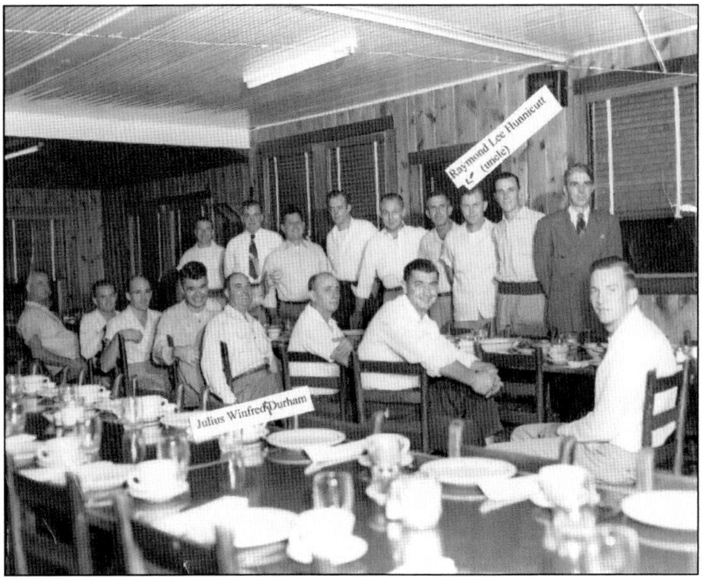

The Piedmont Lion's Club was established about 1951 or 1952 and has served the community since. These are probably the first members. In addition to the two marked, only one other has been identified as Frank Grover, seated in the first row fourth from left. The picture seems to have been taken in what is now the Piedmont Historical Collection room at the Community Building. (Courtesy of Brenda Durham Spearman.)

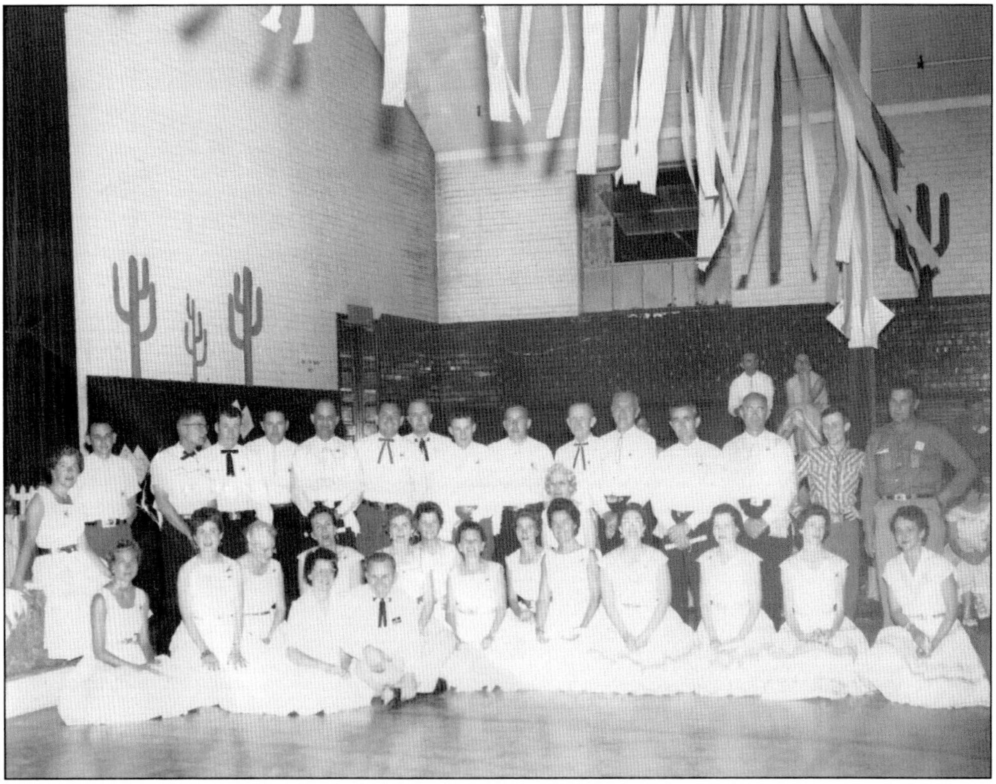

The Square Dancers Club held a cactus walk in the Community Building gym in the 1940s or 1950s. Included in the group are Margie Payne, George and Margaret Buckhiester, Fleet and Mary Bannister, Jessie and Curt Terry, and Margaret Payne. (Courtesy of Margie Payne.)

The Old Time Senior Citizen's Celebration was also sponsored by the Bonnes Amies Club in the 1970s. The ladies pictured at right are, from left to right, Hattie Fisher, Donna Lee Clifford, and Gladys Hughey. The gentlemen below are, from left to right, Roger Norris, Luther Payne, and Ralph Wilson. (Both, courtesy of Betty Davenport.)

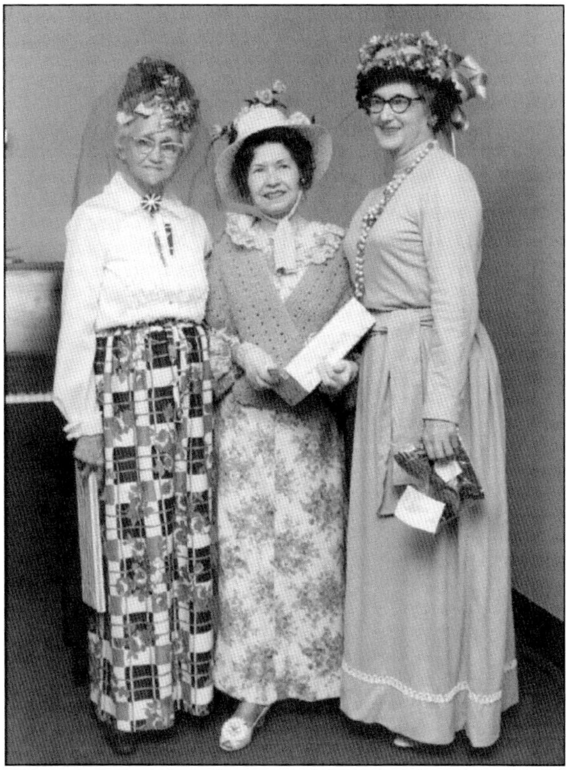

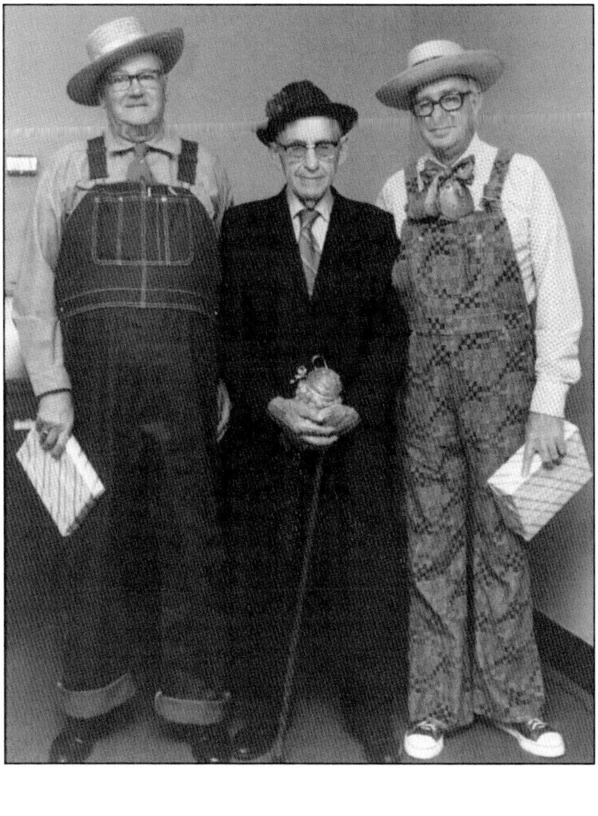

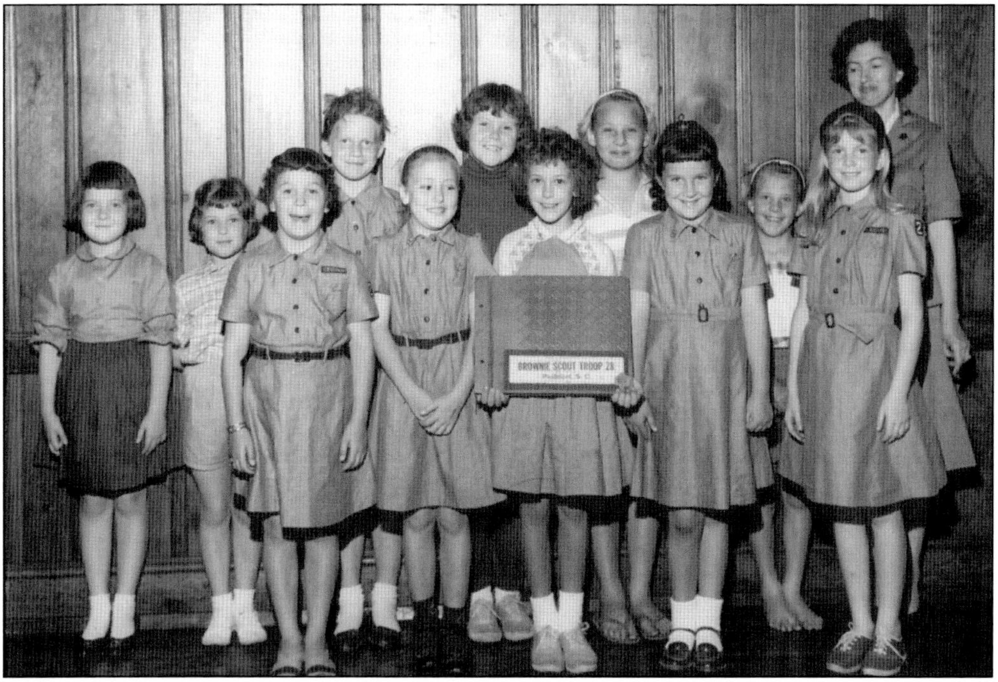

Brownie Scout Troop 28 of Piedmont was led by Betty Davenport. Scout troops met in the Community Building in the 1950s. From left to right are (first row) Marsha Davis, Terri Evans, Tommi Lee Darnell, and Marion Smith; (second row) Dale Grover, Nancy Adkins, Kay Allen, Becky Brown, Diane Oliver, Donna Oliver, and Jane Clifford. (Courtesy of Betty Davenport.)

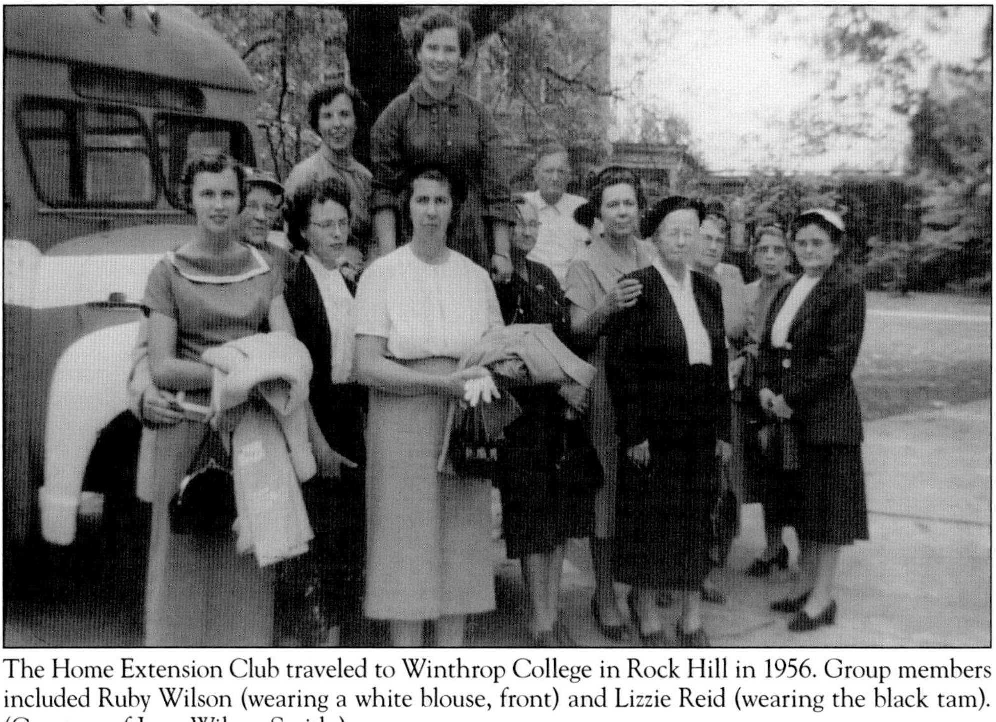

The Home Extension Club traveled to Winthrop College in Rock Hill in 1956. Group members included Ruby Wilson (wearing a white blouse, front) and Lizzie Reid (wearing the black tam). (Courtesy of Joan Wilson Smith.)

Three

The Mill

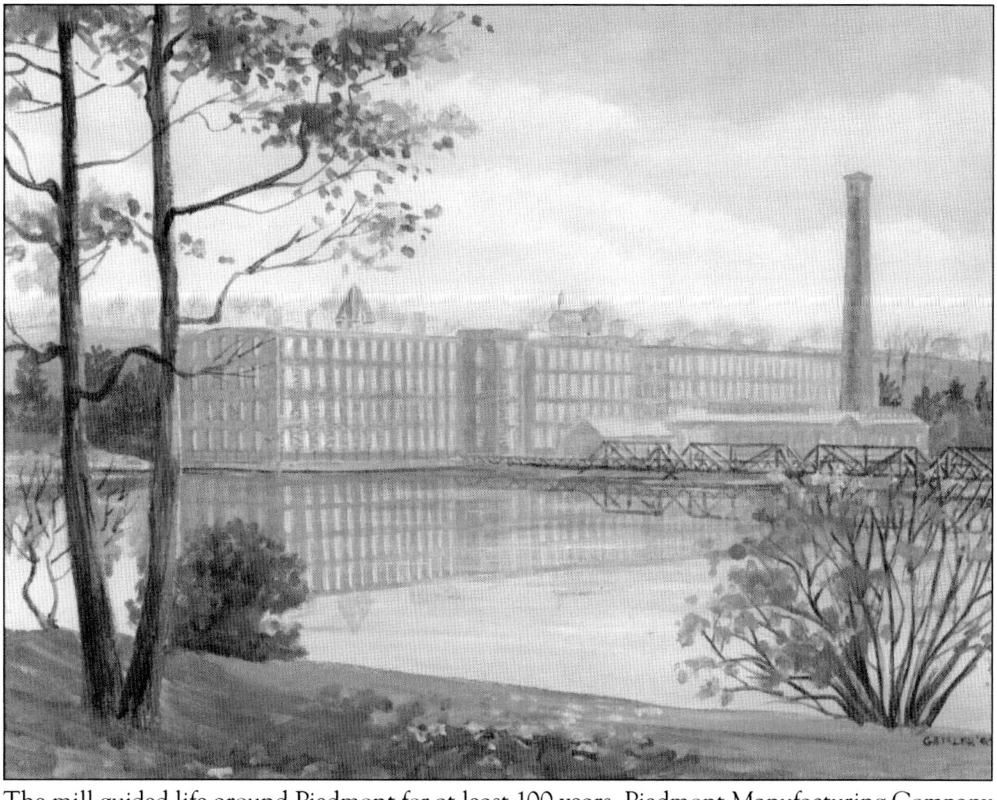

The mill guided life around Piedmont for at least 100 years. Piedmont Manufacturing Company opened in 1874 after much planning and many delays. H.P. Hammett, the first president, worked for many years—including through the Civil War and an economic downturn in the early 1870s—before he was finally able to fund his dream of a textile mill at Garrison Shoals. When Hammett and his board named the company, they also planned to call the mill village the same, so by the opening, Piedmont was founded. (Courtesy of the Bonnes Amies Club.)

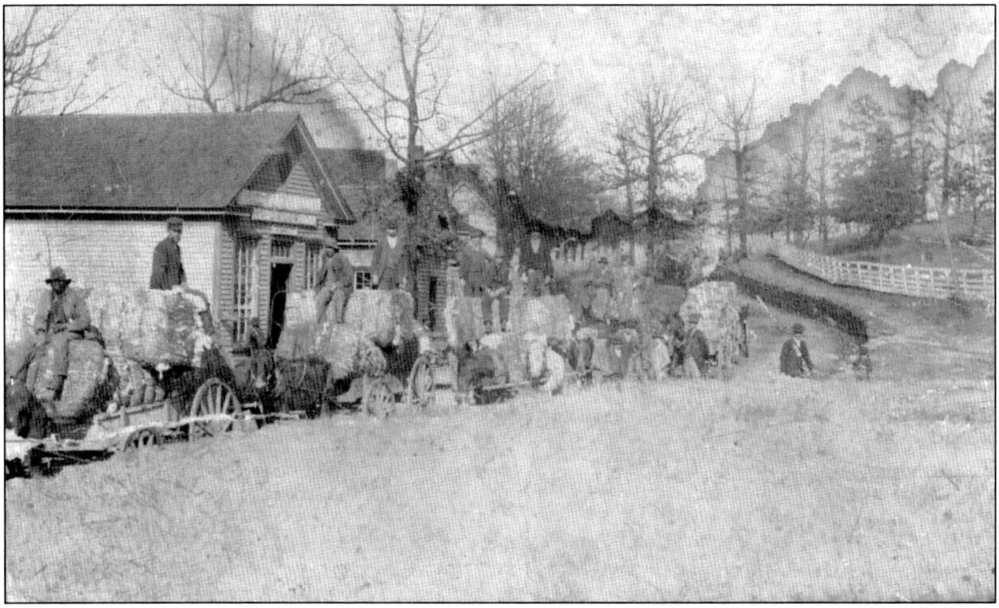

Wagons line up at the Piedmont Manufacturing Office to sell the fall harvest of cotton. Silas F. Trowbridge of the Grove Station community sold the first bale of cotton to Piedmont Manufacturing Company in 1874. He in turn purchased the first roll of cloth for his mercantile store. His youngest daughter was Sue Trowbridge Cleveland. (Courtesy of Piedmont Historical Collection.)

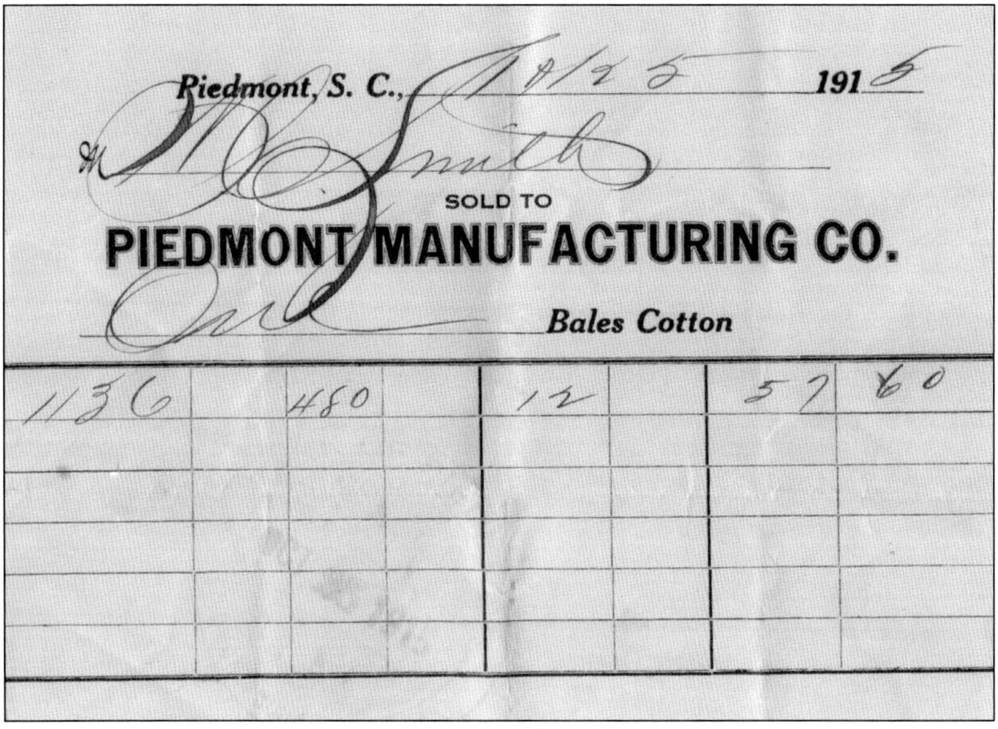

Piedmont, S. C., 191

SOLD TO

PIEDMONT MANUFACTURING CO.

Bales Cotton

In 1915, Walter C. Smith Sr. sold 12 bales of cotton for $4.80 per bale to the Piedmont Manufacturing Company. This original receipt is held by his great-granddaughter Gayle Smith Payne. (Courtesy of Gayle Payne.)

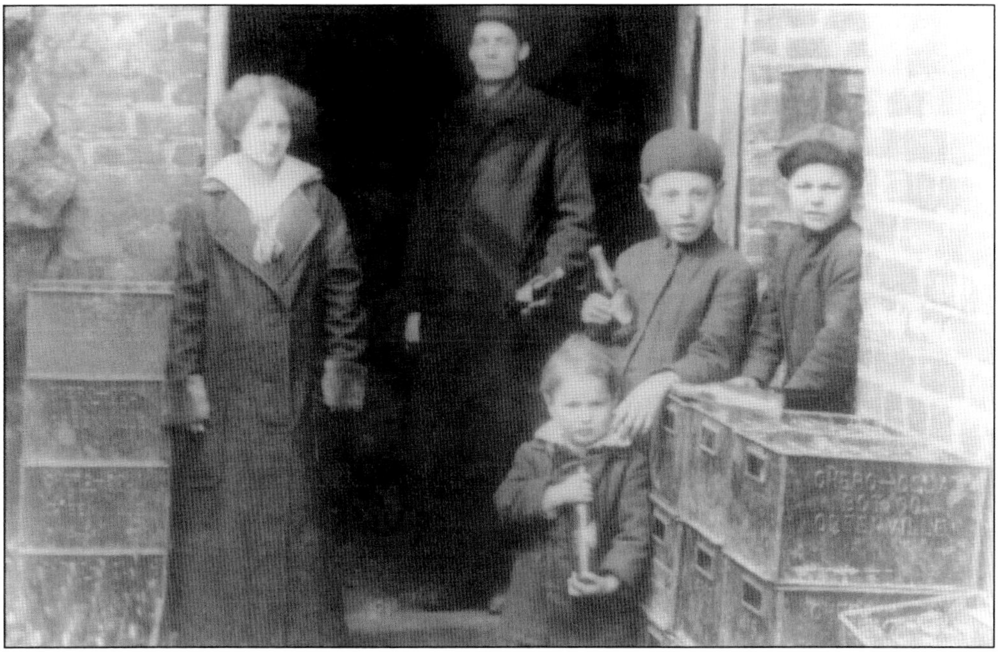

In 1914, the mill canteen entrance was a meeting place for Essie Brown Reeves and "Doc" Reeves, who managed the canteen. The children pictured are Bennett, Roy, and Willie Reeves. The stacks of drink crates hold Chero-Cola, which was created in 1913 in Georgia and was distributed from several bottlers locally. Chero-Cola later became known as RC Cola. (Courtesy of Dan Reeves.)

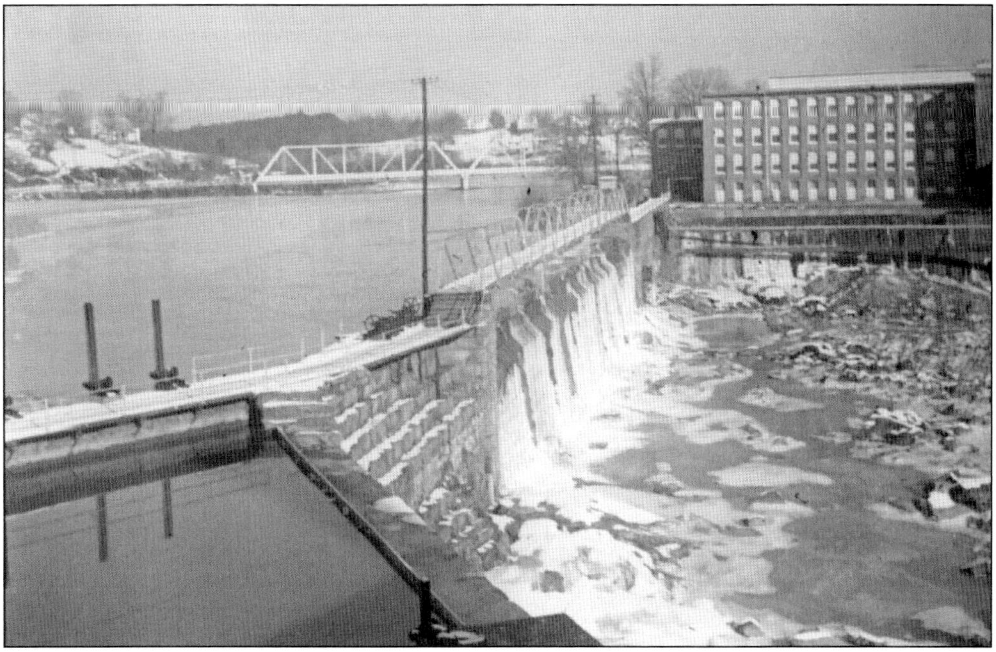

This view overlooking Mill No. 1 shows the footbridge and the surrounding area covered in snow. The dam was built in 1888, and the steel bridge in the background was replaced in 1948 with a concrete structure that still remains over the Saluda River. (Courtesy of Phil and Becky Buckheister.)

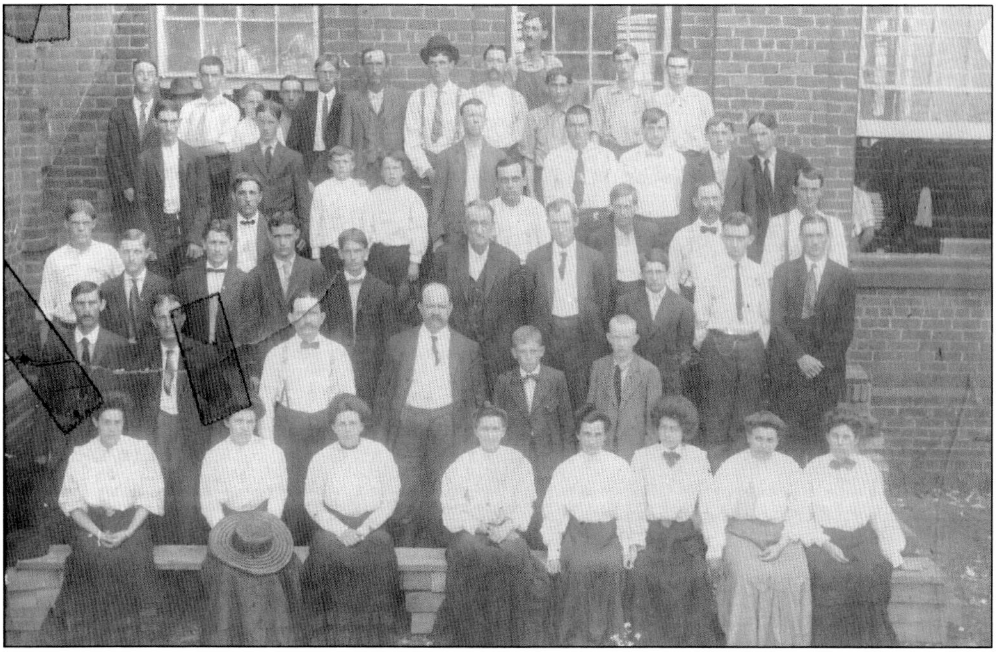

These mill workers in the mid-1880s labored in the spinning room, card room, cloth room, and weave room. Children would go to work in the mill as young as six to eight years of age. Their salary would be between $3 and $5 monthly. Frank Shirley went to work at the age of six and worked until he was 86. (Courtesy of Phil and Becky Buckheister.)

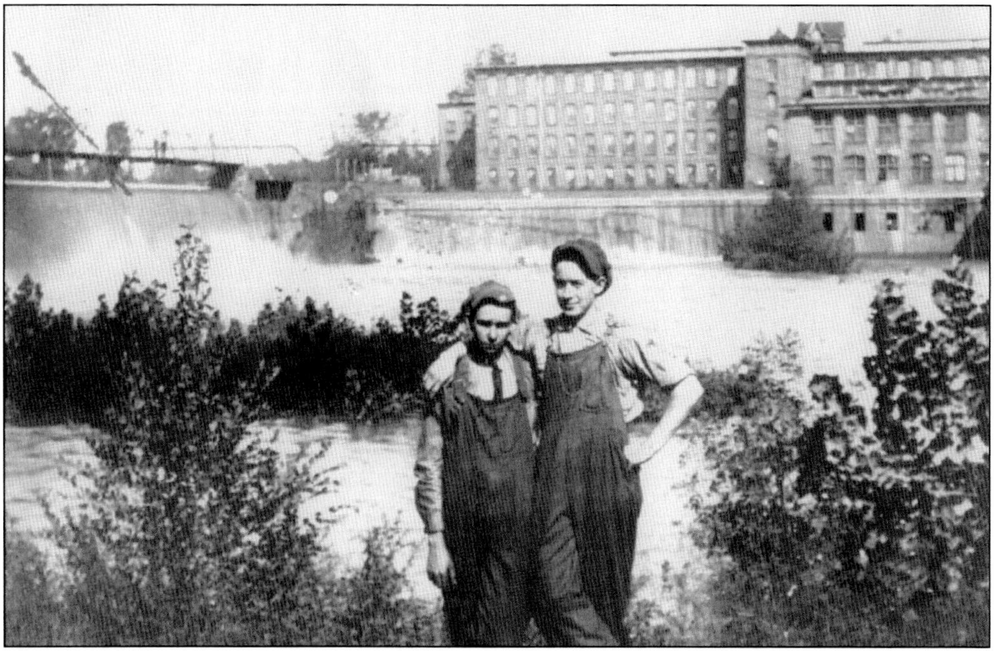

Standing below the dam in the 1930s are J.D. Hughey (left) and J.W. Fletcher. Mill No. 1 in Greenville County and Mill No. 3 in Anderson County were connected by the historic footbridge. The Greenville County mill burned down in 1983, and the Anderson County mill closed in February 1985 and was demolished in 1996. (Courtesy of Shirley T. Elrod.)

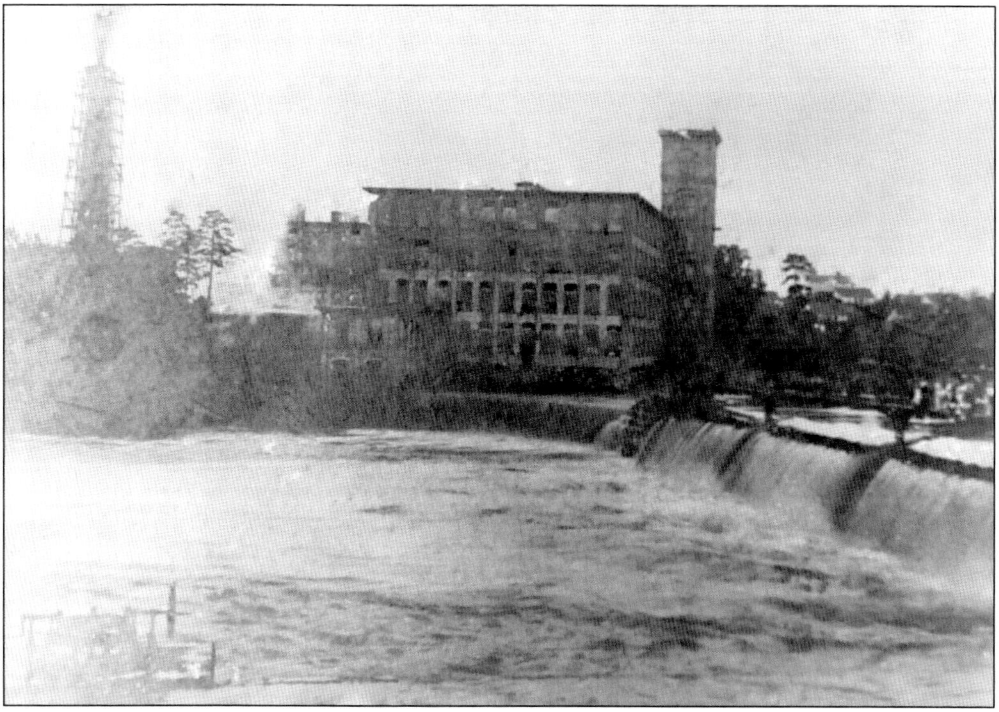

Looking from Greenville County across the imposing Saluda River as it rushes over the dam, the Anderson County mill known as Mill No. 3 is visible. The site of this mill is now a vacant lot; however, the cotton warehouse still stands. (Courtesy of Betty Davenport.)

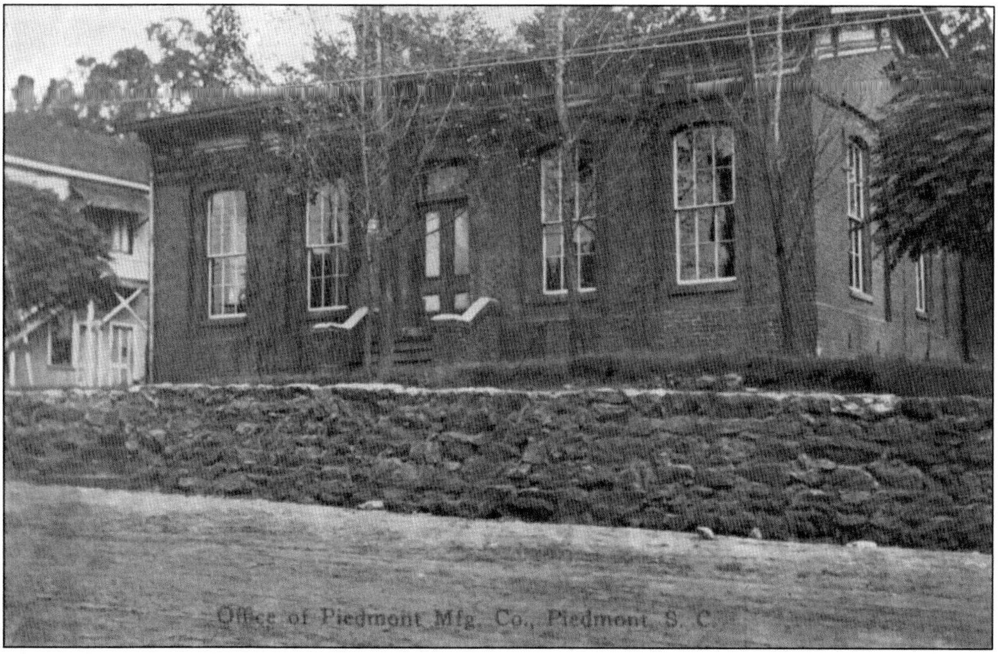

The Piedmont Manufacturing mill office was located on Main Street beside the present Community Building. The mill office housed the superintendent's office and the payroll department. This building is no longer standing. (Courtesy of Margaret Payne.)

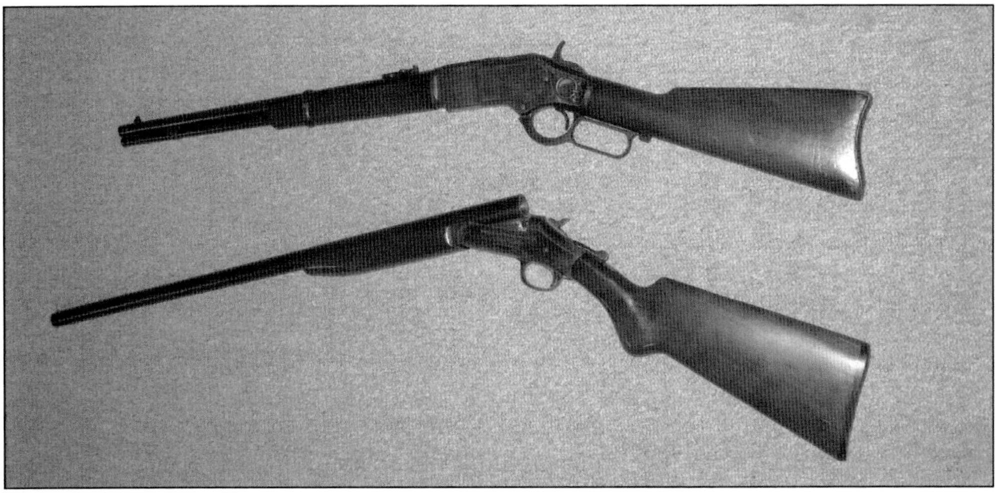

In early 1934, the first hint of unionization crept into the Piedmont Manufacturing Company. W.E. Beattie, the mill's president, ordered "any Yankee-inspired organizing activity to be nipped in the bud." The mill gave Mr. E.V. "Slick" Trammell this Winchester Model 1873 rifle and Walter E. Gaillard this Harrington & Richardson 12 gauge single-shot shotgun. Along with these guns came the orders to "shoot if necessary." The overseers and trusted employees watched from the top of buildings as the unionizers arrived in Piedmont. The procession circled downtown Piedmont, proceeded up Main Street, and headed back to Greenville without ever stopping. (Courtesy of Anne Peden.)

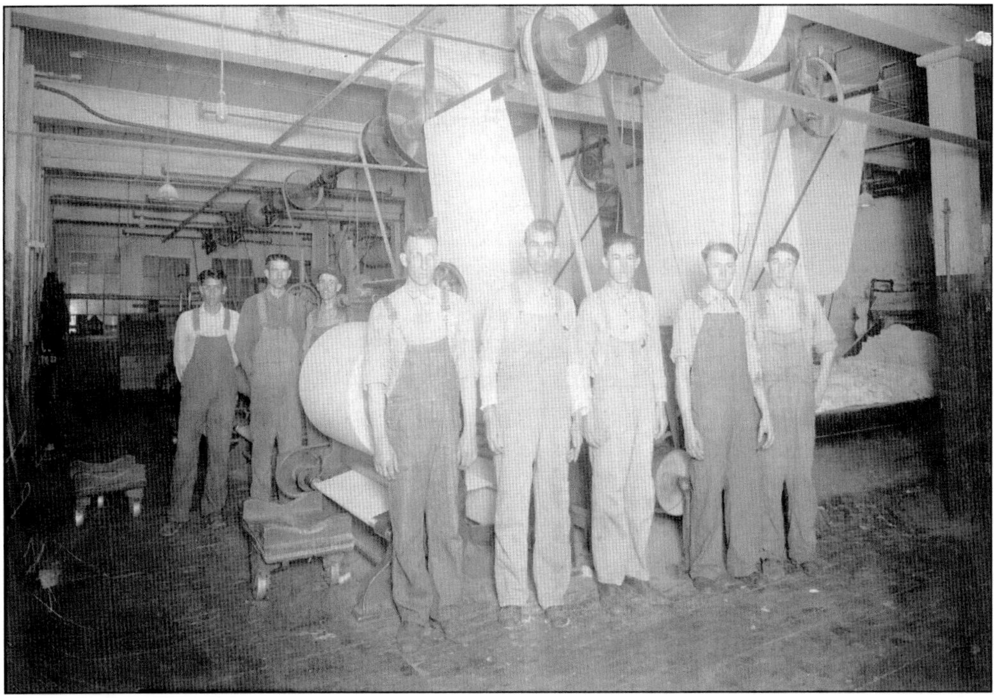

In this 1936 photograph, employees of Piedmont Manufacturing Company's Mill No. 1 stand around huge rolls of cloth. From left to right are (first row) Heyward Davenport, Olander McCall, Clyde Bowen, Luther Cason, and William Tollison; (second row) Lionel Roper, Guy Owens, and Cliff White. (Courtesy of Piedmont Historical Collection.)

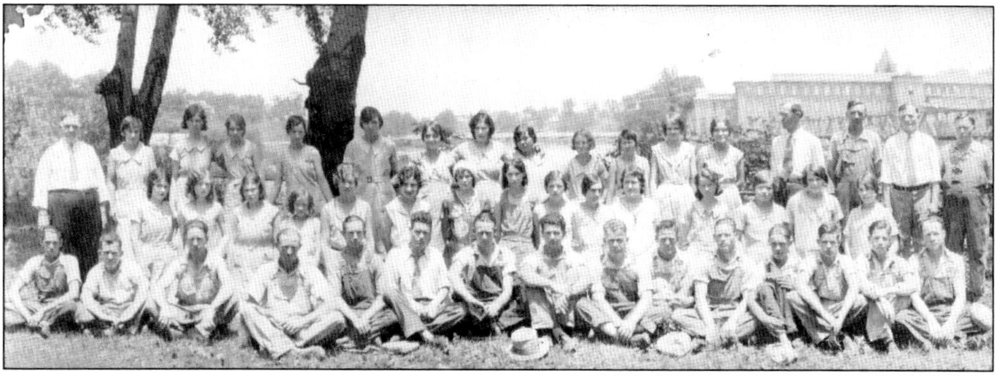

With the mill and the footbridge in the background, the workers from the spinning room of Mill No. 3 in Anderson County pose for a photograph in the 1930s. (Courtesy of Robert Elrod.)

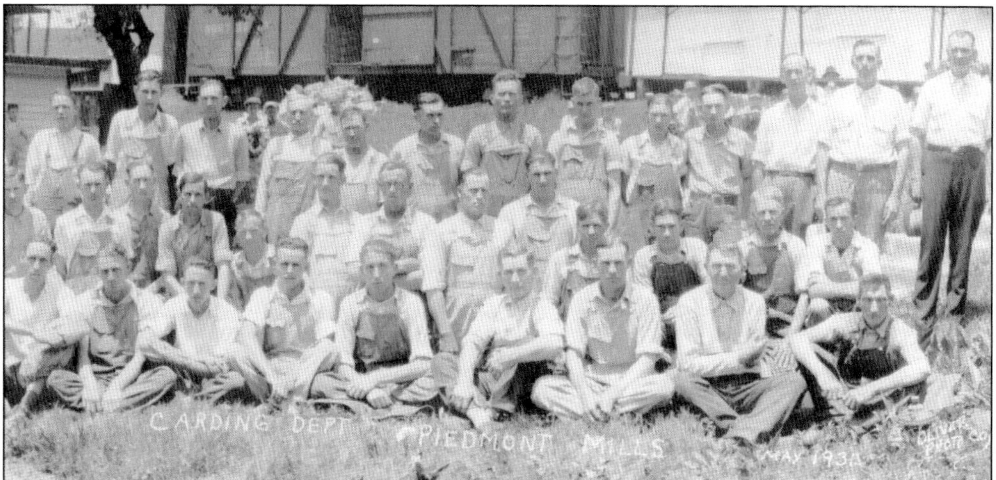

In 1931, workers in the carding department of Piedmont Manufacturing Company gathered for a photograph beside the railroad tracks that ran to the mill. Among those pictured are Floyd Woodson and Milton Glenn. (Courtesy of Frances Evans.)

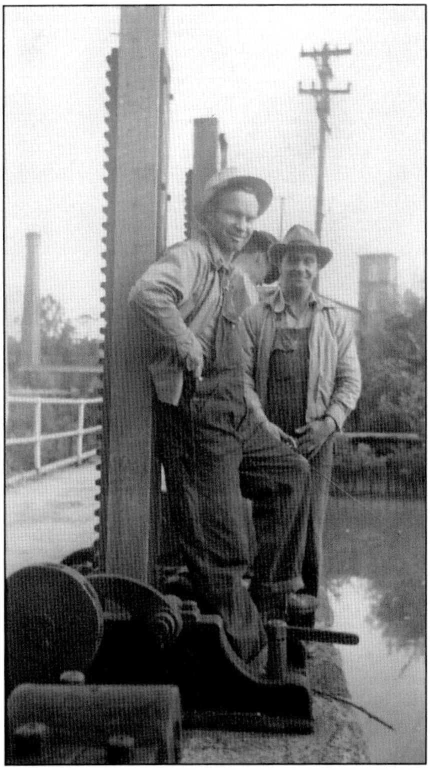

These three men were getting ready to raise the gates to allow water to flow over the dam. This was part of their job at Piedmont Manufacturing Company when excessive rain caused the river to rise too high. Note the Anderson County mill's smokestack on the right and the Greenville County mill's smokestack on the left. (Courtesy of Pert Clifford.)

The bridge at Brickyard Lake was used in transporting all of the bricks that were produced for the construction of Piedmont Manufacturing Company. Mr. Sauls was in charge of brick production, and Brickyard Lake was sometimes referred to as "Sauls Lake." This bridge was constructed across a portion of the brick pond to enable the handcrafted building blocks to be moved more easily to the mills and town, where they were used to create the most up-to-date cotton town in the area. The brick pond was located north of the current bridge, up the Saluda a couple hundred yards on the Anderson side, along River Road. (Courtesy of Betty Davenport and Piedmont Historical Collection.)

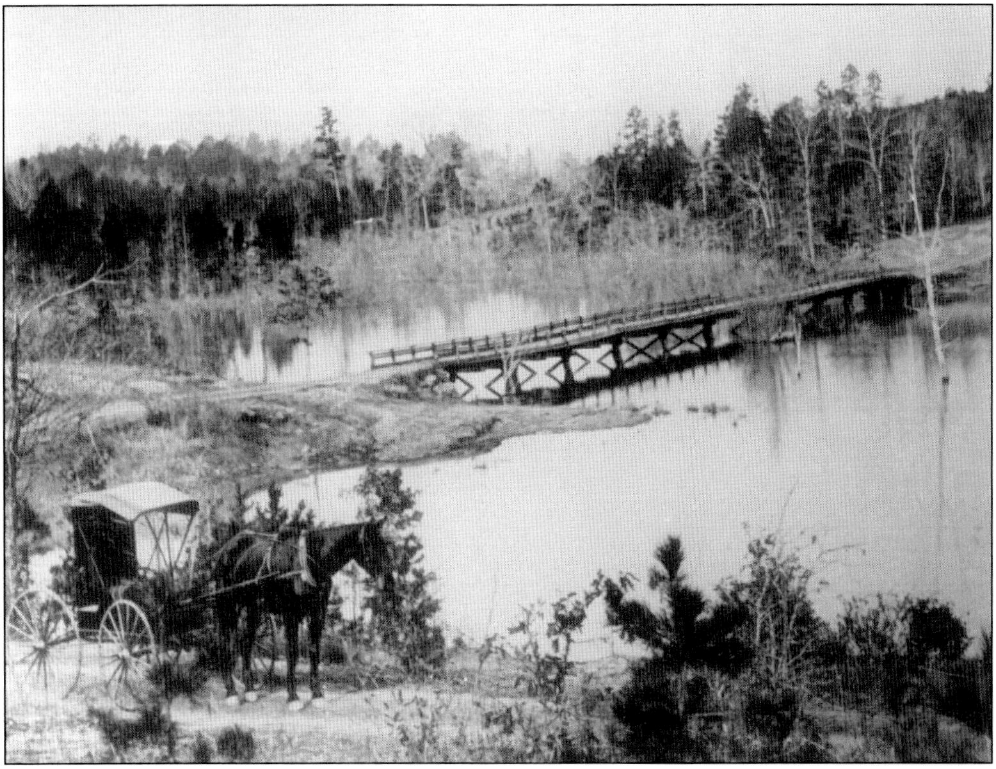

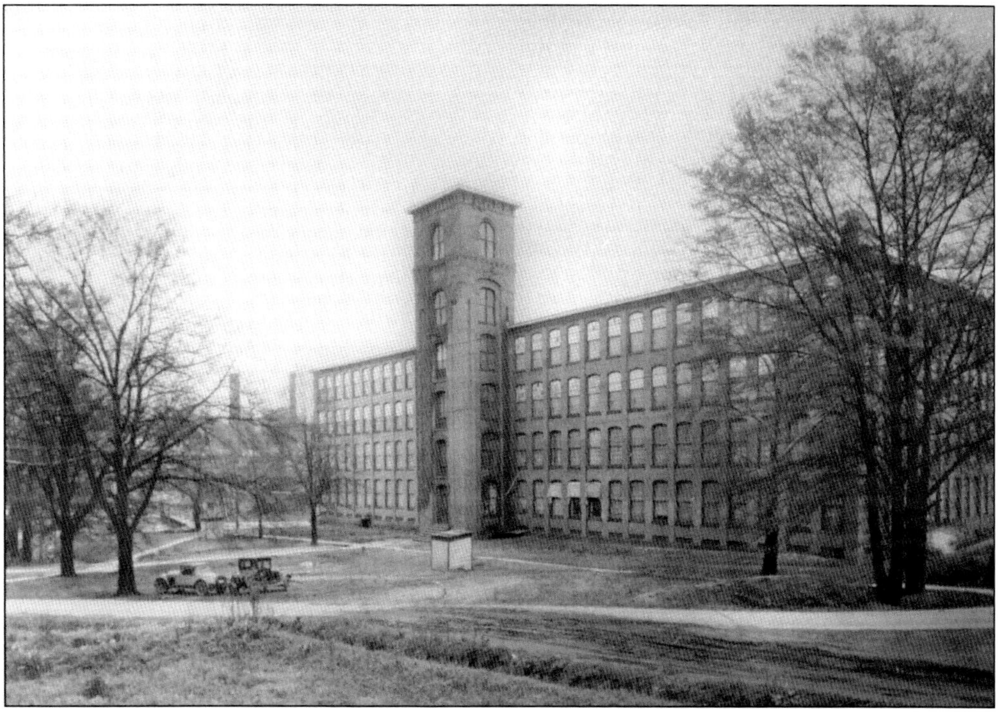

In 1882, Piedmont Manufacturing enlarged its production by constructing a mill on the west bank of the Saluda River in Anderson County. It was referred to as Mill No. 3. In the triangle between the sidewalks, a sign informs workers of the movie being shown at the Village Theater. (Courtesy of Piedmont Historical Collection.)

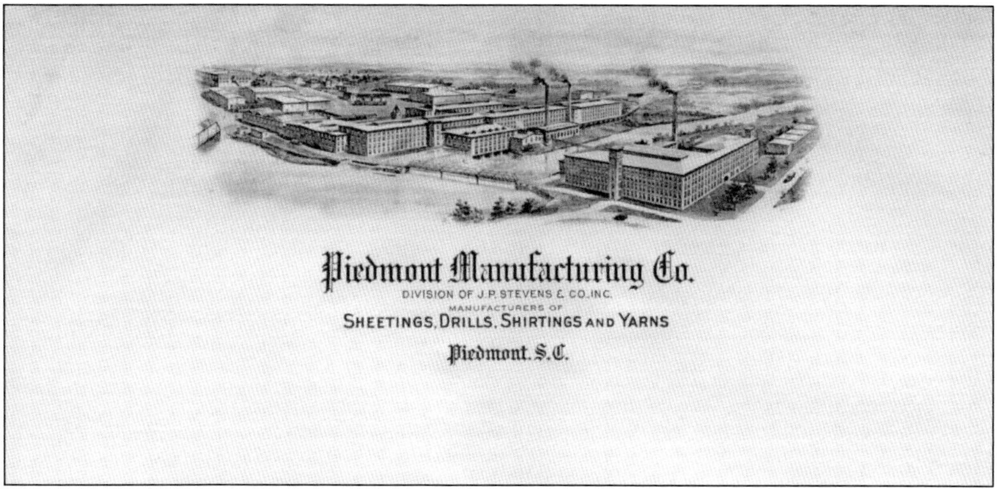

This photograph was taken between 1918 and 1925; however, it was used as the letterhead for the mill's stationery after J.P. Stevens purchased the plant in 1946. (Courtesy of Piedmont Historical Collection.)

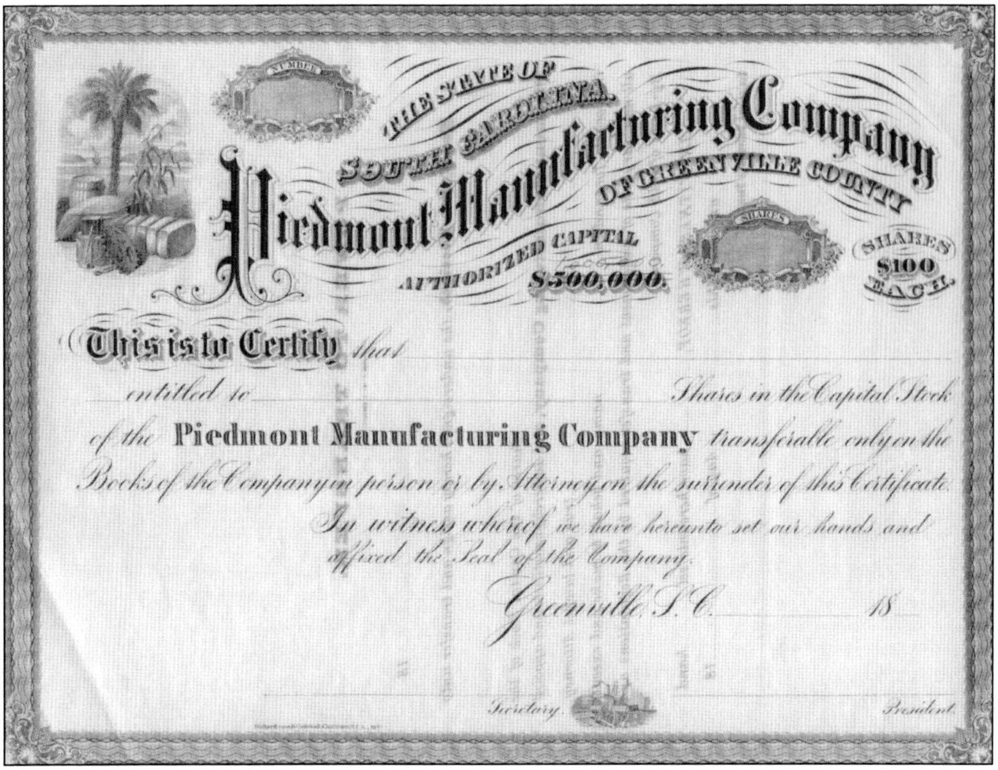

This is a copy of one of the original shares of stock from Piedmont Manufacturing Company in the 1800s. Notice that the cost was $100 and the capital was $500,000. By the 20th century, the cost had gone down to $20 and the capital had risen to $1.6 million. (Courtesy of the Shuler Jones family.)

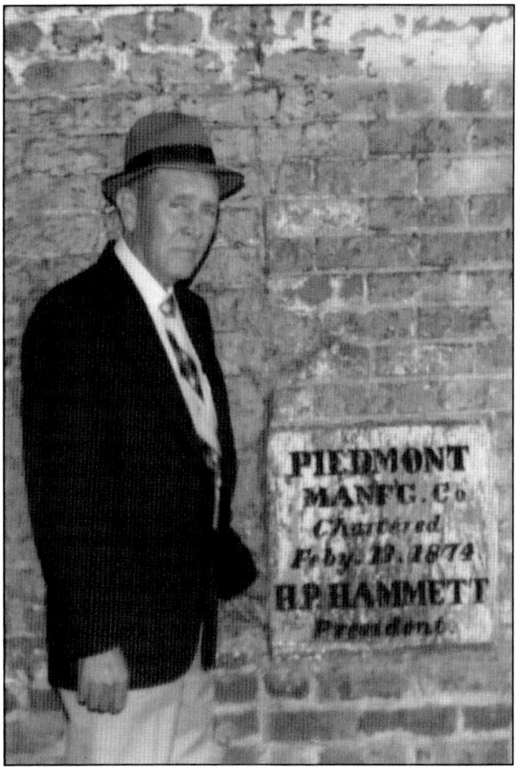

Piedmont Manufacturing Company has left its mark on business history. Truman Jenkins, longtime superintendent of Piedmont Manufacturing Company, was born and raised in Piedmont. He began his textile career as a cloth doffer and sweeper in the weave room and worked his way up through the ranks. Here, he is pictured beside the cornerstone of Mill No. 1 in Greenville County. This stone was removed and placed in the Piedmont Community Building along with other Piedmont manufacturing artifacts. (Courtesy of Piedmont Historical Collection.)

Although the original Piedmont plant, Mill No. 1, was designated a National Historical Landmark in 1978, it lost that designation when it burned down. This plaque is displayed in the Community Building. (Courtesy of Piedmont Historical Collection.)

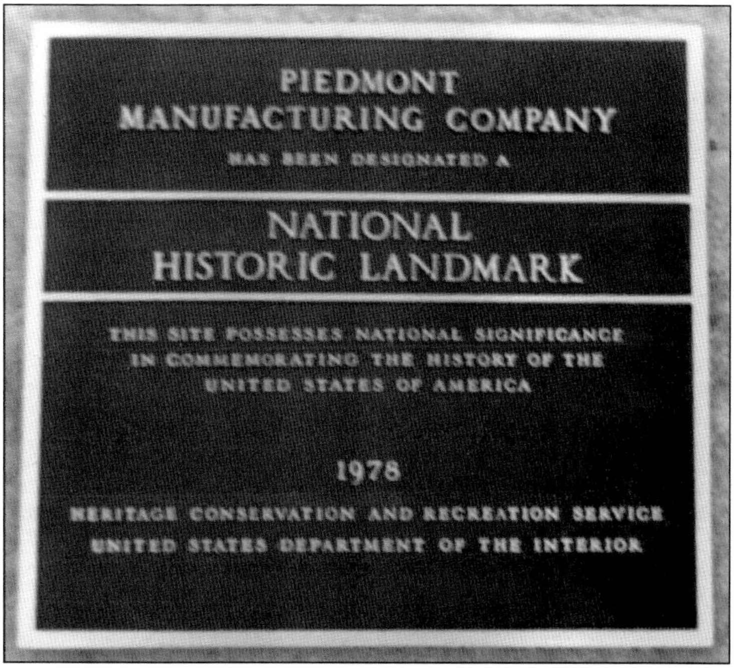

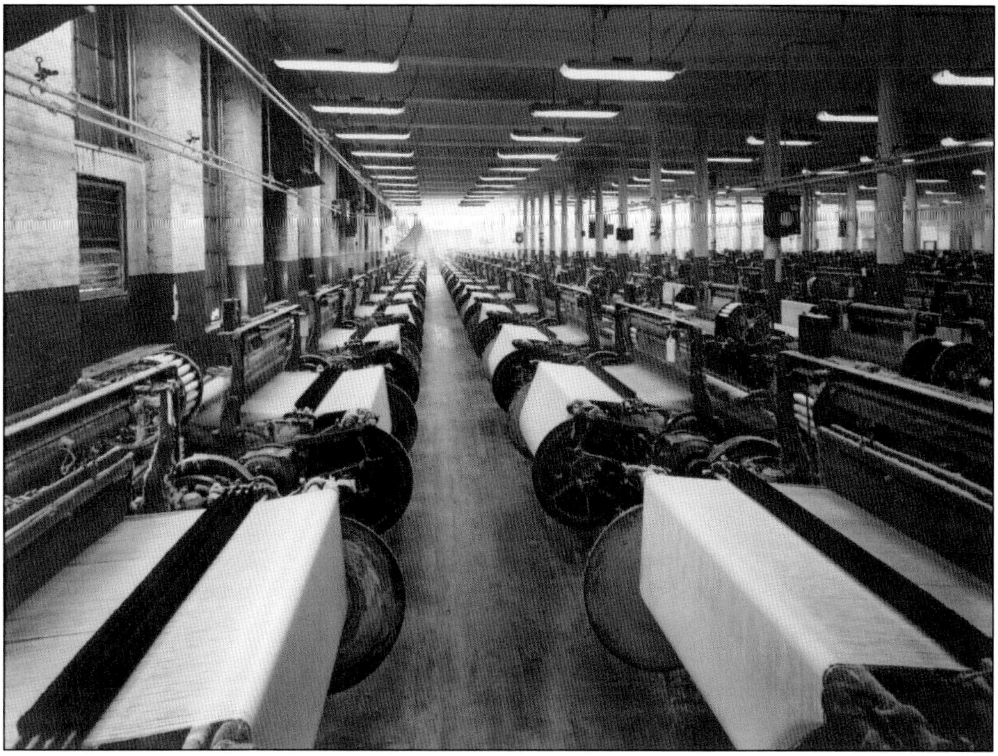

This 1950s photograph of the first-floor weave room in Mill No. 3 shows the update from narrow to wide looms. This weave room produced cloth from 1888 to 1996. Mill No. 3 was one of the first plants to export cloth to China, and the China market dominated its sales for two decades. (Courtesy of Piedmont Historical Collection.)

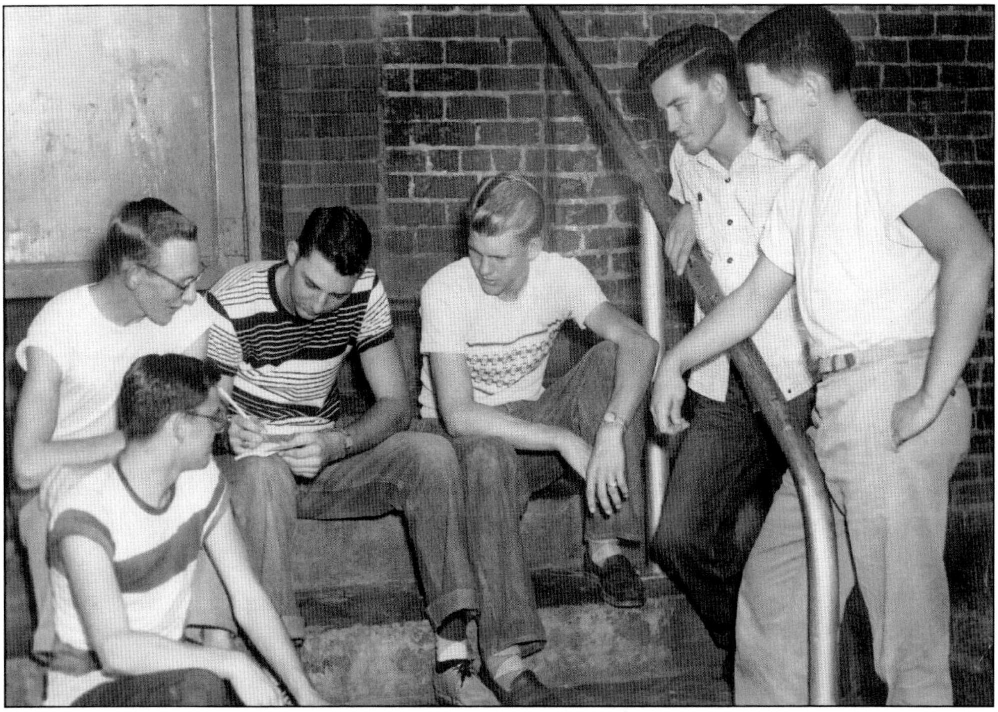

The summer help (clockwise from front left)—Stanley Gilreath, Jimmy Richey, Bill Burden, Charles Blackston, Bill Golden, and Marion "Pick" Picklesimer—take a break from their jobs on the steps of Piedmont Manufacturing Company in 1953. (Courtesy of Jimmy Richey.)

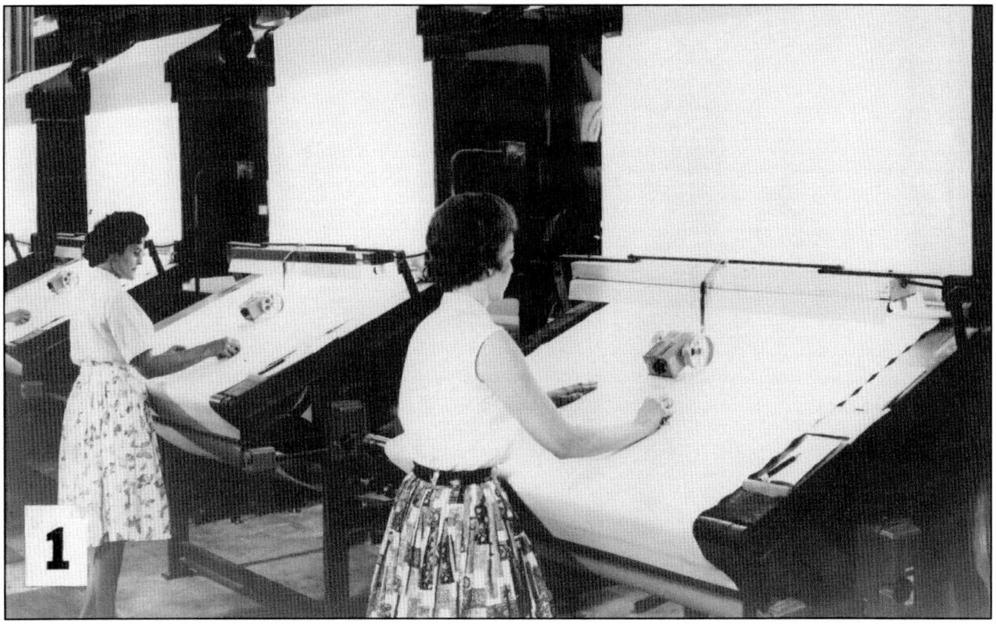

In 1964, a new plant owned by J.P. Stevens began manufacturing. Here, Shirley Norris (left) and Polly Reeves inspect cloth at the new Estes Plant. In 1965, the Estes Plant was named a top 10 plant in the United States. It operated as a J.P. Stevens facility until June 30, 1986, when it was sold to Delta Mills. (Courtesy of Piedmont Historical Collection.)

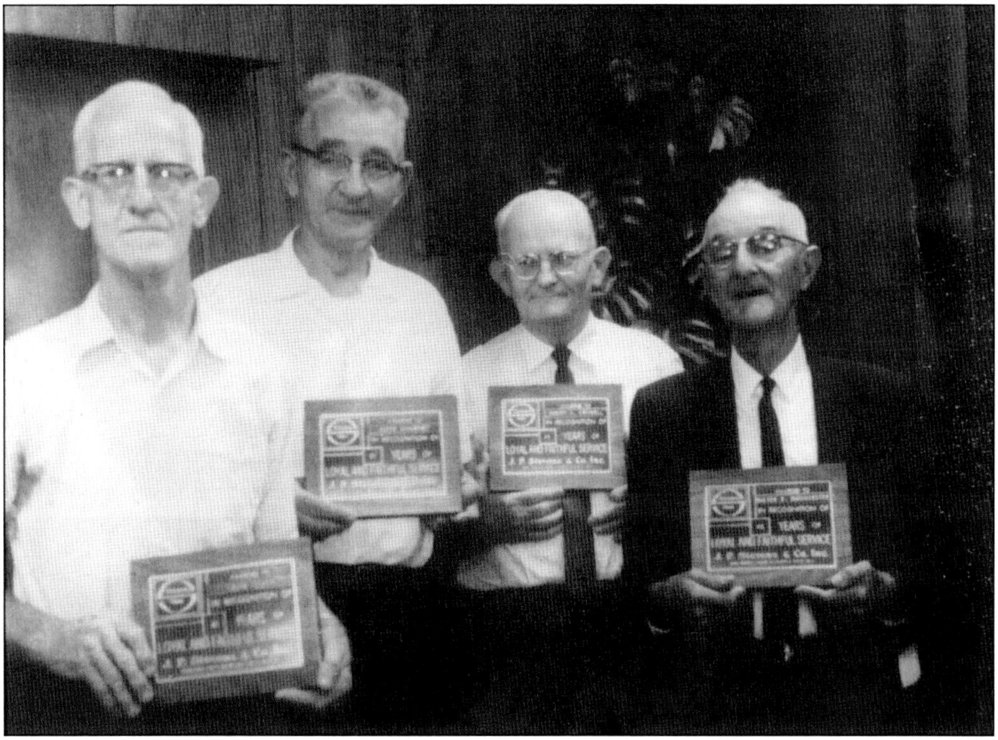

From left to right, Mr. Looper, Robert Creswell, Oscar Davenport, and William Walter Buckhiester receive plaques for 63 years of service at J.P. Stevens. (Courtesy of Phil and Becky Buckhiester.)

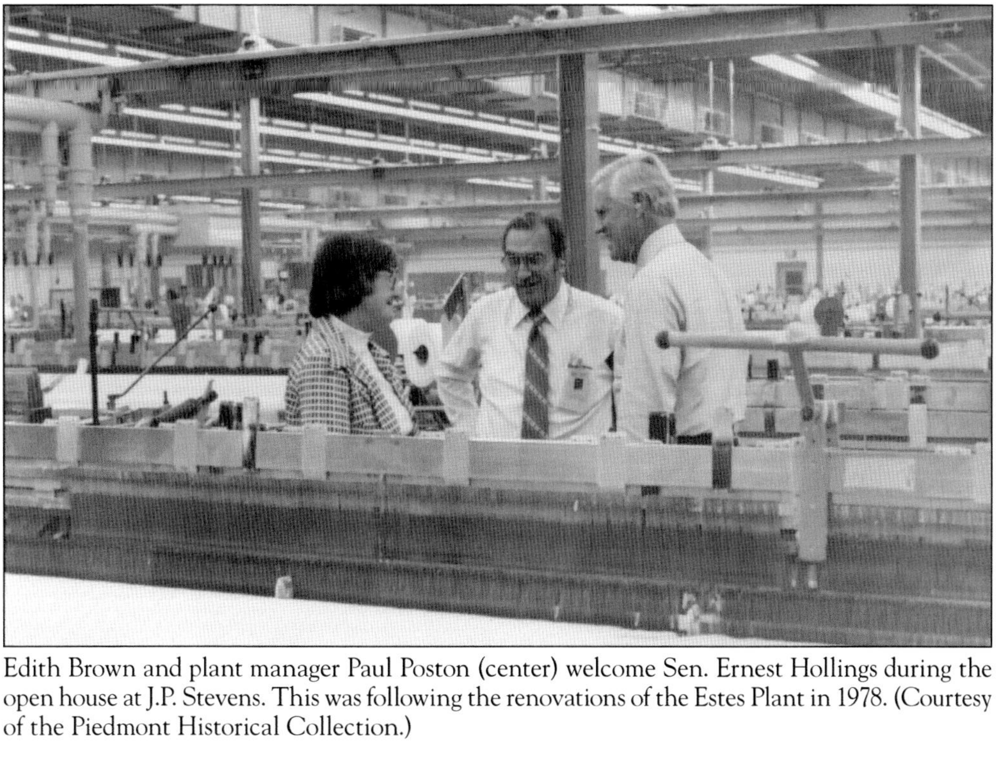

Edith Brown and plant manager Paul Poston (center) welcome Sen. Ernest Hollings during the open house at J.P. Stevens. This was following the renovations of the Estes Plant in 1978. (Courtesy of the Piedmont Historical Collection.)

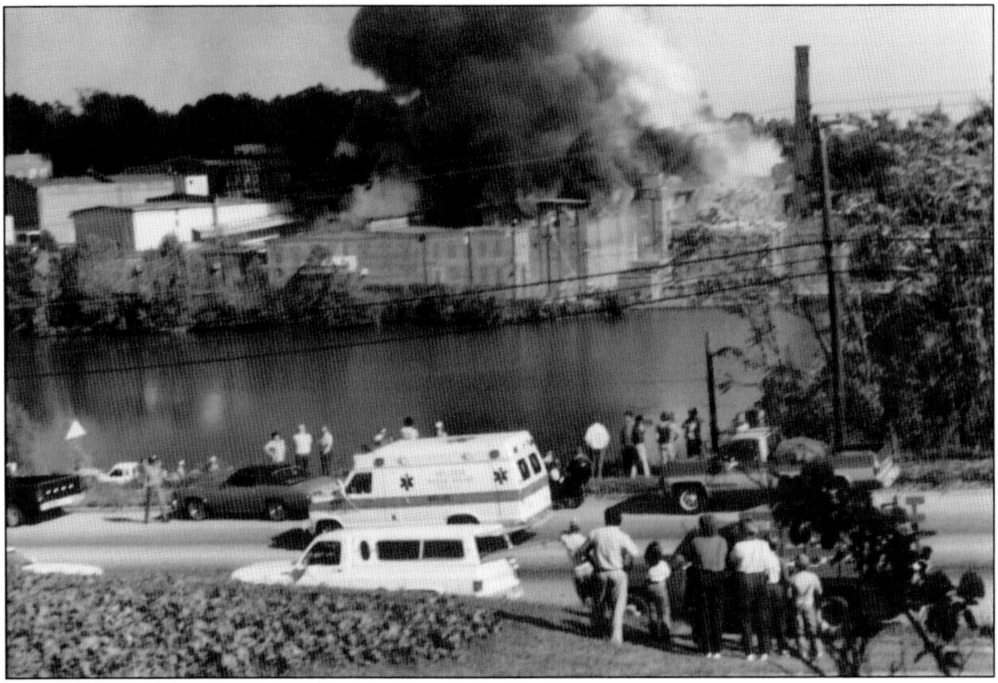

On October 26, 1983, life in Piedmont changed forever. The buildings that once made up one of the largest textile mills in the world burned as the town watched. The four-story structure with three-foot-thick plaster walls and oil-soaked maple floors was soon reduced to rubble. (Courtesy of Betty T. White.)

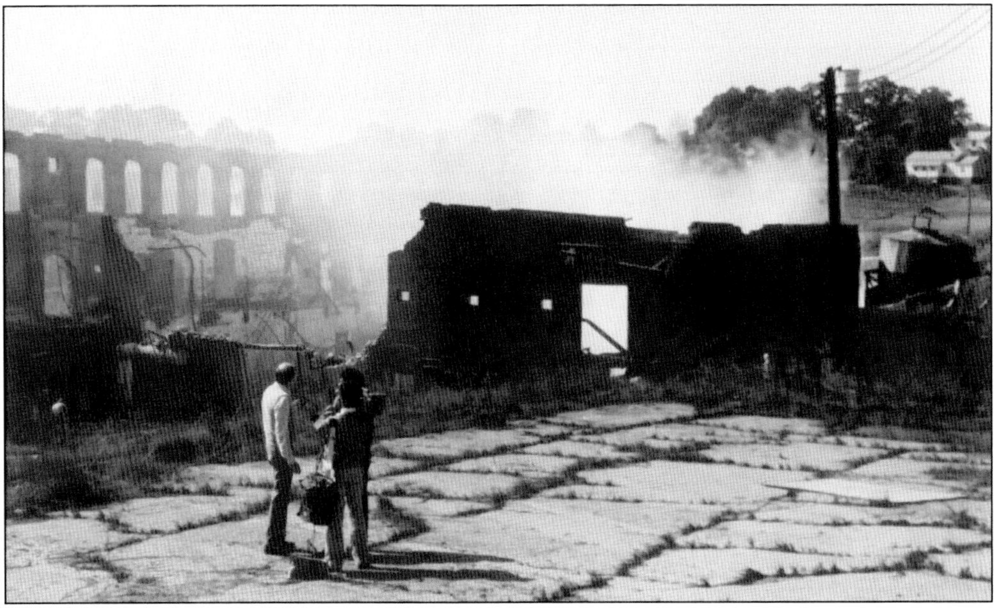

Fire Chief Doug Cowart (left) and a photographer view the smoking ruins of Piedmont Manufacturing. (Courtesy of Pert Clifford.)

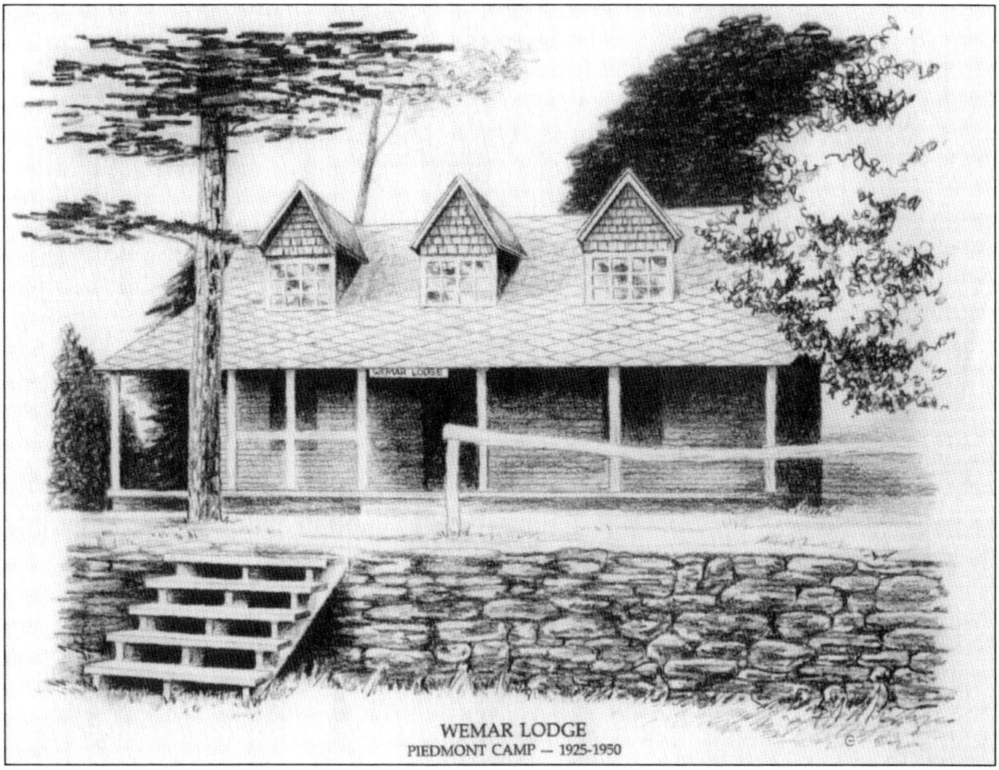

In addition to supporting the everyday lives of its workers, the mill also provided recreation. A Fourth of July celebration was always held, and a camp was established at Cedar Mountain, North Carolina. Mill employees and their families were able to enjoy the facilities at Wemar Lodge free of charge. (Courtesy of Pert Clifford.)

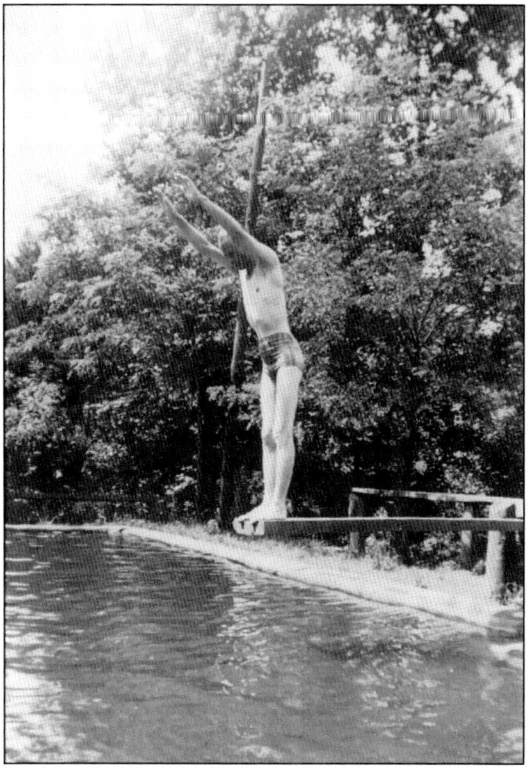

"Ham" Williams prepares to dive into the swimming pool at Piedmont Camp. In the 1990s, Frances Evans and Glen Shirley wrote a book about Piedmont Camp called *Mountain Memories*. The camp was located near the North Carolina border, and employees enjoyed vacationing there for several weeks each year. (Courtesy of Betty White.)

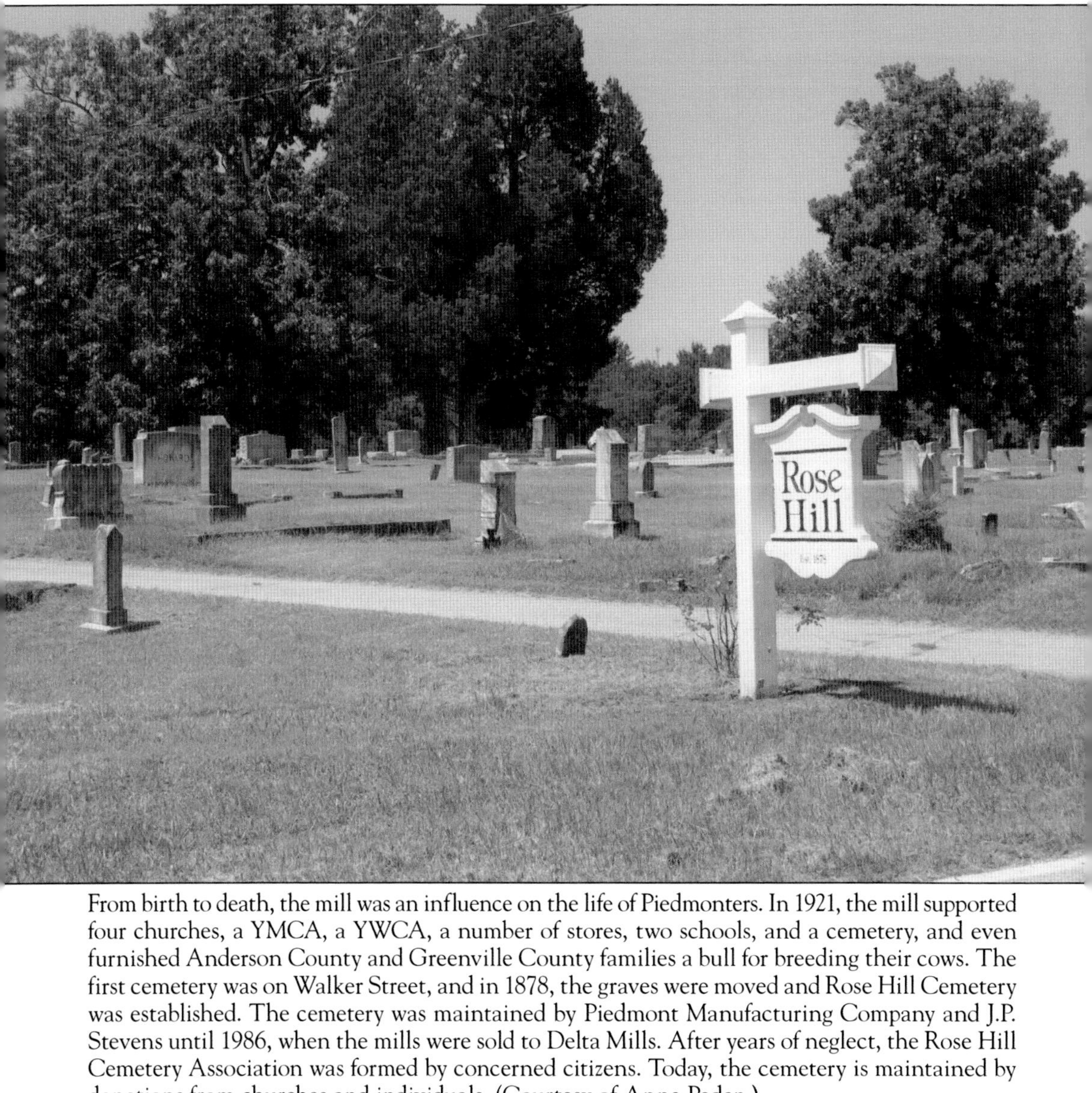

From birth to death, the mill was an influence on the life of Piedmonters. In 1921, the mill supported four churches, a YMCA, a YWCA, a number of stores, two schools, and a cemetery, and even furnished Anderson County and Greenville County families a bull for breeding their cows. The first cemetery was on Walker Street, and in 1878, the graves were moved and Rose Hill Cemetery was established. The cemetery was maintained by Piedmont Manufacturing Company and J.P. Stevens until 1986, when the mills were sold to Delta Mills. After years of neglect, the Rose Hill Cemetery Association was formed by concerned citizens. Today, the cemetery is maintained by donations from churches and individuals. (Courtesy of Anne Peden.)

Four

Businesses

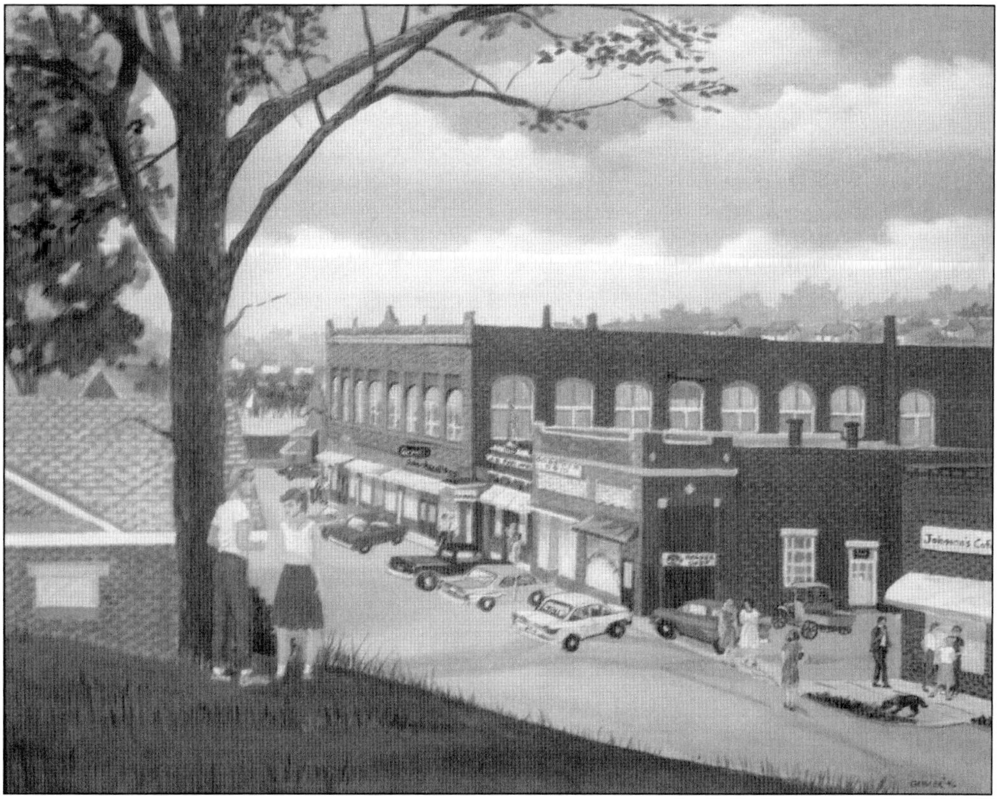

Downtown Piedmont, in its brick form as it exists today, was completed approximately a year after the 10 original stores burned in 1903. In the style of the early 20th century, the storefronts sport iron columns and recessed doorways. This painting represents Main Street around the 1930s. (Courtesy of the Bonnes Amies Club.)

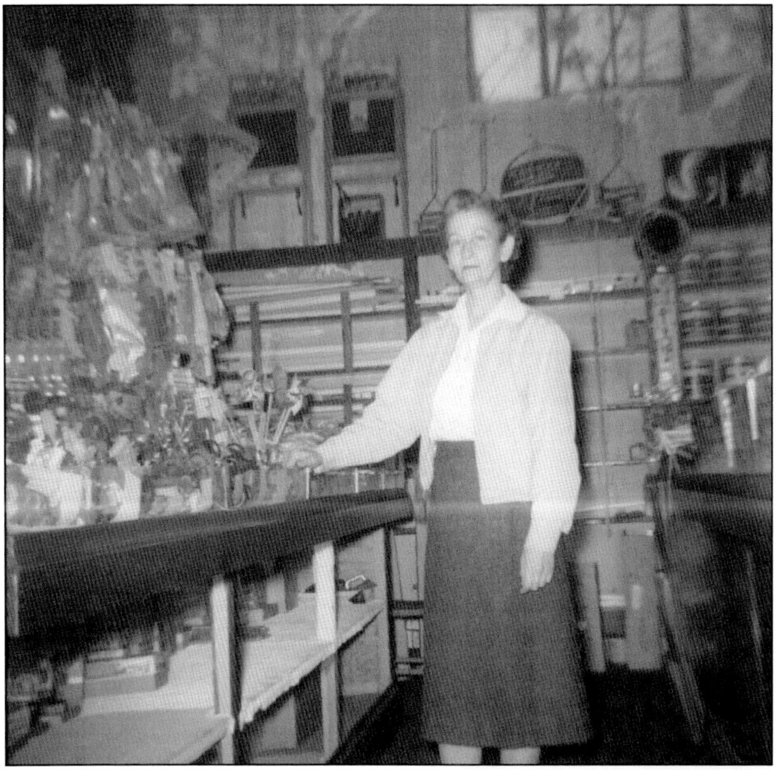

Saleslady Louise T. Evans displays some of the wares of Goldsmith's 5 & 10 store. Located in the downtown area of Main Street, the "Dime Store," as locals called it, was a place where one could find most anything, especially a dime's worth of candy carefully measured out and put in a bag. (Courtesy of Betty White.)

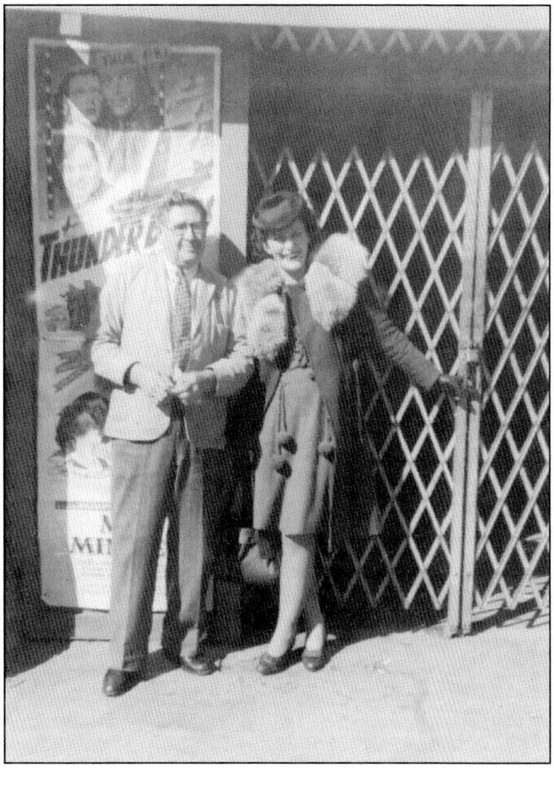

Dr. Barr, Piedmont's druggist, poses with Reba Hollingsworth in front of the Star Theater. Hollingsworth is quite fashionable in her fur-trimmed coat. The poster advertises the popular movie *Thunder Road*, which was currently showing at the Star Theater. The theater provided the people of Piedmont with the latest movies for many years before closing in the early 1960s. (Courtesy of Pert Clifford.)

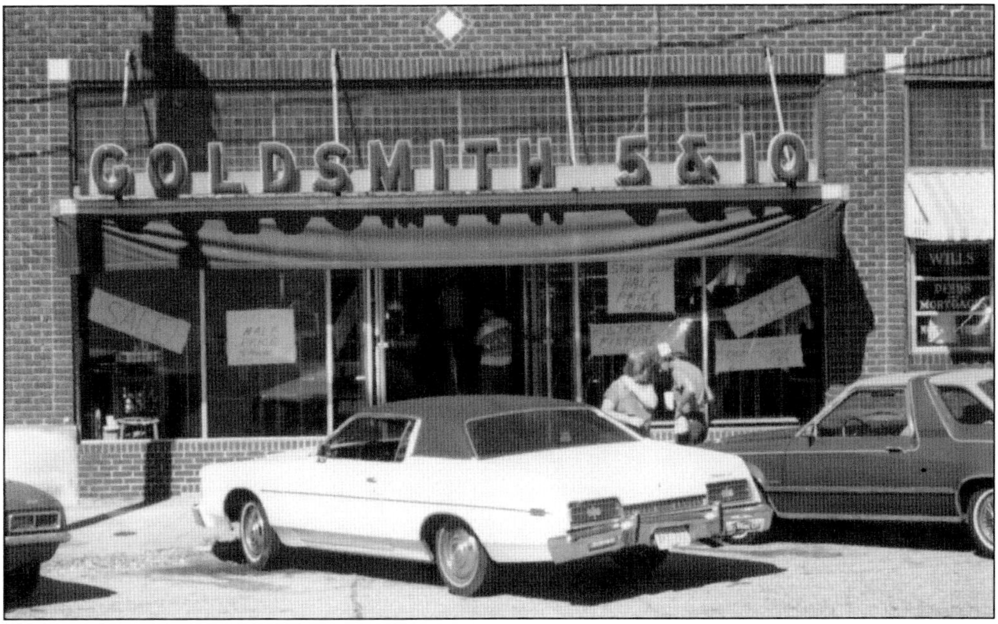

Goldsmith's 5 & 10 store on Main Street is shown here in the 1970s. Signs in the windows indicate that the store was going out of business. The Dime Store was the place all the children wanted to go after their parents completed their business at the bank across the street or one of the many other businesses nearby. Goldsmith's sold toys, candy, housewares, and other miscellaneous items. (Courtesy of Pert Clifford.)

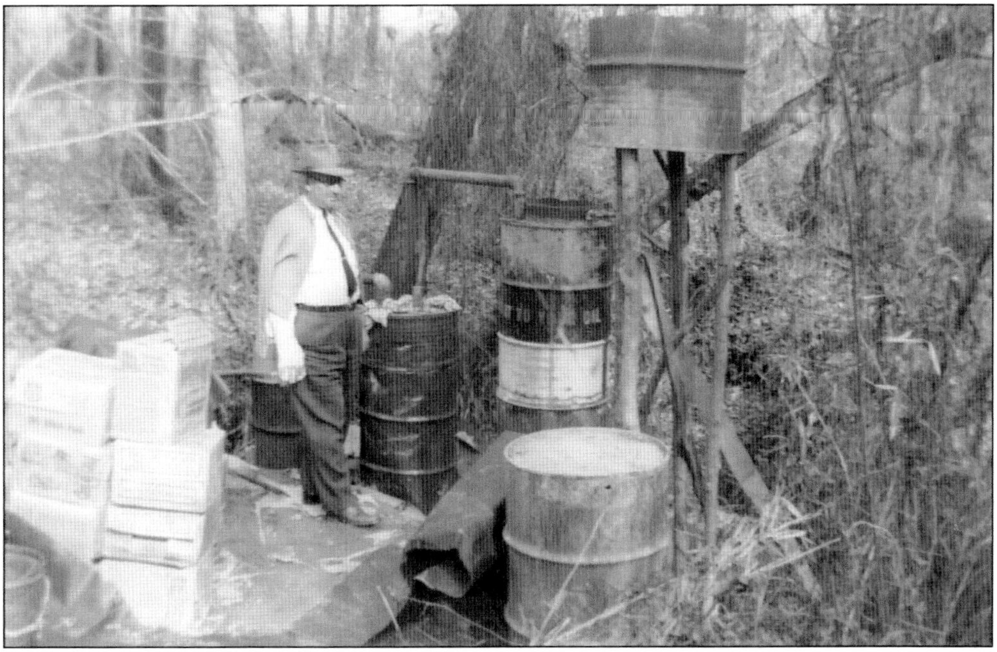

Piedmont's police chief Clarence Hammonds investigates a liquor still found in the mid-1960s. When the leaves fell from the trees in the fall, the still was more exposed and could be easily identified by anyone in the area. The cardboard boxes of jars in the foreground indicate plans to bottle the moonshine after brewing. (Courtesy of Pert Clifford.)

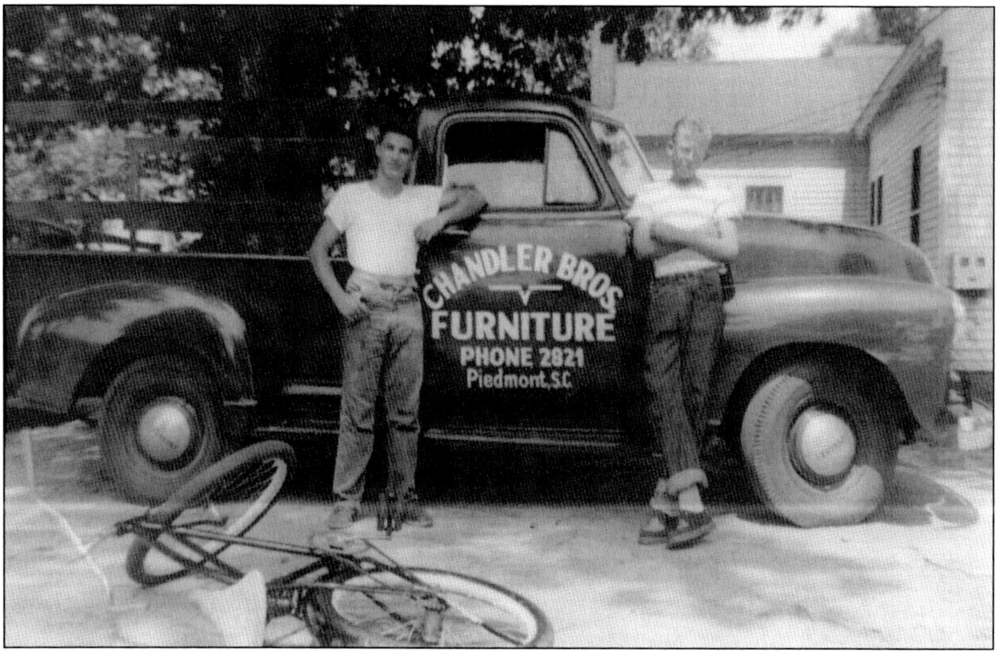

Mike Neal (left) and David Chandler lean against a Chandler Brothers furniture truck. This c. 1950s photograph was taken in the Chandlers' backyard while the boys took a break from their delivery duties. Chandler Brothers was known for its quality furniture, which still graces the homes of many today. (Courtesy of Piedmont Historical Collection.)

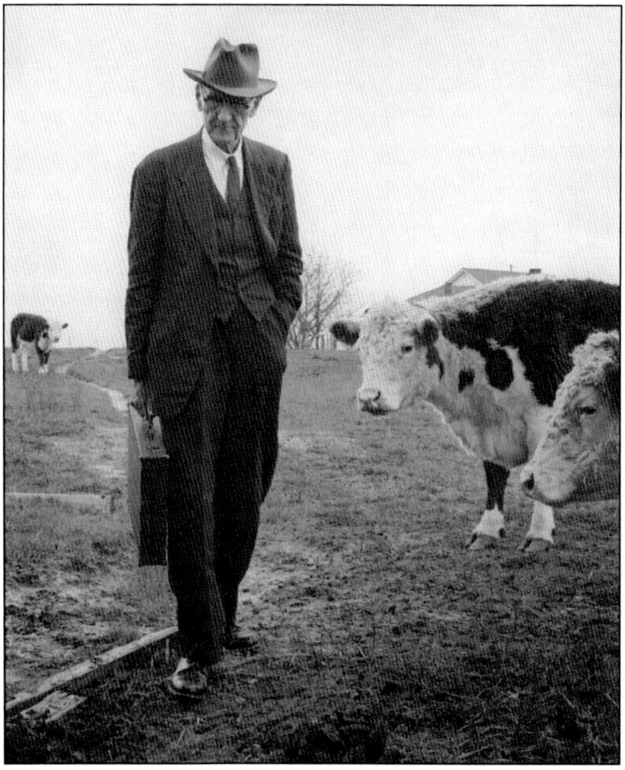

Wid Cason, the local veterinarian, was self-taught and did not have an office. If a sick animal needed care, owners came to his home. Always dressed in a suit with his medicine bag in hand, he is pictured here in the cow pasture of the Gillespie farm. "Doctor" Wid was highly regarded in the village and surrounding area. (Courtesy of Carolyn Reeves.)

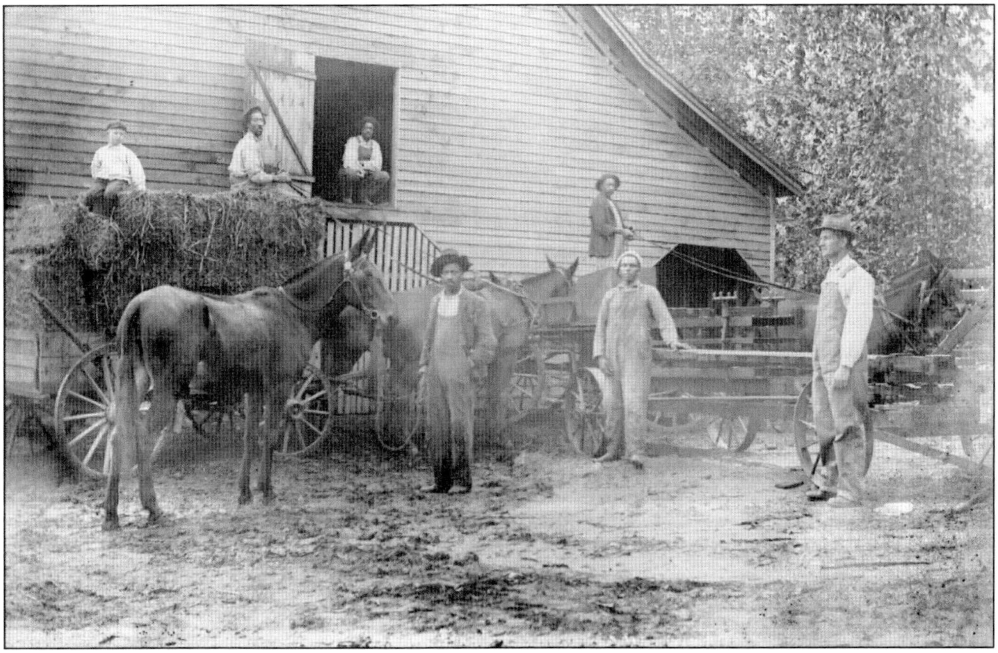

In this 1912 photograph, workers are getting ready to go out into the field to pick cotton. The cotton would then be stored until the price went up (a good price in 1950 was 42¢ per pound). Edward King is pictured on the right, and Sam King is the boy sitting atop the hay. The other men are sharecroppers who lived on the property. (Courtesy of Jo King Hood.)

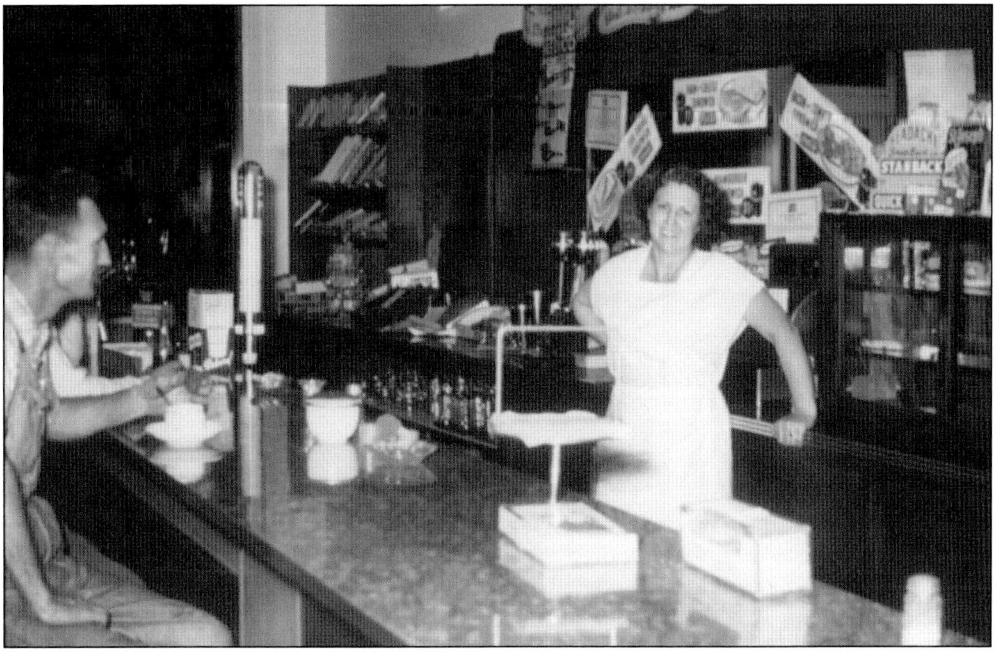

Ruby Peden White ran a successful café on Main Street. In the early 1940s, it was located in the row of businesses near the grocery store. White later moved up the street, where the Downtown Café is currently located. She is pictured in the 1950s serving local customers after the move. (Courtesy of Margaret Payne.)

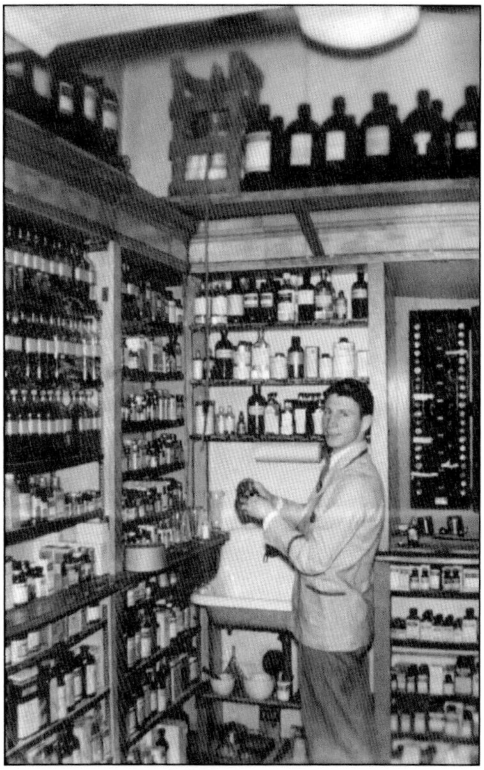

Willard Bishop is hard at work in Suber's Drug Store on Thanksgiving Day in 1941. Rows and rows of elixirs, potions, and pills for every ailment are at hand to serve the people of the mill village. Located on Main Street, Suber's was also known for fountain drinks, ice-cream cones, banana splits, and ice-cream sundaes. (Courtesy of Gayle Payne.)

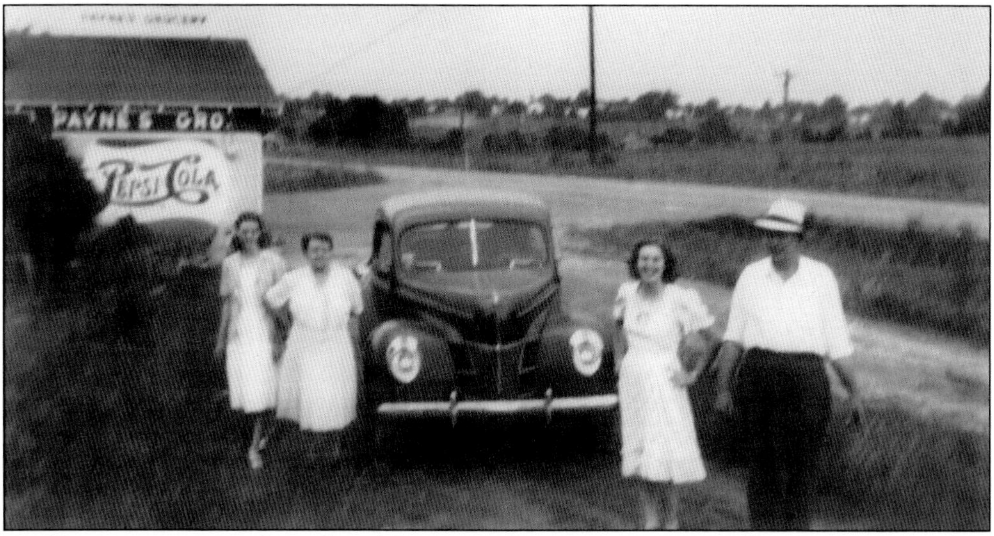

Small groceries were vital to village life. Payne's Grocery was on Bessie Road in 1945. From left to right, Margaret, Blanche, Lillian, and Jim Payne stand next to their car. The store was owned by John Payne, Jim's brother. The family-owned grocery was a convenient stop in Piedmont for locals to buy food and staples with their war ration stamps. Another small store just down the road near New Golden Grove Church was active until the 1970s. It was run by Mae Peden, whose husband, T.K., was a relative of the Paynes. When Mae closed the store, she disposed of boxes filled with note cards that recorded outstanding charges for groceries and gas. Asked why she never collected the debts, she said that folks had babies to feed. (Courtesy of Gayle Payne.)

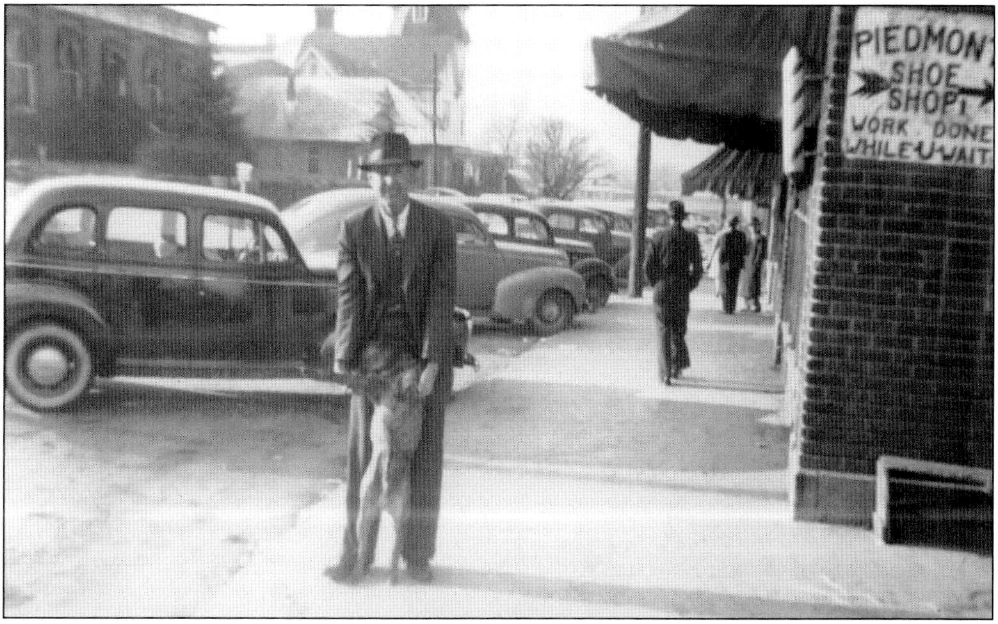

Carl Finley was Piedmont's resident taxi driver. He is pictured here in 1941 with Butch, Margaret Buckhiester's dog. Among the buildings in the left background is the Men's Building before the fire destroyed it in 1943. As evidenced by the many parked cars and the people on the street attending to their shopping and business, it was a busy day in the village. (Courtesy of Phil and Becky Buckhiester.)

Carhop Jack Hart sits at Pete's Drive-In Restaurant on Greenville Street (Highway 20) listening to the latest hits on the jukebox while waiting for customers to drive up. Pete's was a local gathering place for teenagers to hang out and eat. The table and chairs are made of the stylish chrome and Formica that were so popular in the 1950s. (Courtesy of Joe Evans.)

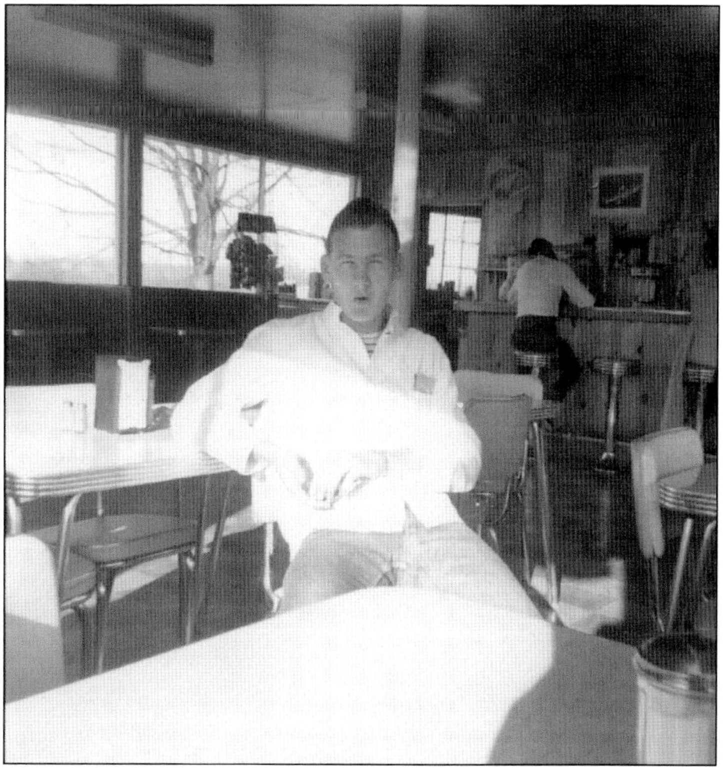

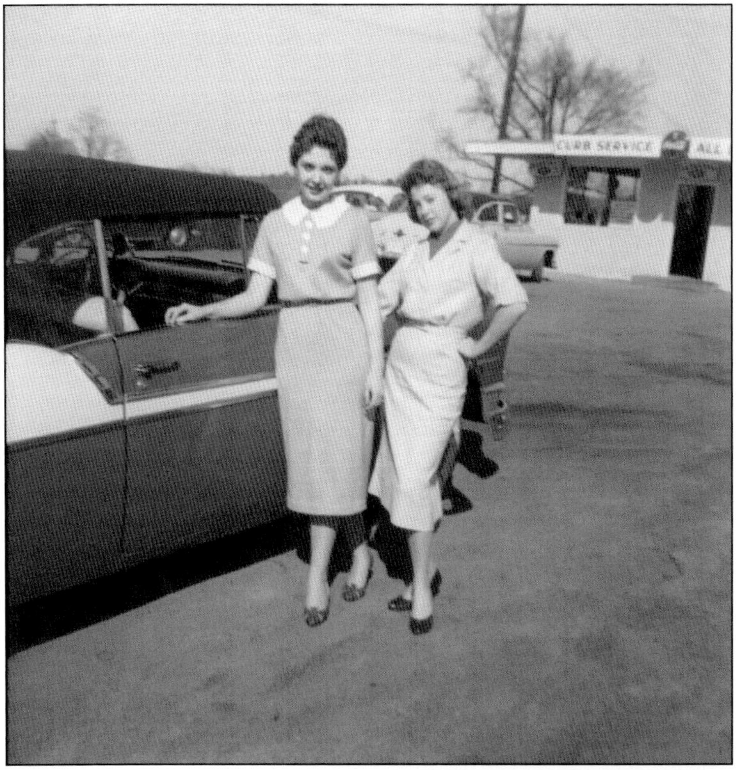

Local beauties Peggy Jenkins (left) and Doris Calvert stand beside a two-toned Chevrolet convertible. Both of these young ladies are stylish in the latest 1958 fashions. Pete's Drive-In Restaurant, where many of the young people ate and socialized, is in the background. (Courtesy of Joe Evans.)

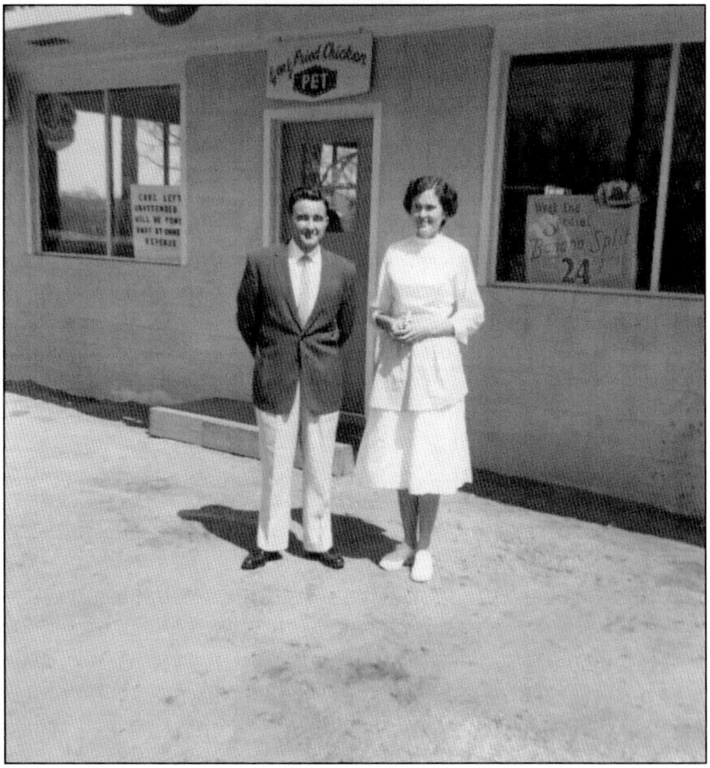

The owners and operators of Pete's Drive-In Restaurant, Pete and Mildred Davis, pose in 1958. Their establishment was a great place for the young people to meet, eat, and enjoy each other's company. Pete's featured curb service, a soda fountain, and a jukebox. Many younger kids celebrated their birthdays at Pete's with all of their friends. (Courtesy of Joe Evans.)

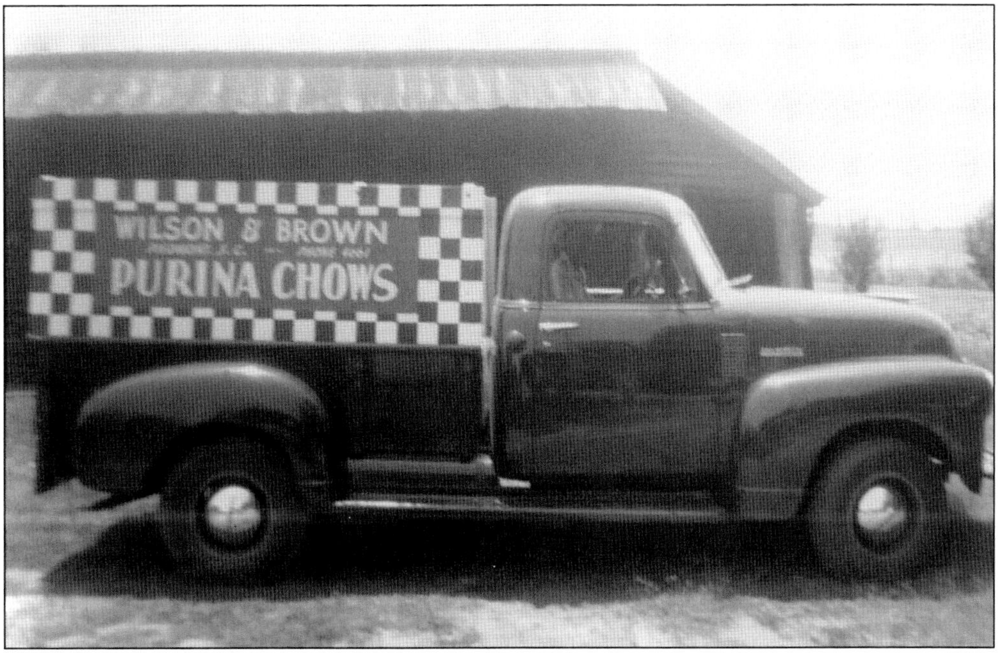

In this 1952 photograph taken at the farm of James and Ruby Wilson, a delivery truck advertises Wilson & Brown feed and seed store. The store later became Wilson's Feed and Seed, and residents of Piedmont and the surrounding area were frequent customers, buying seed for their gardens along with farm implements. (Courtesy of Betty Wilson Burdett.)

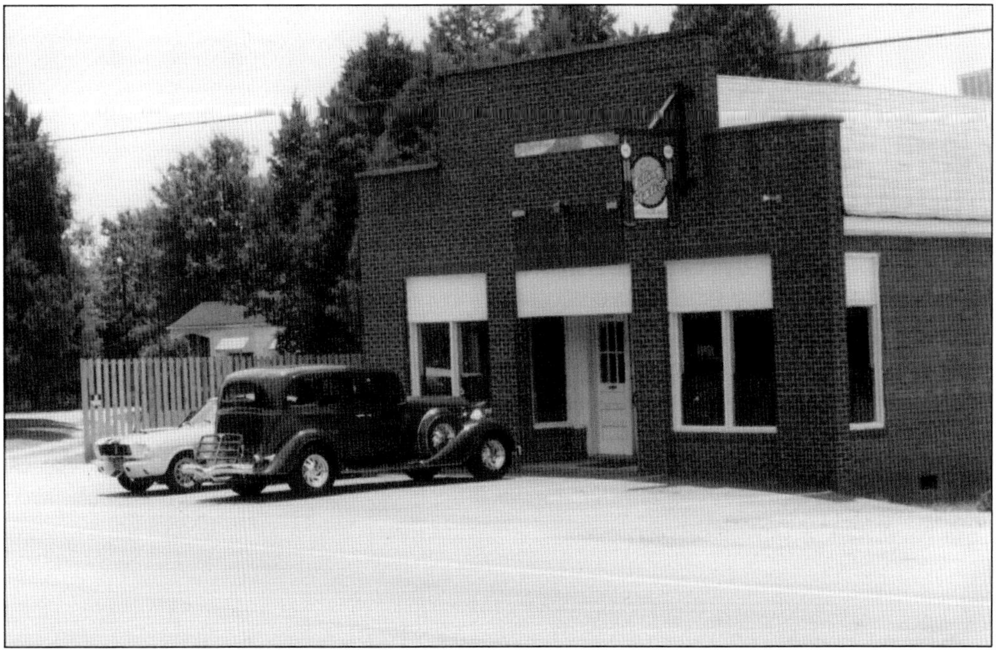

Moore's Store, located on Highway 86 in Piedmont, was built in the 1940s. This photograph was taken when Dan and Carolyn Reeves opened the Filling Station Restaurant in 1991. The building is currently Cancun Mexican restaurant, one of the most successful businesses in Piedmont. (Courtesy of Carolyn Reeves.)

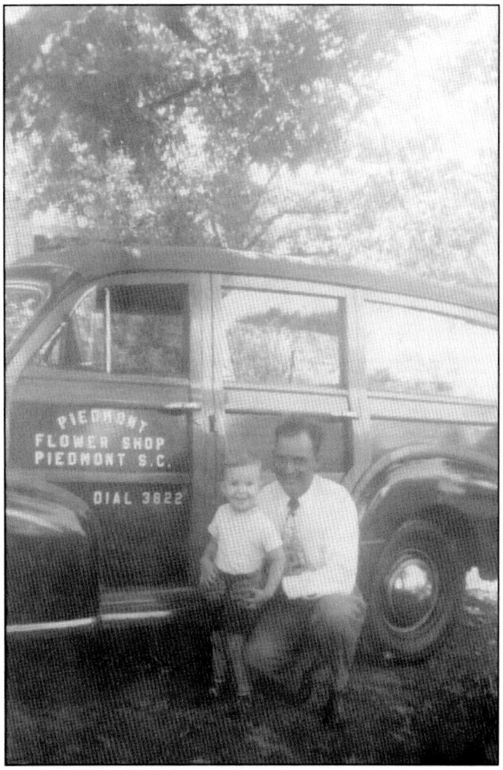

Piedmont Flower Shop was owned and operated by Margaret Buckhiester. Her husband, George, and son Phil are shown here in 1950 beside the Chevy station wagon used to deliver flowers. Notice the short telephone number on the side of the car. (Courtesy of Phil and Becky Buckhiester.)

Jackson Co. was advertised as an "Up-To-Date Store." From left to right, Roy Gresham, W.E. McConnell, Ollie Bagwell, and Earl Moore are pictured in the interior of the brick mercantile, probably during the 1920s. Jackson Co. was the largest and most popular company store. If one was running short on cash, they could go to the mill payroll office and purchase coins known as "Looies." These coins were then used to purchase goods at the store. Other stores also had Looies. When the town's wooden buildings burned down in 1903, they were quickly replaced by Piedmont Manufacturing and rented to the merchants. Rent receipts have been found showing payments of $69.25 four times per year. (Courtesy of Sandra Wood.)

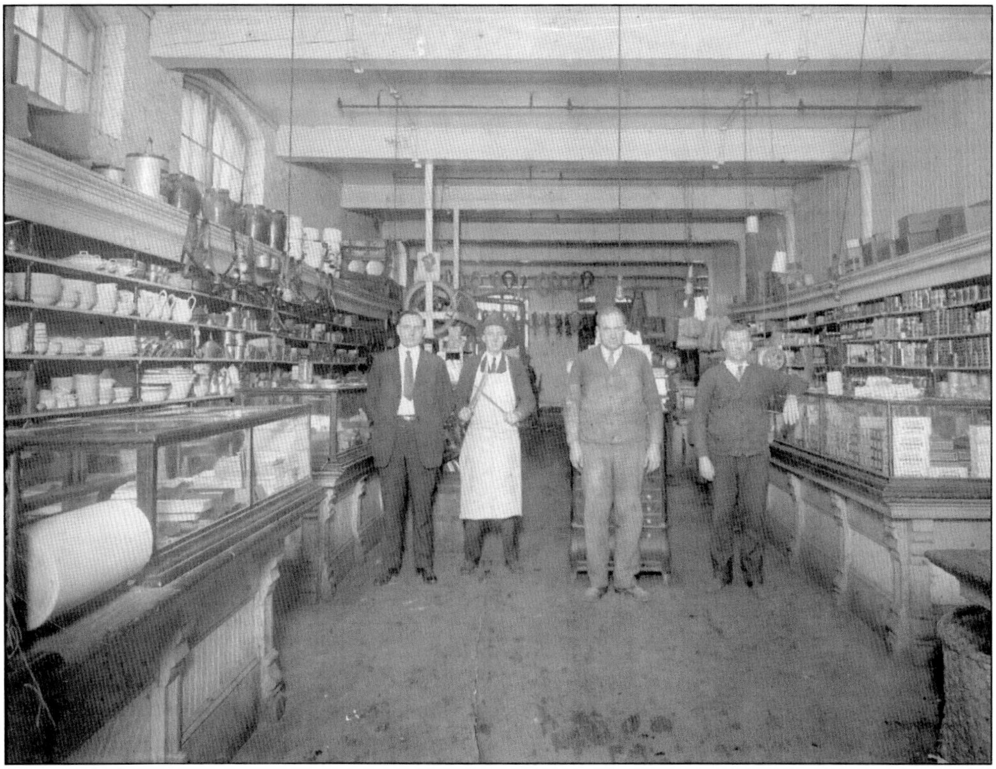

Mr. and Mrs. Louie Guest receive a contest prize from Purina in 1950. Louie Guest filled out a form to enter the contest at Wilson's Feed and Seed. The contest was run all across the country, and 10 prizes were given away—Guest was one of the lucky 10. He received a cage house with 1,000 pullets (young hens ready to lay eggs). When the cage house was set up, they had a big open house for the community, and the Purina people came to the event. Guest was then able to quit his job in the cotton mill and work for himself the rest of his life selling eggs. (Courtesy of Betty Burdett.)

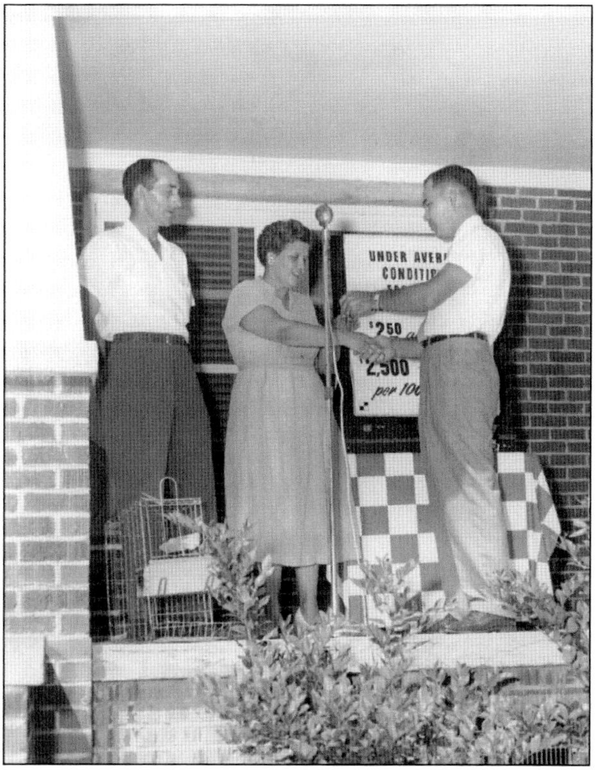

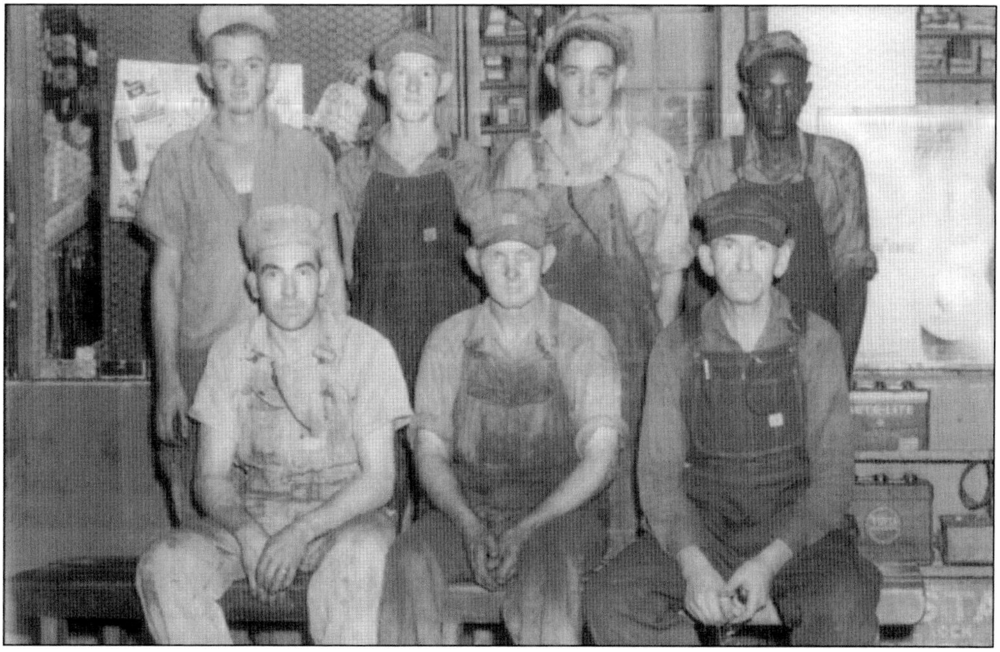

This photograph was taken in the mid- to late 1940s at Wigington's Shop, located on Highway 86. From left to right are (first row) Dennis Sherman, Newt Freeman, and Elihu Wigington; (second row) Jim Greeman, Junior Wigington, Johnny B. Lee, and Hickey Todd. Wigington's worked on farm equipment and other machinery. (Courtesy of Jimmy Wilson.)

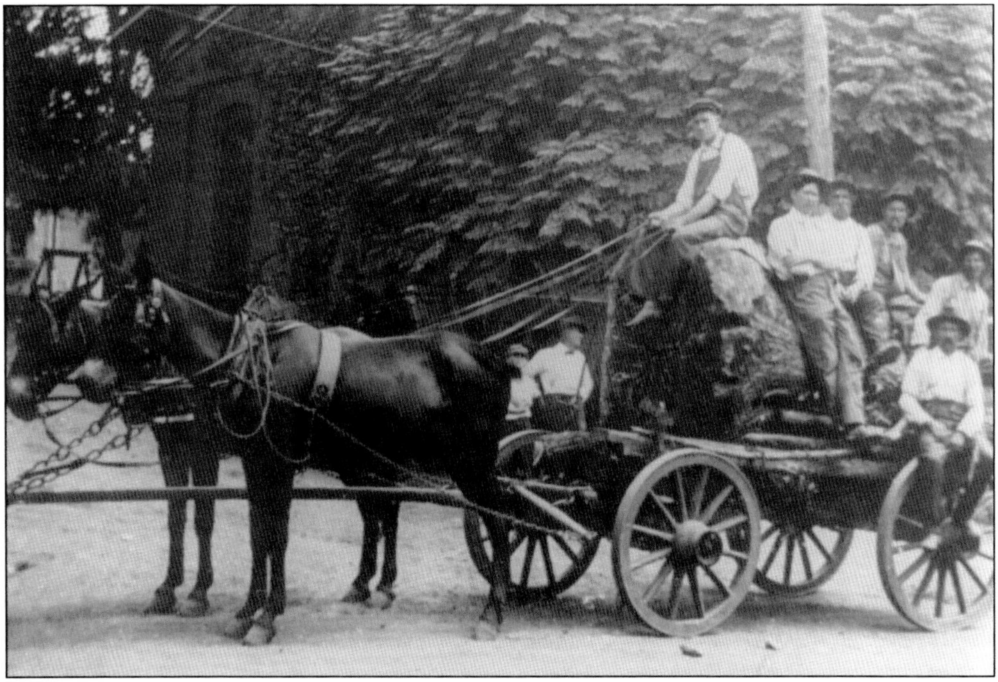

A mule team pulls a wagon filled with cow and horse hides at the corner of Main Street and Hotel Hill in 1920. Among the men pictured are Arthur Williams (driving the rig), Clan Campbell, and Walter Buckhiester in the background. (Courtesy of Piedmont Historical Collection.)

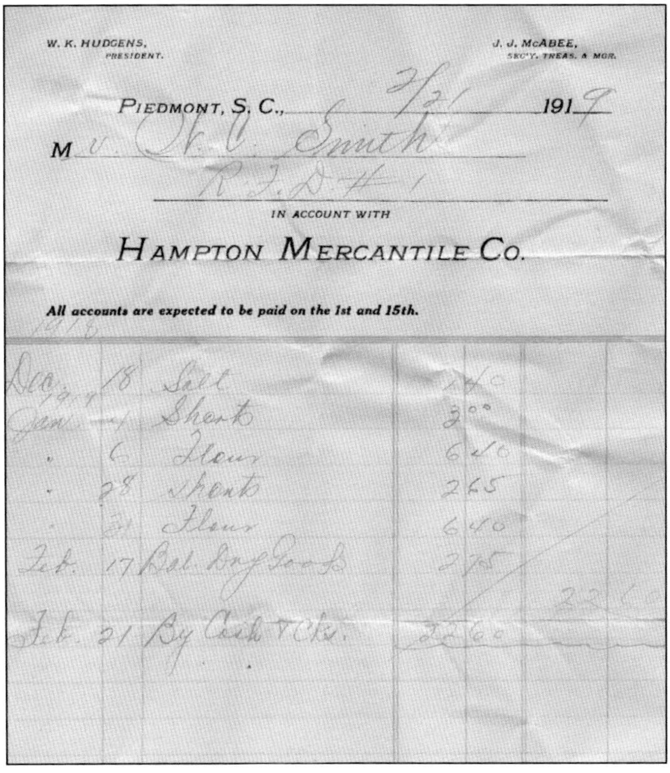

W. K. HUDGENS, PRESIDENT. J. J. McABEE, SEC'Y, TREAS. & MGR.

PIEDMONT, S. C., 2/21 1919

M N. C. Smith
R. F. D. # 1

IN ACCOUNT WITH

HAMPTON MERCANTILE CO.

All accounts are expected to be paid on the 1st and 15th.

1918			
Dec.	18	Salt	1.40
1919 Jan	4	Shorts	2.00
	6	Flour	6.40
	28	Shorts	2.65
	31	Flour	6.40
Feb.	17	Bal. Dry Goods	2.75
			22.60
Feb.	21	By Cash & Cks.	22.60

Pictured here is a receipt from Hampton Mercantile Company. The mercantile was located on the Anderson County side of Piedmont. The building later became A.C. McAbee's Grocery Store and Leopard's Barber Shop. It is now Piedmont Industrial Supply. (Courtesy of Gayle Payne.)

Lionel Roper stands at the service station beside Ballentine's Grocery Store on the Anderson County side of Piedmont in the 1950s. This store eventually became A.C. McAbee's Grocery Store. (Courtesy of Piedmont Historical Collection.)

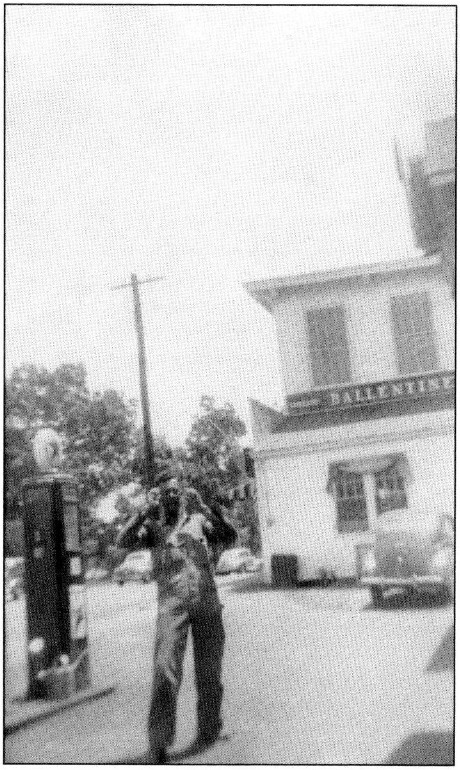

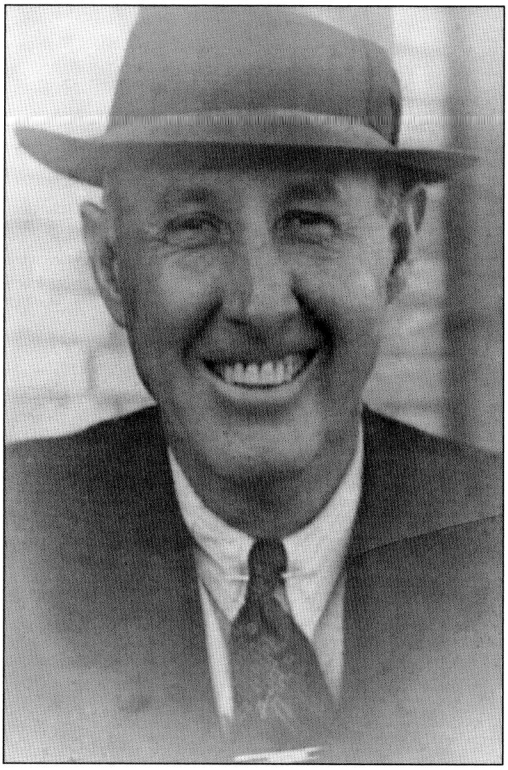

Carl Finley could be found parked at the top of the Main Street storefronts, always available to taxi anyone who needed a ride. He was a happy and friendly man who knew everyone, and everyone knew him. Carl started his taxi service by using a buggy to meet the train. (Courtesy of Phil and Becky Buckhiester.)

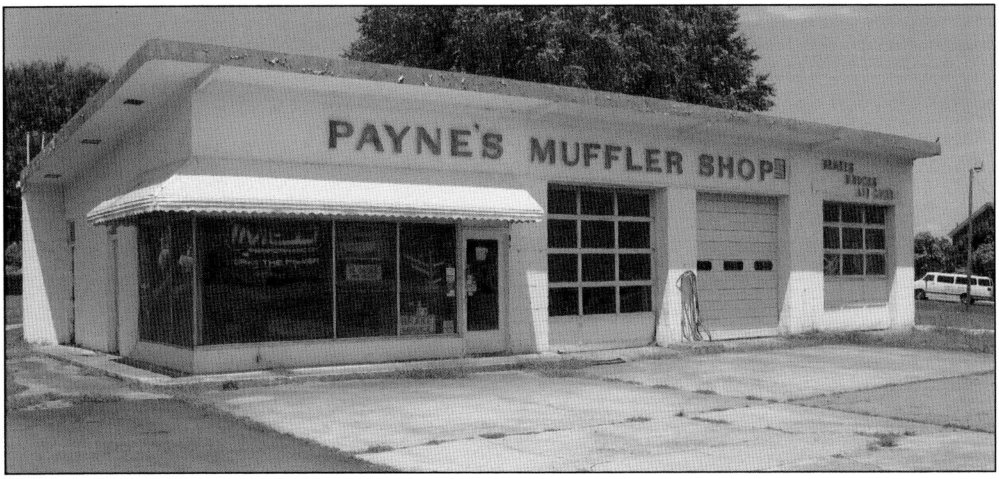

Originally a Shell service station, Joe and Inez Spearman built this building in the 1950s on Highway 86 on the Anderson County side of Piedmont. It was owned by the Spearmans but had different tenants. Jimmy Payne purchased the station in 1974 and operated it. He later turned it into Payne's Muffler Shop. (Courtesy of Anne Peden.)

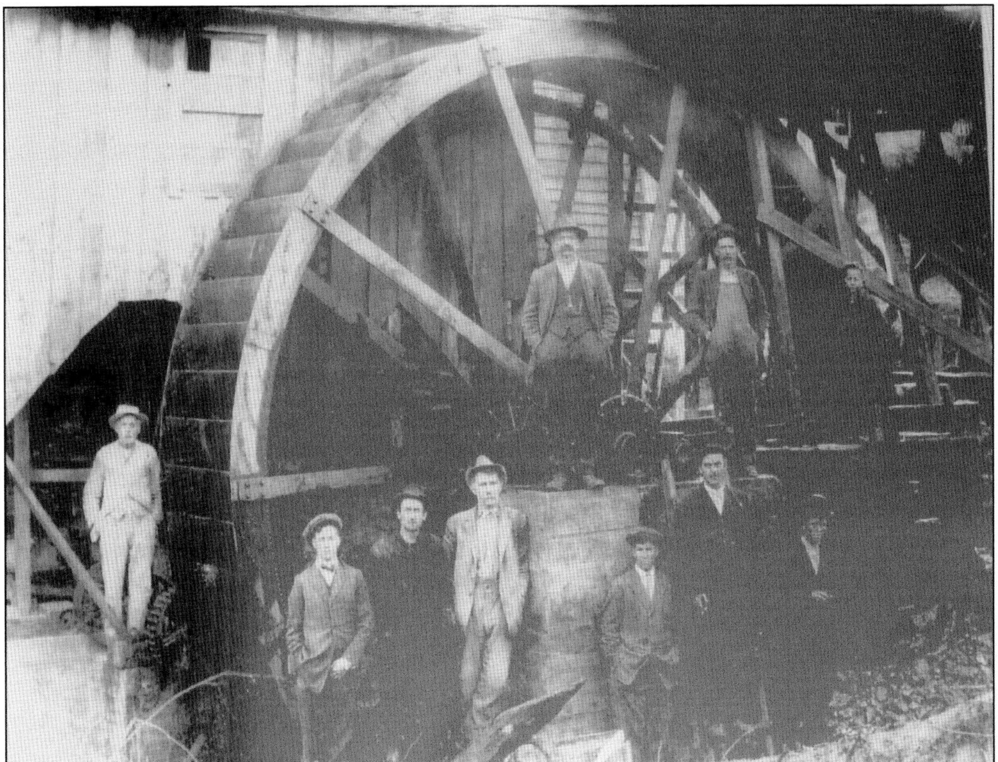

Moore's Mill is pictured here. The steel wheel, manufactured by the Fritz Wheel Company in Pennsylvania, was installed around 1914. Buddy Garrett is on the pilaster, George Hulan Durham and George Washington Durham stand next to the pilaster on the left, and on the right of the pilaster are three Garretts, who were all blacksmiths and probably helped put the wheel together. (Courtesy of Society of Old Mills and Jesse Adkins.)

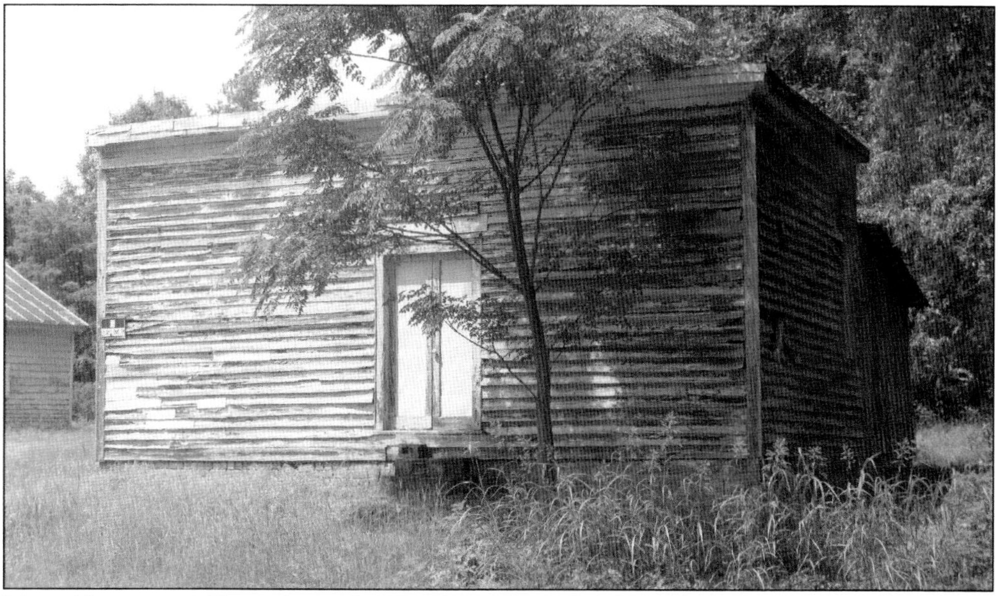

This old printing office is located on Highway 86 in the Wren community. It was owned and operated by John Thomas Wigington and his father, Elihu Wigington. A community newspaper was printed here in the early 1900s. (Courtesy of Bessie Wigington.)

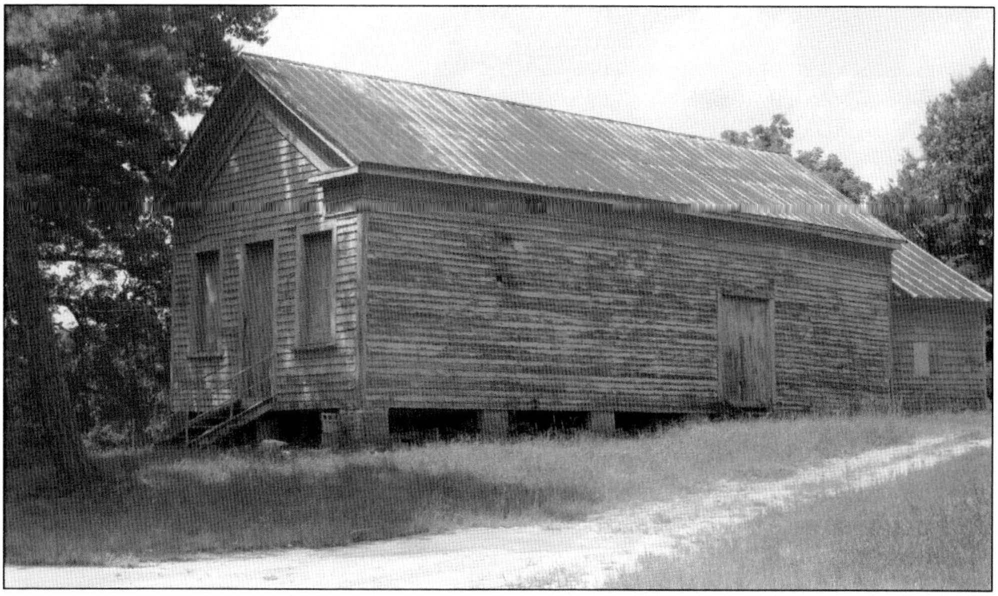

Elihu Wigington owned and operated the mercantile pictured here on Highway 86 in present-day Wren, right beside the printing office. Customers could purchase a wide variety of merchandise here, including clothing, farm equipment, food, furniture, and candy. Peanut butter was sold by the ounce from barrels. Wigington was also a watch repairman. Customers often brought in chickens or eggs to barter for the supplies they needed. Inside the mercantile was the Newell post office, where customers could post a letter or pick up their mail. John Thomas Wigington, Elihu's son, assisted his father in the store and print shop and eventually took over after his father retired. Elihu Wigington kept detailed journals that were written in beautiful calligraphy. The store closed in the early 1920s. (Courtesy of Bessie Wigington.)

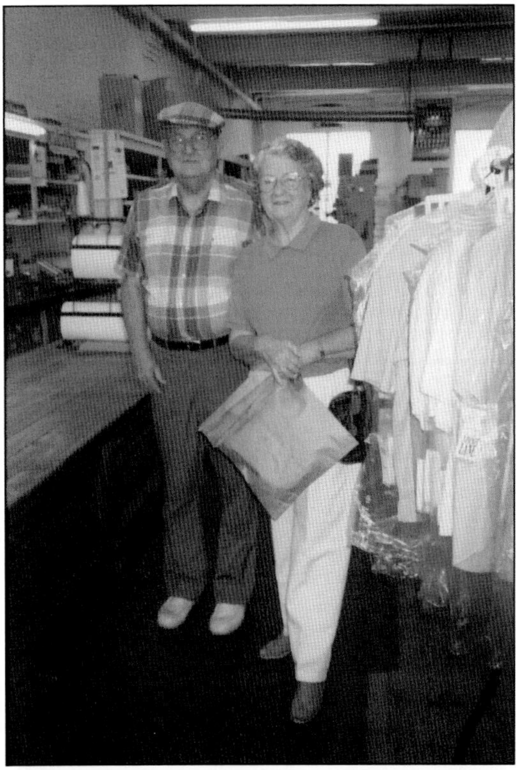

Proprietor M.J. "Dolly" Cooper and clerk Cecil Spearman pose inside Piedmont Economy Store at left. The below view of downtown from 1990 shows that Dolly sold Nunn Bush shoes. He always had fine suits, and when a gentleman needed one for a special occasion, he would just say he had to "go see Dolly." Dolly was a member of the state legislature for many years, and the Saluda River Bridge is dedicated to him, as well as a park in Powderville and a veterans' nursing home. (Left, courtesy of Beth and Dan Cooper; below, courtesy of Frances Ward.)

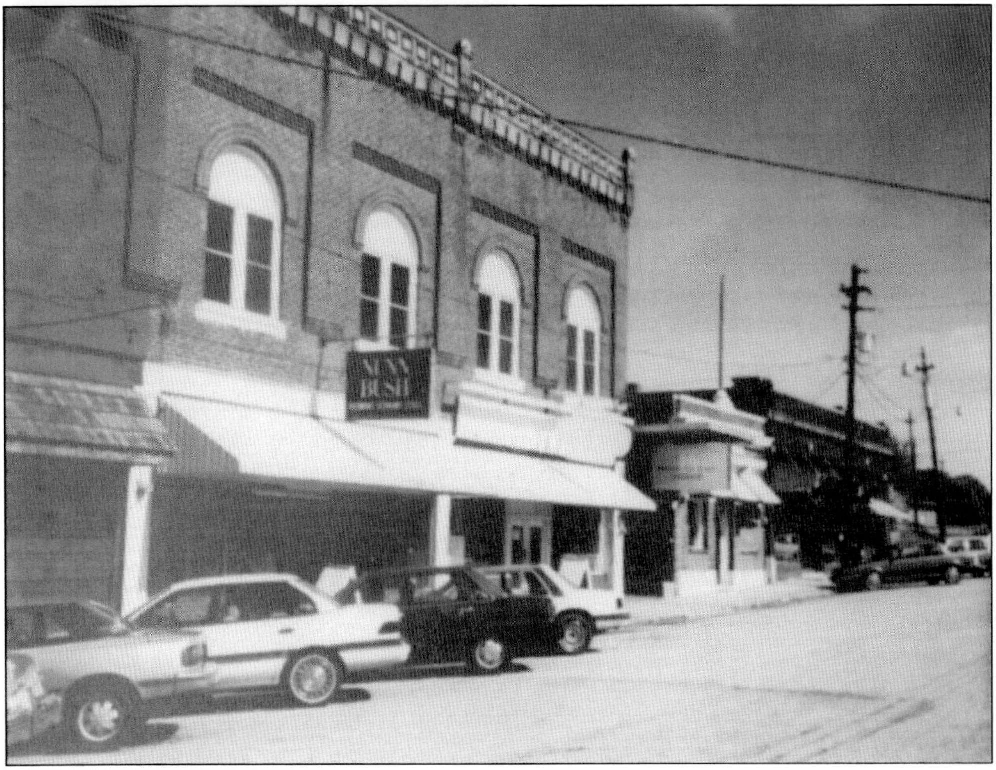

Five

SCHOOLS

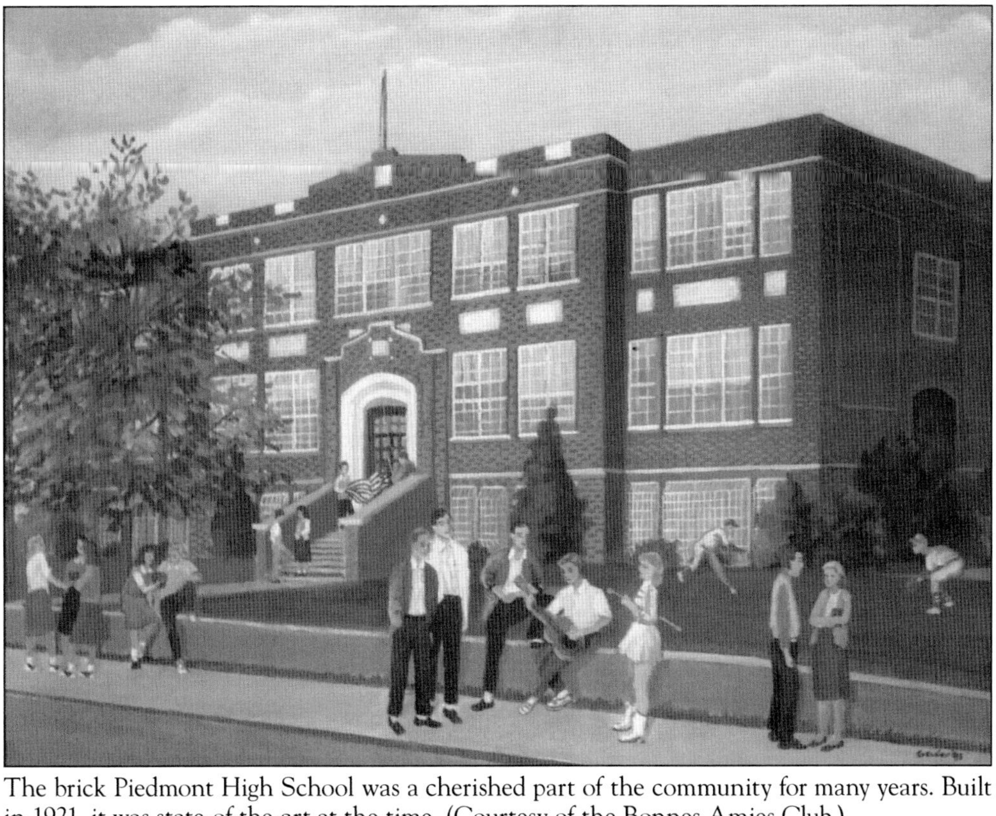

The brick Piedmont High School was a cherished part of the community for many years. Built in 1921, it was state-of-the-art at the time. (Courtesy of the Bonnes Amies Club.)

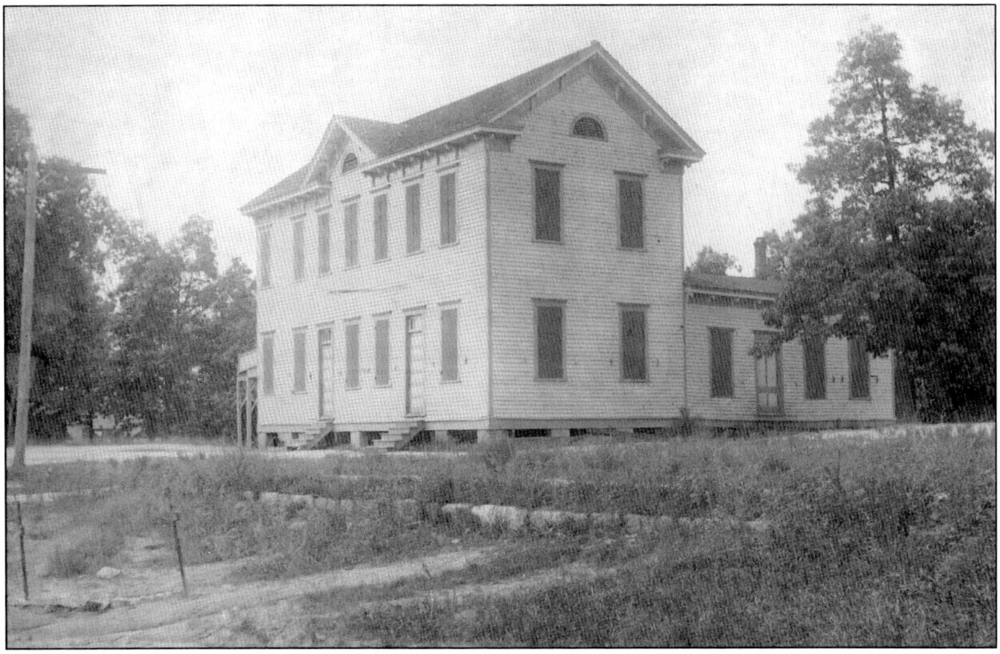

The Union School in Piedmont was built near the mill around 1878. That first school had 80 students. This later two-story wooden structure was raised somewhere in the vicinity of the intersection of Highways 20 and 86. The last graduating class was in 1921, when the brick Piedmont High School was opened. (Courtesy of Linda Smith.)

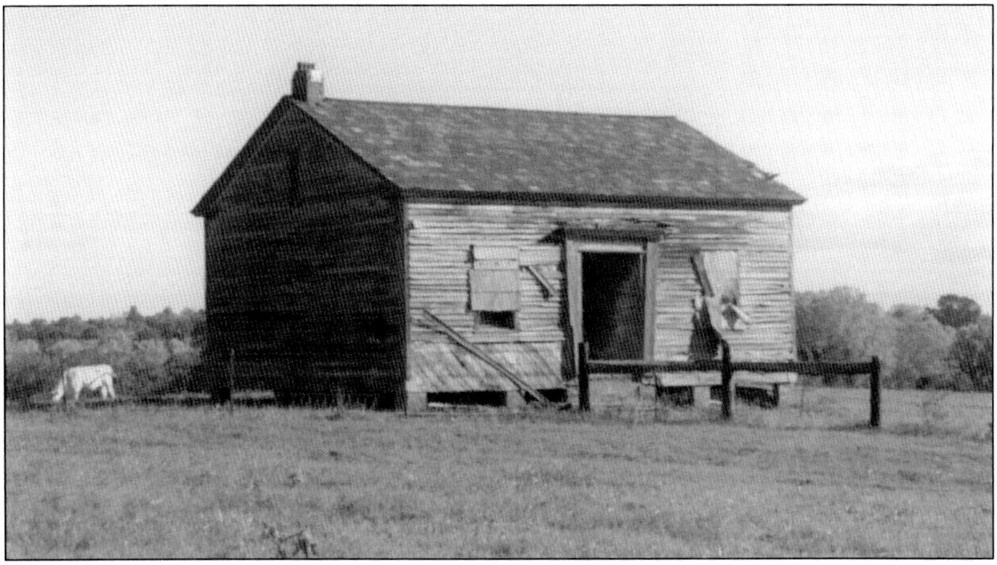

Waco School was built in 1890, and the first teacher was John Watson. The school was initially for white children, but after Rock Hill School was built, it was converted to a school for black children. The school was then named New Mount Bethel, or, as it was nicknamed, "Who Would'a Thunk It." That school still stands today on a hill off Highway 86. In 1957, Anderson School District 1 built Spearman School, which held kindergarten through 12th grade. Hazel Bolden Loveless started in the first grade that year and graduated in 1969, the last year of Spearman High School. (Courtesy of Carolyn Reeves.)

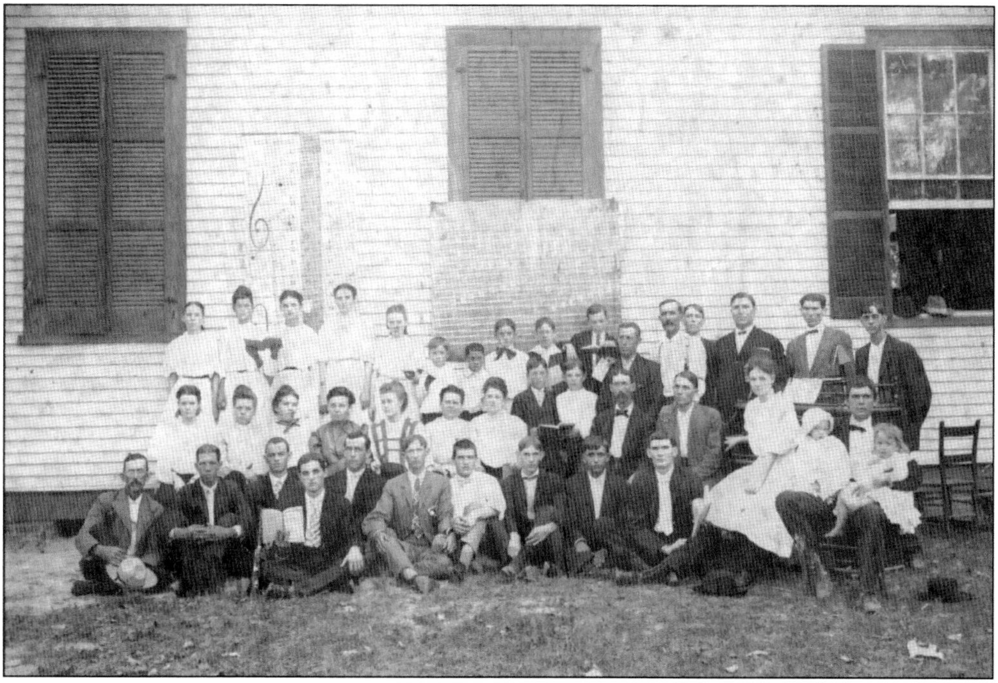

Mountain Springs High School was built in 1857 and was used as a meeting place for Mountain Springs Baptist Church until the first church building was constructed. The music class at Mountain Springs was a vital part of the school. The building burned down in 1941. (Courtesy of Carolyn Reeves.)

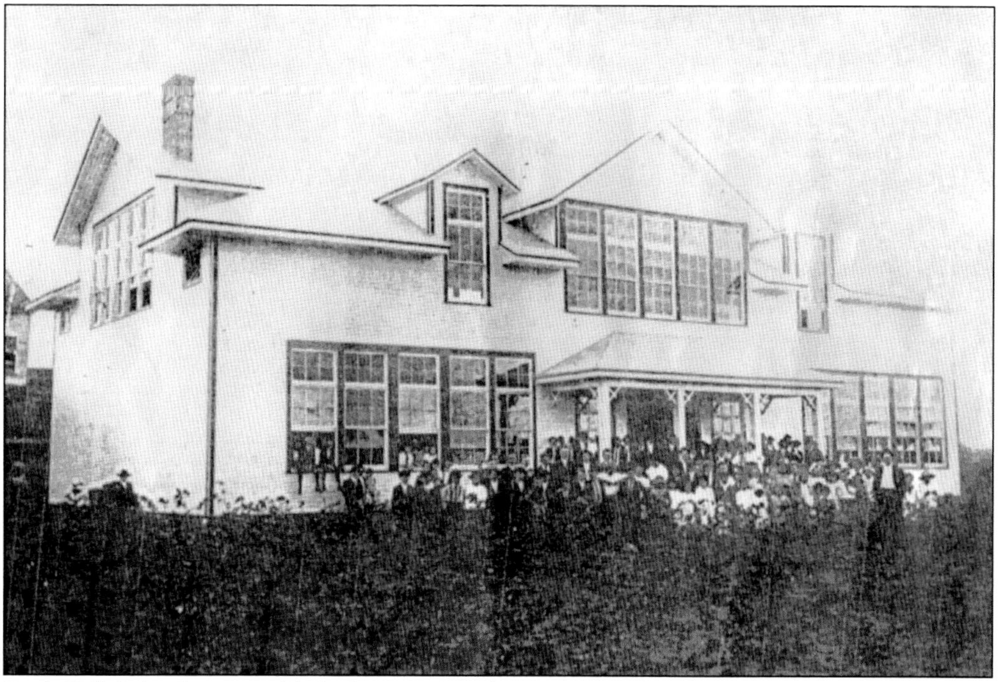

Rock Hill School was established in 1915 in the Simpsonville section of Piedmont. (Courtesy of Gayle Payne.)

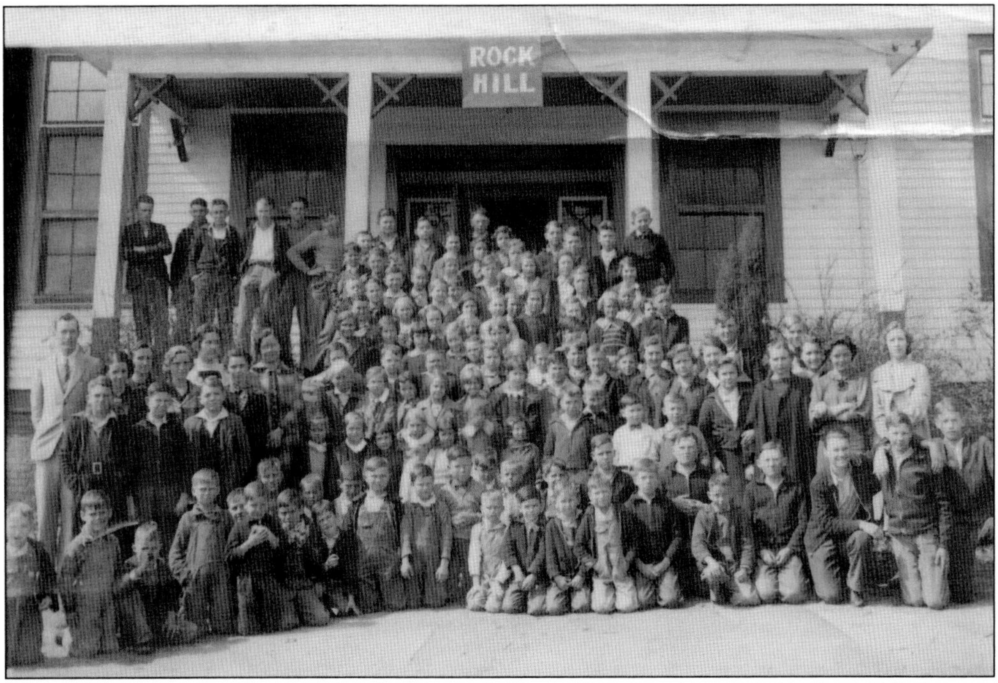

This photograph of Rock Hill School in the early 1930s shows teachers C.L. Dodson, Effie Harris, and Barbara Traynham. Some of the students pictured include Charles Aiken, James Cason, Bruster Reid, J.C. Traynham, Louise Adkins, Mary Ayers, Albert Capps, Louie Smith, Mary and Margaret Roper, Pat Rogers, James Blackston, and J.T. Davis. (Courtesy of Gayle Payne.)

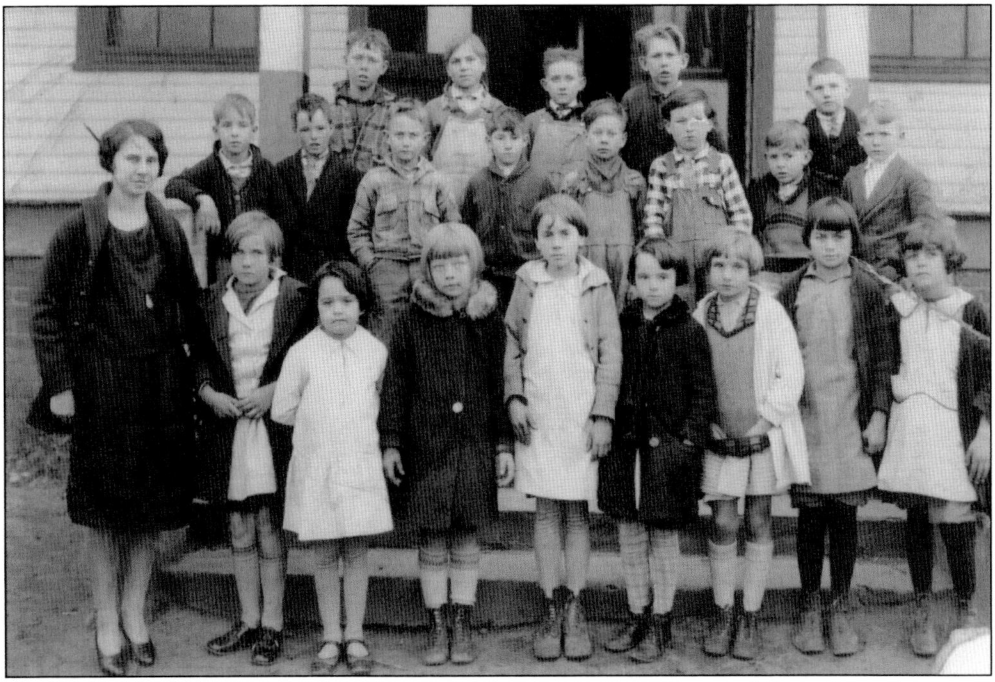

Rock Hill School's 1928 second-grade class is pictured here. (Courtesy of Gayle Payne.)

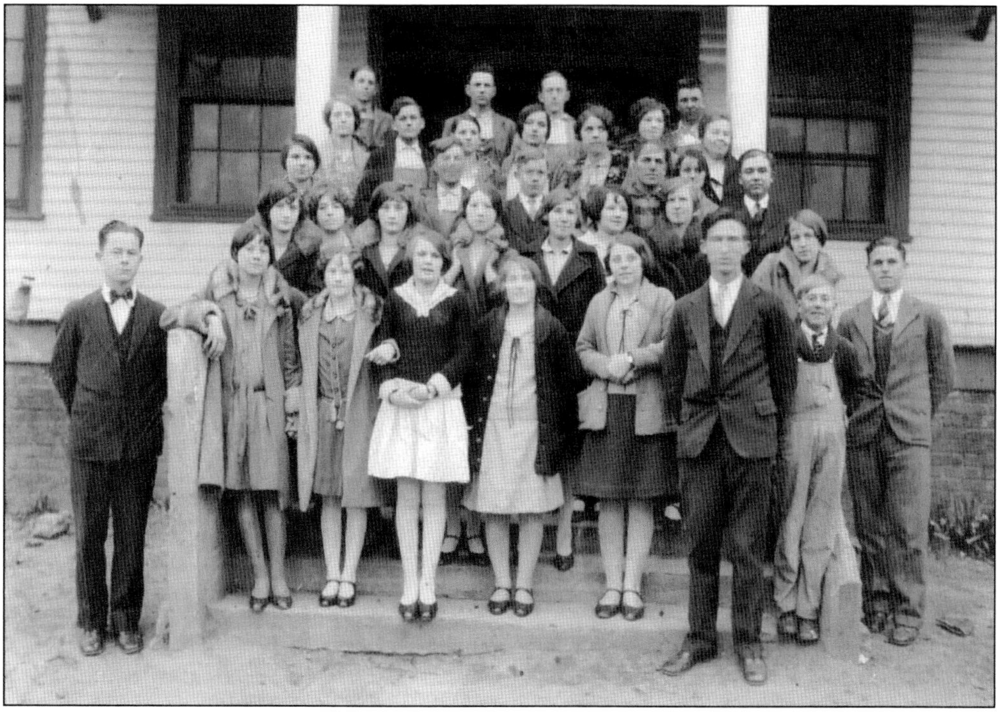

Among the students in this photograph of Rock Hill School in the 1920s are twins Montez and Inez Moore and Clara Gillespie. (Courtesy of Carolyn Reeves.)

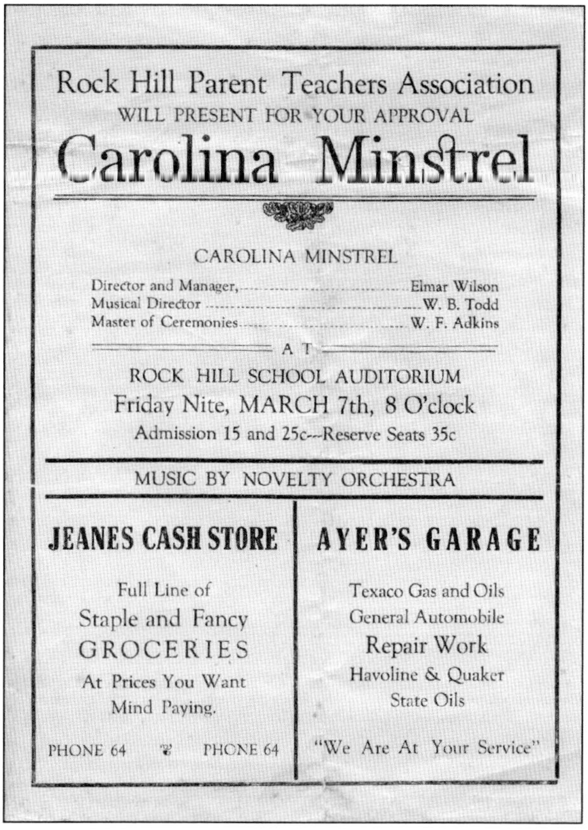

Rock Hill Parent Teachers Association
WILL PRESENT FOR YOUR APPROVAL

Carolina Minstrel

CAROLINA MINSTREL

Director and Manager, ... Elmar Wilson
Musical Director .... W. B. Todd
Master of Ceremonies .... W. F. Adkins

AT

ROCK HILL SCHOOL AUDITORIUM
Friday Nite, MARCH 7th, 8 O'clock
Admission 15 and 25c—Reserve Seats 35c

MUSIC BY NOVELTY ORCHESTRA

JEANES CASH STORE

Full Line of
Staple and Fancy
GROCERIES
At Prices You Want
Mind Paying.

PHONE 64 PHONE 64

AYER'S GARAGE

Texaco Gas and Oils
General Automobile
Repair Work
Havoline & Quaker
State Oils

"We Are At Your Service"

Pictured here is a program from Carolina Minstrel, which was sponsored by the Rock Hill Parent Teachers Association on March 7 sometime prior to 1950. The admission charge was 15¢ and 25¢, with reserved seats costing 35¢. (Courtesy of Linda Smith.)

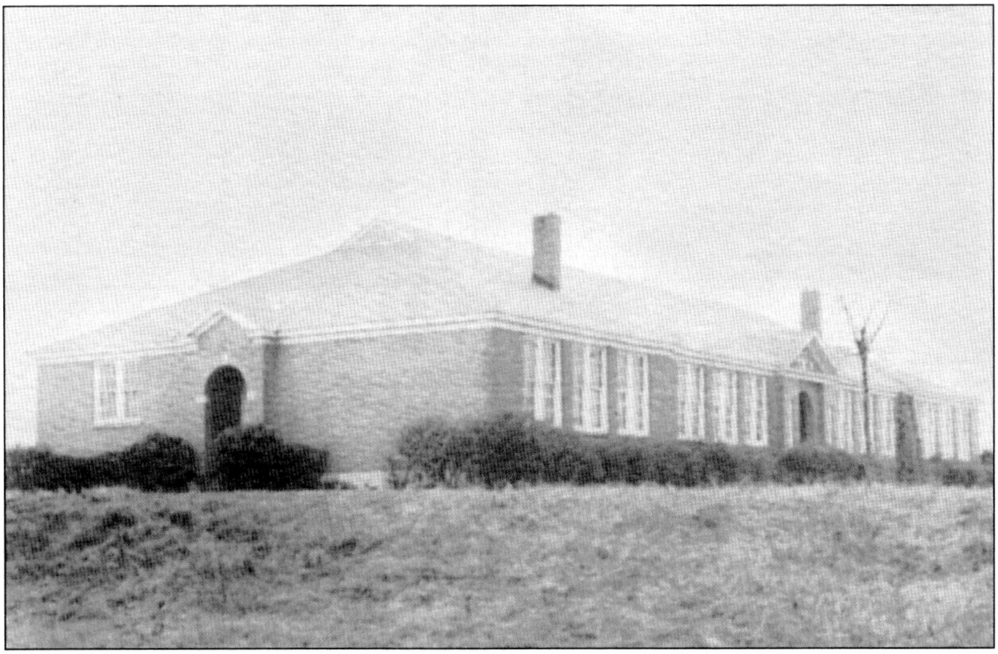

The brick Rock Hill School is shown here. Ruby Wilson ran the cafeteria and fixed home-cooked meals that the students still remember today. It closed in 1958, and the students and teachers were transferred to Wren. (Courtesy of Carolyn Reeves.)

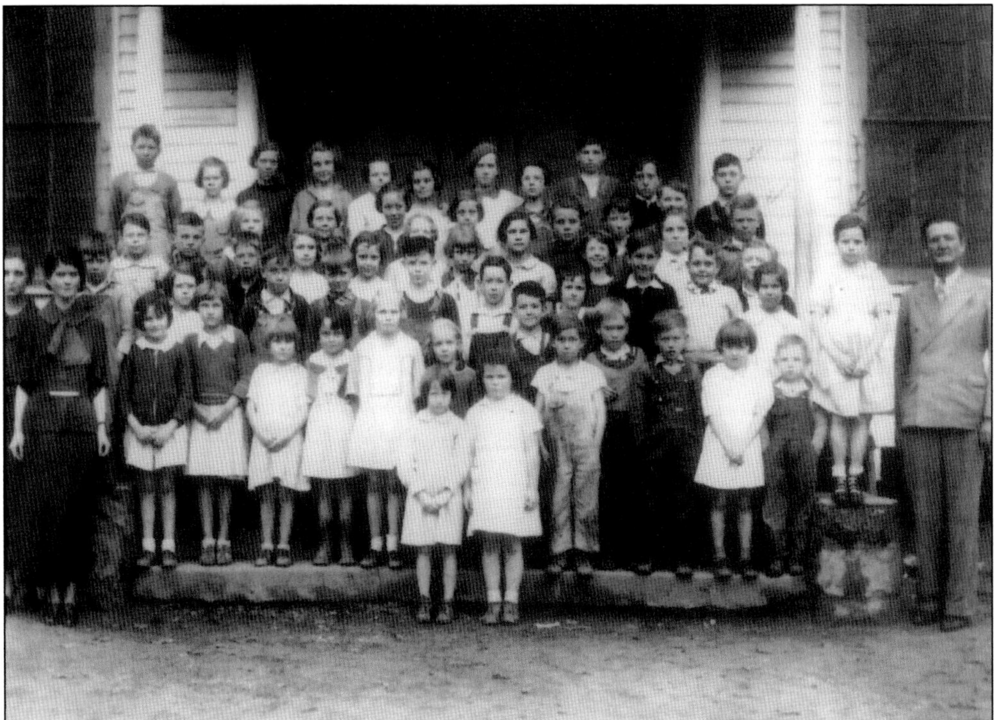

This class stands before the original Grove Station School in the 1920s or early 1930s. (Courtesy of Jimmy Richey.)

Pictured in the original Grove Station School is James B. Richey, who was a student there in 1920. (Courtesy of Jimmy Richey.)

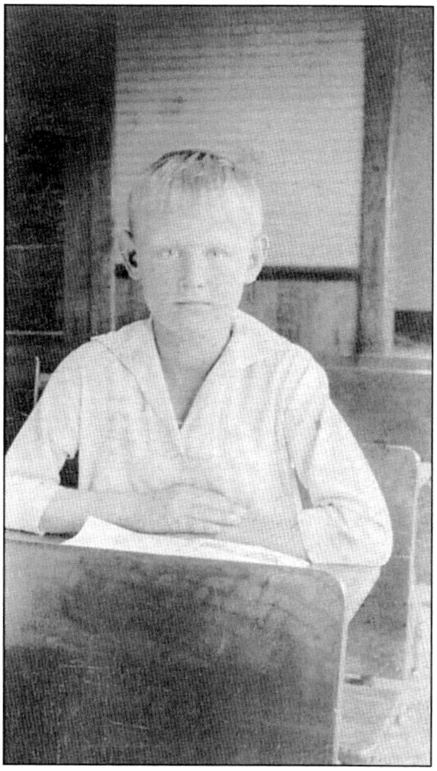

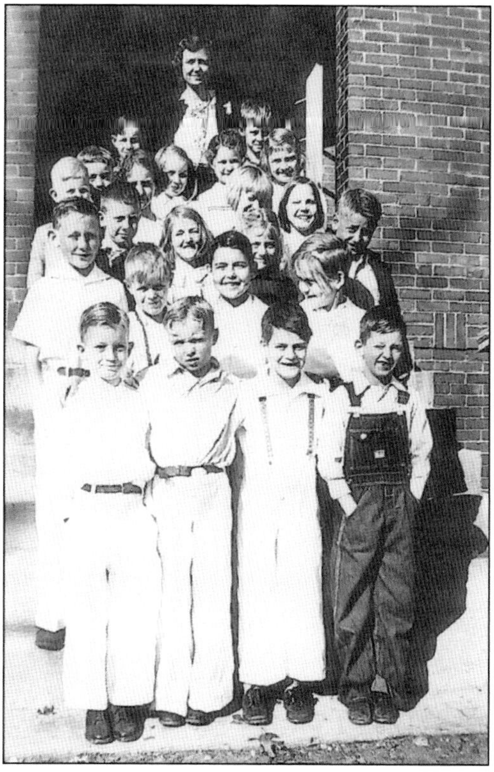

The brick Grove Station Elementary School was built from 1941 to 1942. Ms. Hammett's third-grade class is shown here. (Courtesy of Jimmy Richey.)

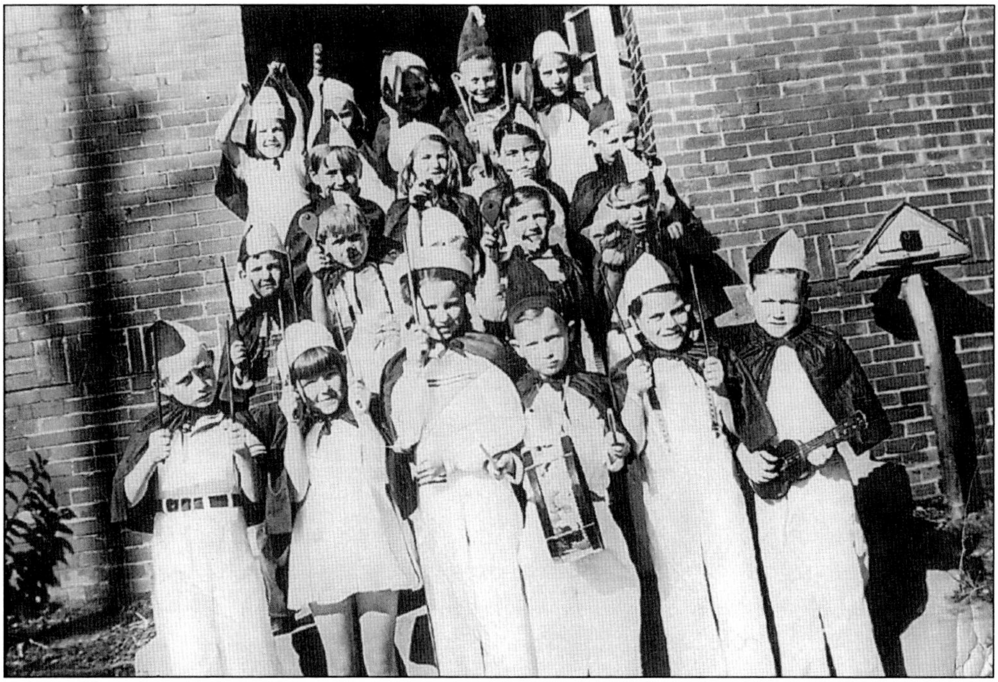

Grove Station Elementary School's orchestra of 1943–1944 stands on the steps, ready to play. (Courtesy of Jimmy Richey.)

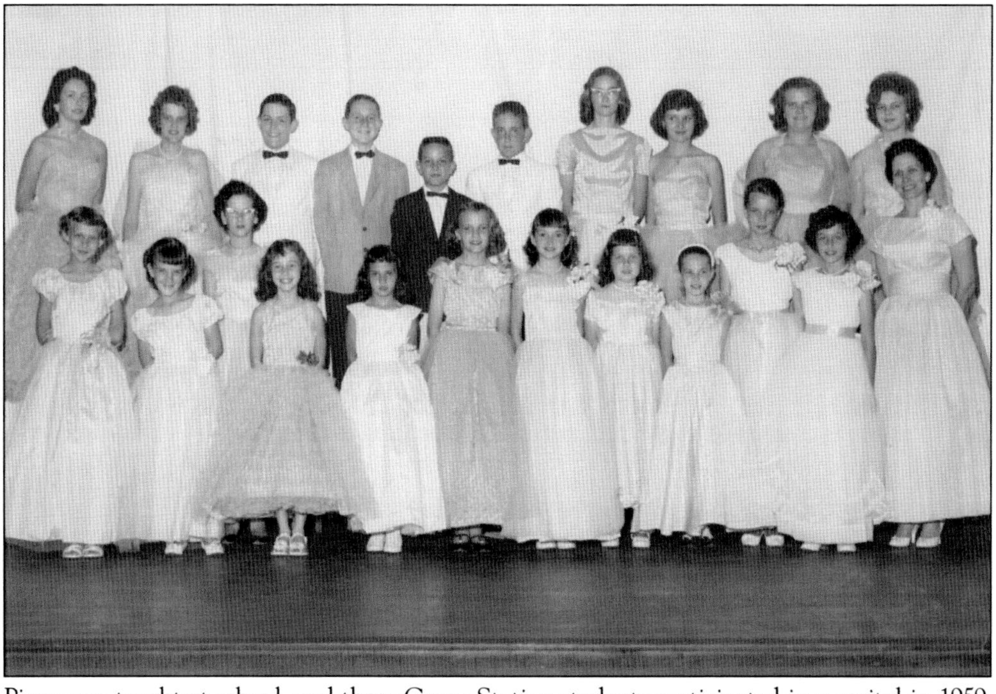

Piano was taught at school, and these Grove Station students participated in a recital in 1959. Inez Hopkins was the teacher. Students pictured here include Becky Richey, Dot Lollis, Debbie Elrod, Liz Robinson, Susan Vinson, Gene Hughes, Yvonne Mitchell, Patsy Davis, Faye Anderson, Dwight Elrod, Janet Blackwell, and Linda Lindsey. (Courtesy of Dot Lollis Evans.)

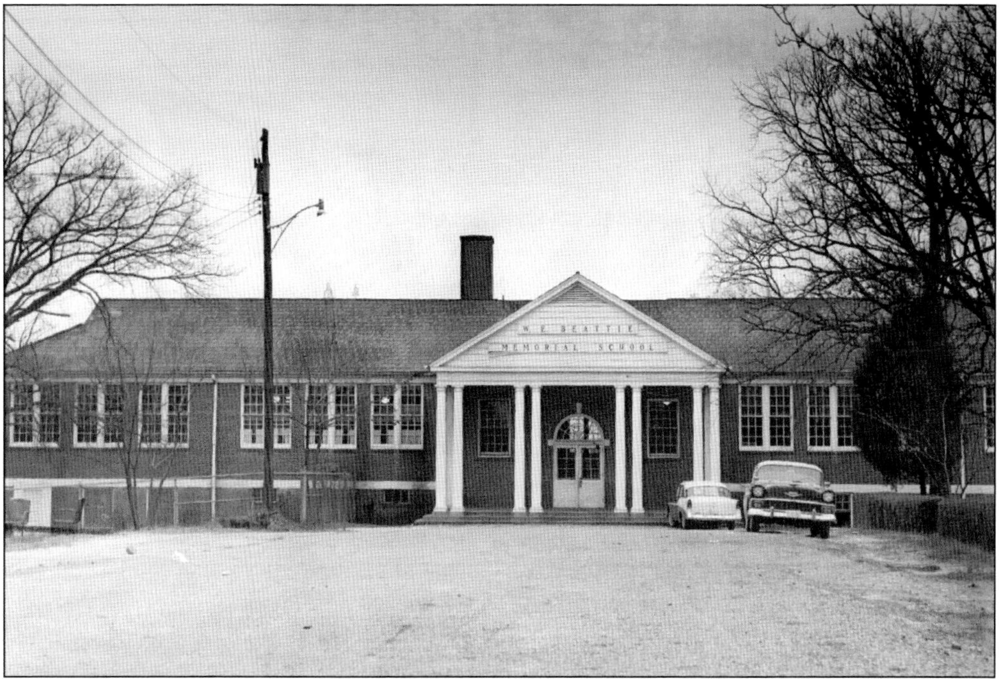

W.E. Beattie Memorial Grammar School was built in 1936 for the Anderson County children of Piedmont. When the school closed in 1962, the Anderson County students went to Wren Elementary School. (Courtesy of Betty Davenport.)

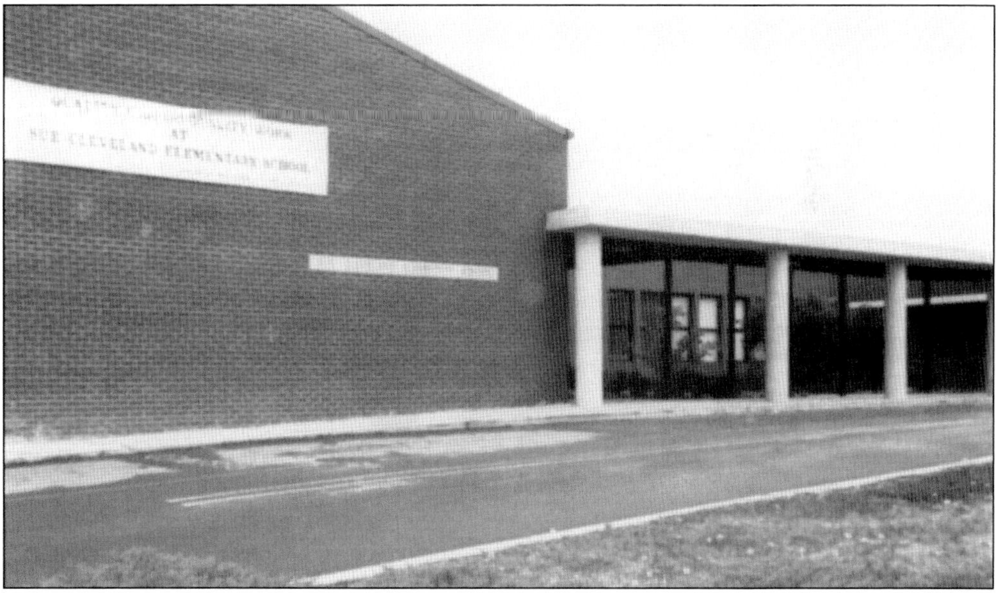

Sue Cleveland Elementary School was built in 1955 for the children of Piedmont who lived in Greenville County. Part of the old high school was used at first as well. Over the years, additions were made, and a new building was eventually built on Bessie Road east of Piedmont. H.A. Loftis was the longtime principal. Piedmont High School students began attending schools in their respective counties in the 1950s, and in the 1960s, Piedmont High merged with Ellen Woodside High to form Woodmont. Anderson students attended Wren High. (Courtesy of Anne Peden.)

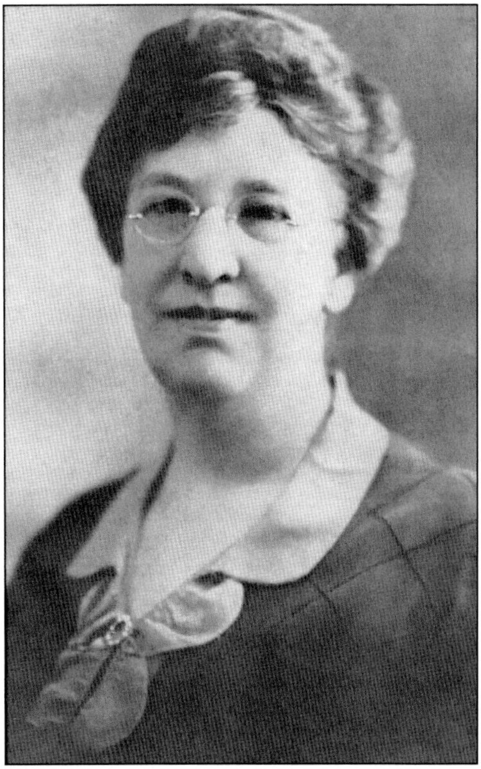

Pictured in 1945 is Sue Cleveland, for whom Sue Cleveland Elementary School was named. Cleveland was born Sue Freddie Trowbridge, the youngest daughter of Silas and Nancy Nesbitt Trowbridge. Her father, Silas Trowbridge, was reported to have sold the first bale of cotton to Piedmont Manufacturing Company. Sue Trowbridge Cleveland taught at Beattie School, Grove Station School, and Piedmont School. (Courtesy of Joe Evans.)

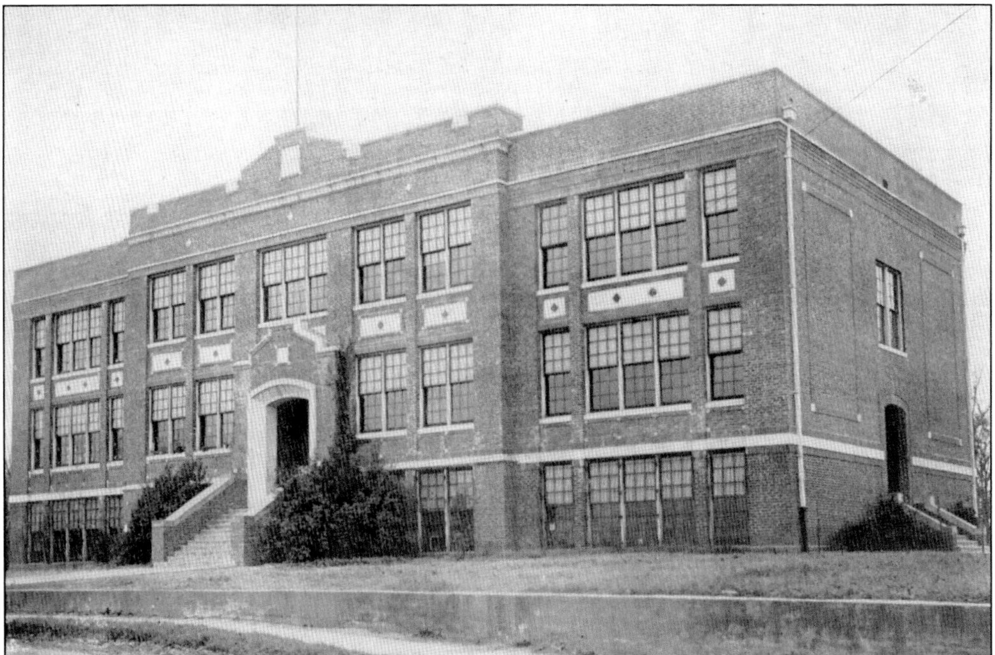

The brick Piedmont School was built in 1920. The school was converted to a junior high school in 1962 and closed in 1965, when the students were transferred to Ellen Woodside or Carolina. The building was destroyed by fire in 1967. (Courtesy of Phil and Becky Buckhiester.)

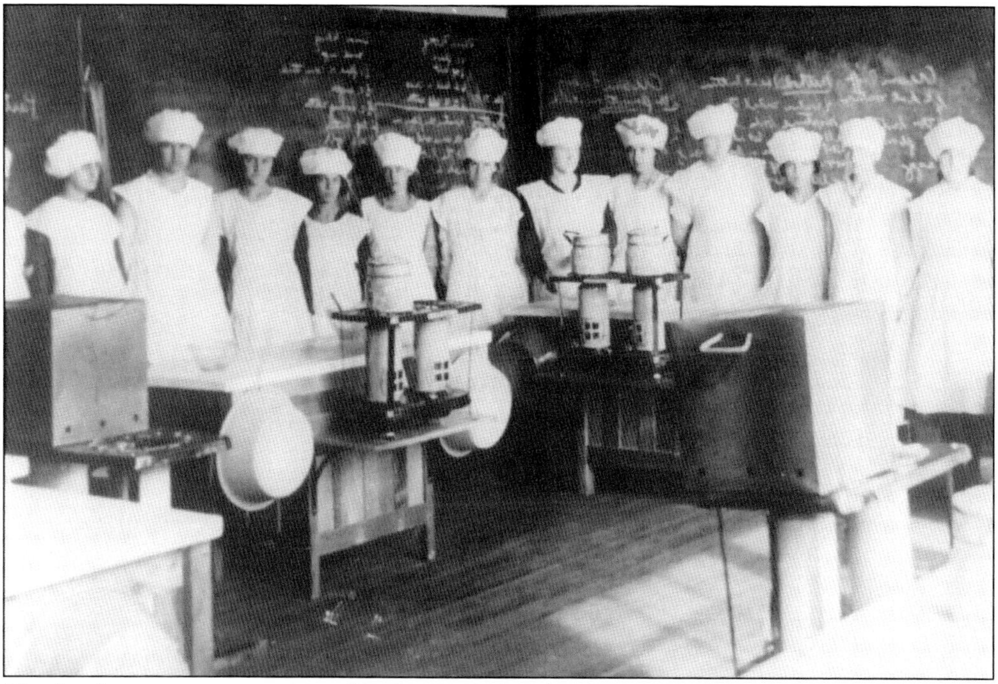

The first home-economics class of Piedmont High School in 1921 is extremely proud of their new school. Fourth from left is Elsie Hawthorne Davenport, mother of Betty Davenport and Frances Davenport Evans. (Courtesy of Betty Davenport.)

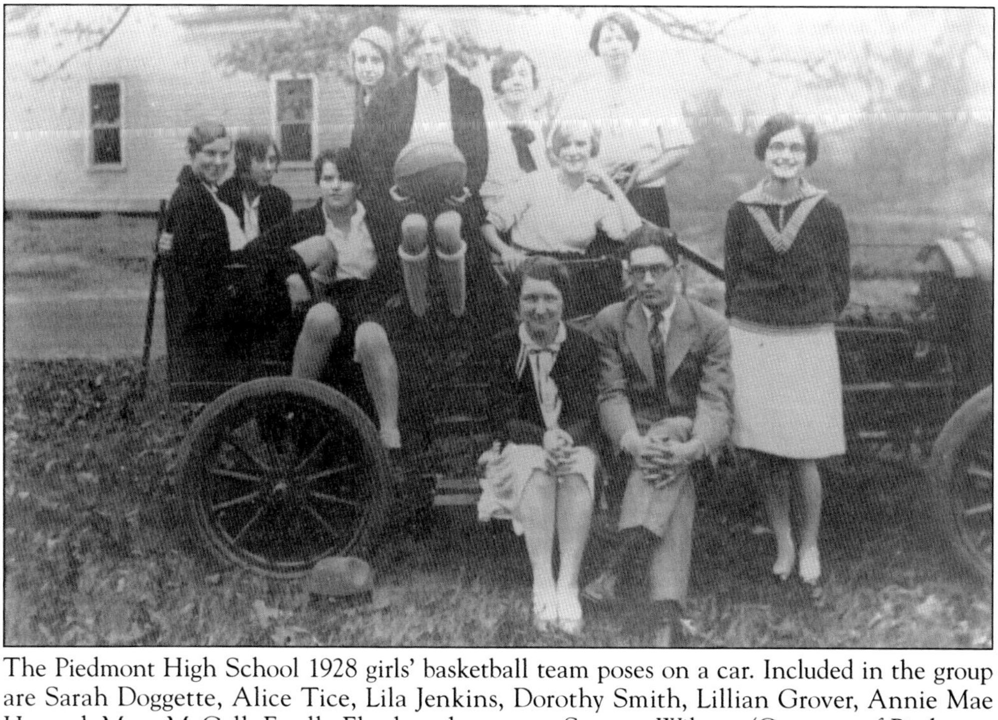

The Piedmont High School 1928 girls' basketball team poses on a car. Included in the group are Sarah Doggette, Alice Tice, Lila Jenkins, Dorothy Smith, Lillian Grover, Annie Mae Howard, Mary McCall, Estelle Elrod, and manager Stewart Wilson. (Courtesy of Piedmont Historical Collection.)

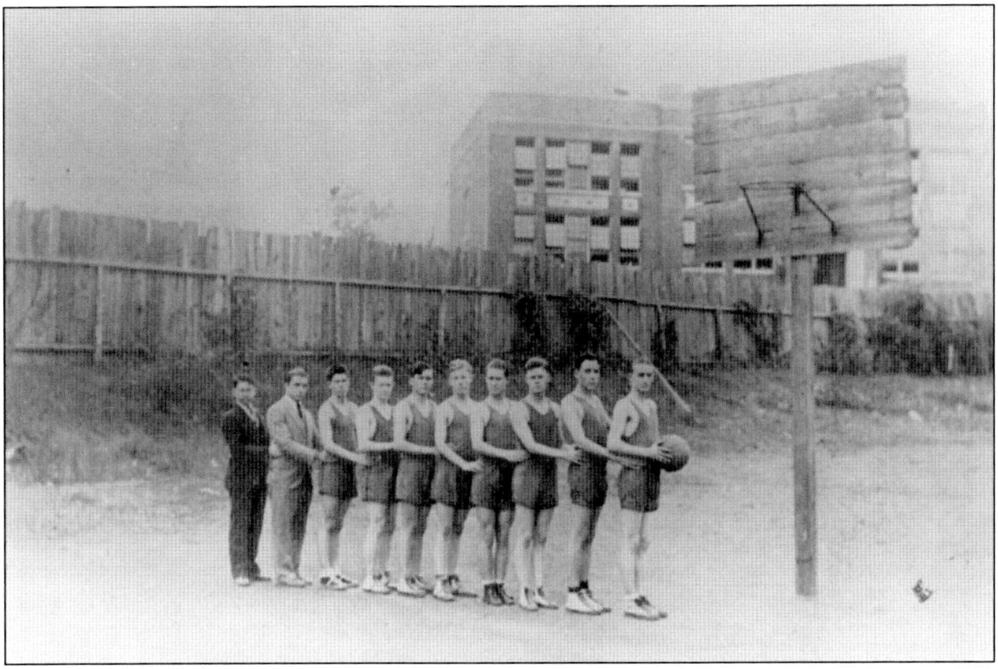

The Piedmont High School 1928 boys' basketball team looks ready to practice dunks. From left to right are unidentified, coach Edward McCall, Clarence Allen, Marvin Stone, Homer Mullikin, Bill Jenner, Clarence Smith, Truman Gilreath, Louie White, and Elmer Herd. (Courtesy of Piedmont Historical Collection.)

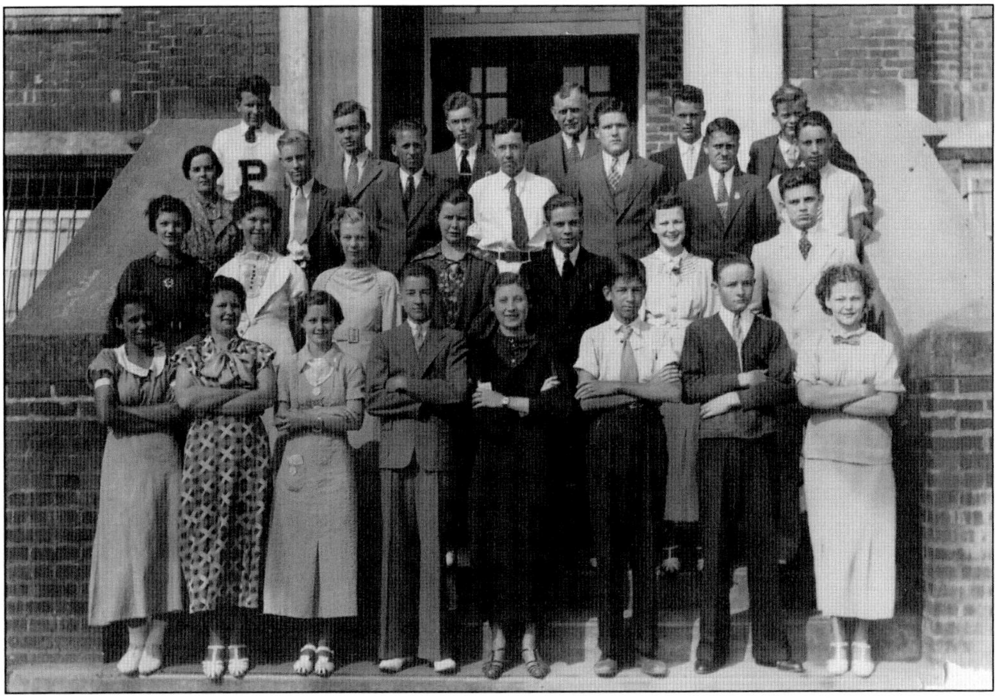

Piedmont High School's senior class of 1936 is pictured here. Some of the students are Vivian Bishop Payne, Helen Jones Austin, and Pat Patterson. (Courtesy of Gayle Payne.)

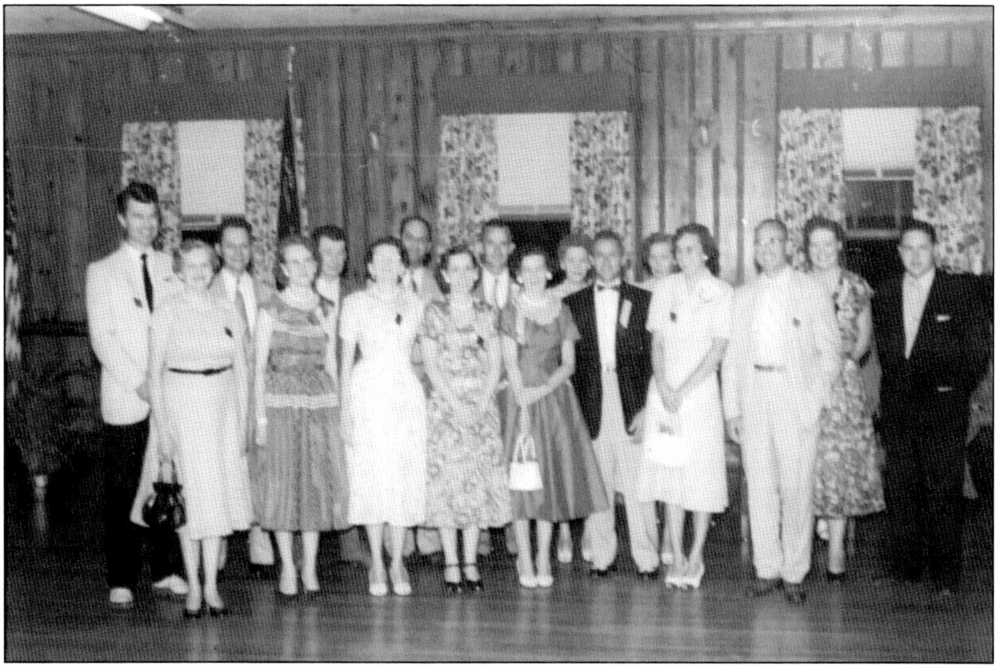

In the 1950s, Piedmont High School's class of 1932 enjoyed a reunion at the Community Building. Some of the folks in attendance were Frank Grover, Harold Payne, George Buckheister, Curt Terry, and Charles Kimbo. (Courtesy of Phil and Becky Buckheister.)

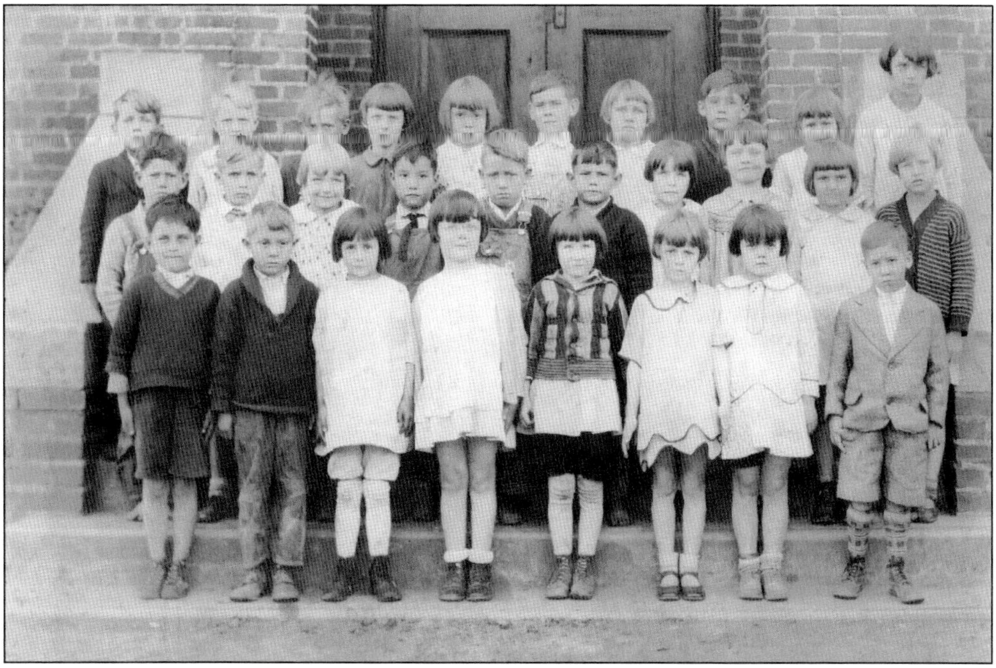

The Piedmont School students pictured here around 1930 look shy. Some of the children are Margie Payne, Helen Trammell Howard, Wilma Clemmons, Mary Bowers, Charles Anderson, Harry White, Dot Porter, Evelyn Aiken, Velma Burrell Morgan, J.T. Buckheister, Hodge Evans, and Virginia Babb. (Courtesy of Margie Payne.)

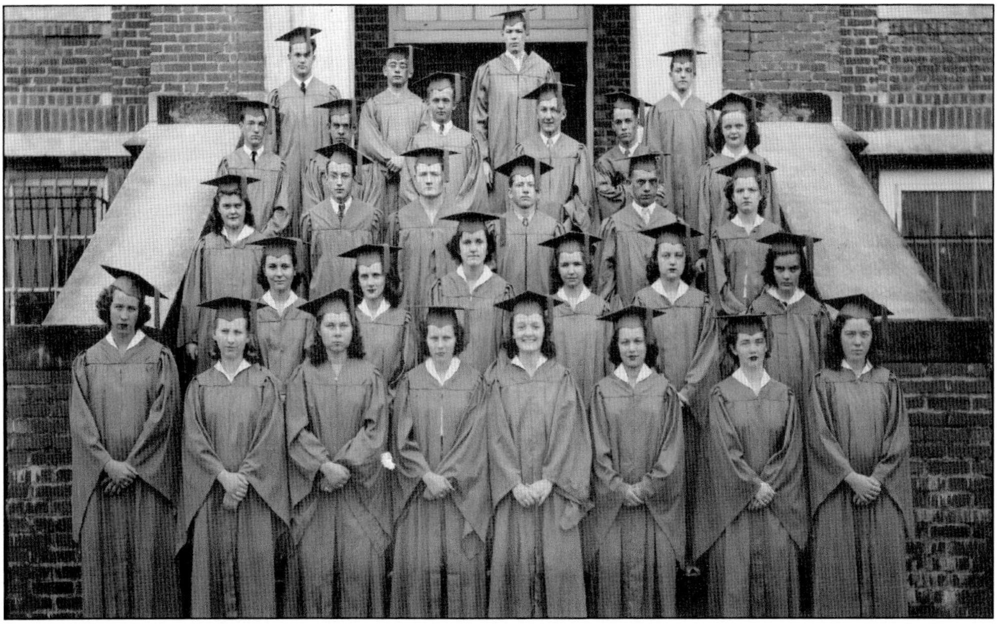

Graduating just months after the bombing of Pearl Harbor, the Piedmont High School class of 1942 was not able to take the annual senior class trip to Washington, DC, due to gas shortages. Instead, the seniors were dismissed early one day, took the train to Pelzer, walked to the drugstore, had ice cream, re-boarded the train, and returned home to Piedmont. From left to right, the students are (first row) Frances Sweat, Edna Galloway, ? McCoy, Lottie Davis, Dorothy Anderson, Roxie Reeves, Ruth Allen, and Lillie Lollis; (second row) Mary Smith, Evelyn Wynn, Marcell Bowman, ? Huff, Mildred Fletcher, and Malzima Smith; (third row) Ailene Payne, Ray Smith, Fred Shackelford, Wade Mitchell, Shuler Jones, and Carmel Duke; (fourth row) ? Smith, unidentified, J.C. Blackstone, Billy Holcombe, Charles Garrison, and Margie Payne; (fifth row) Dillard Burrell, Harry Terry, Bobby Bowen, and Ed Fowler. (Courtesy of Margie Payne.)

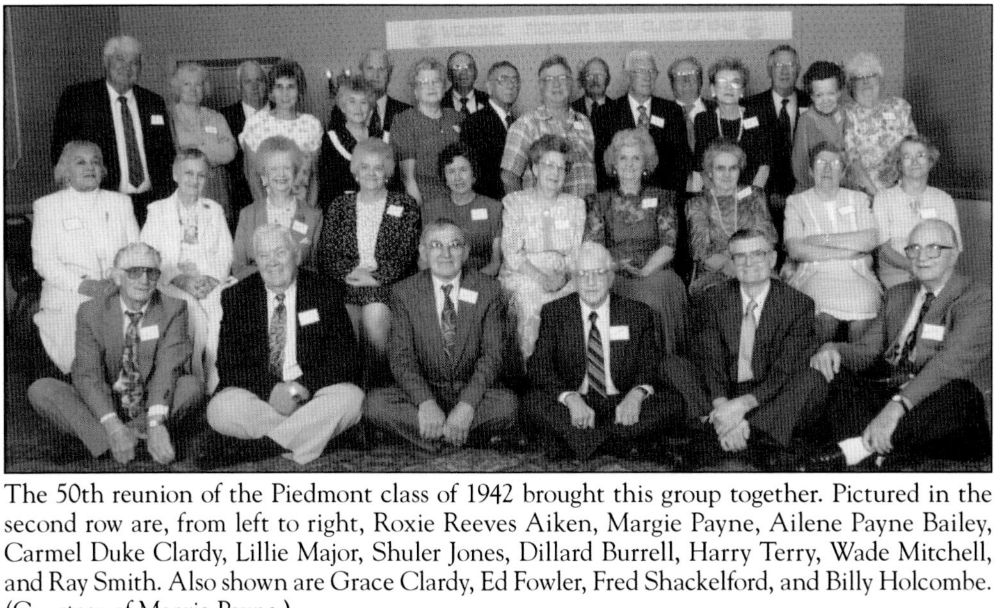

The 50th reunion of the Piedmont class of 1942 brought this group together. Pictured in the second row are, from left to right, Roxie Reeves Aiken, Margie Payne, Ailene Payne Bailey, Carmel Duke Clardy, Lillie Major, Shuler Jones, Dillard Burrell, Harry Terry, Wade Mitchell, and Ray Smith. Also shown are Grace Clardy, Ed Fowler, Fred Shackelford, and Billy Holcombe. (Courtesy of Margie Payne.)

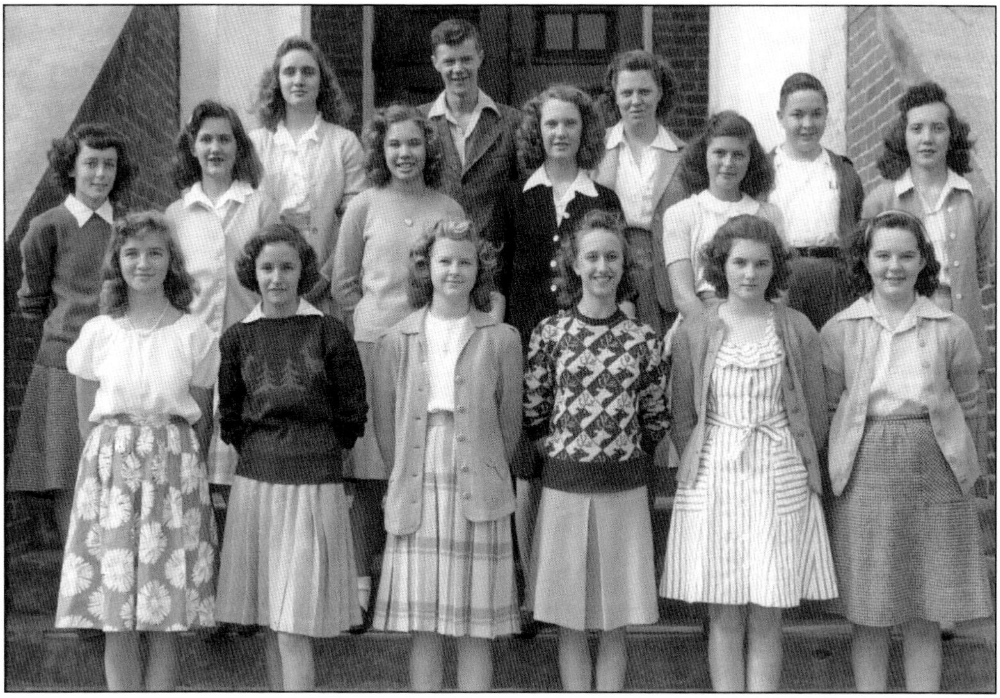

The Piedmont High School music club is pictured in the 1950s. Some of the students are Nancy Hawthorne, Pat Drennon, Toby Boiter, Evelyn Hooper, Betty Reeves, and Fred Payne. (Courtesy of Margie Payne.)

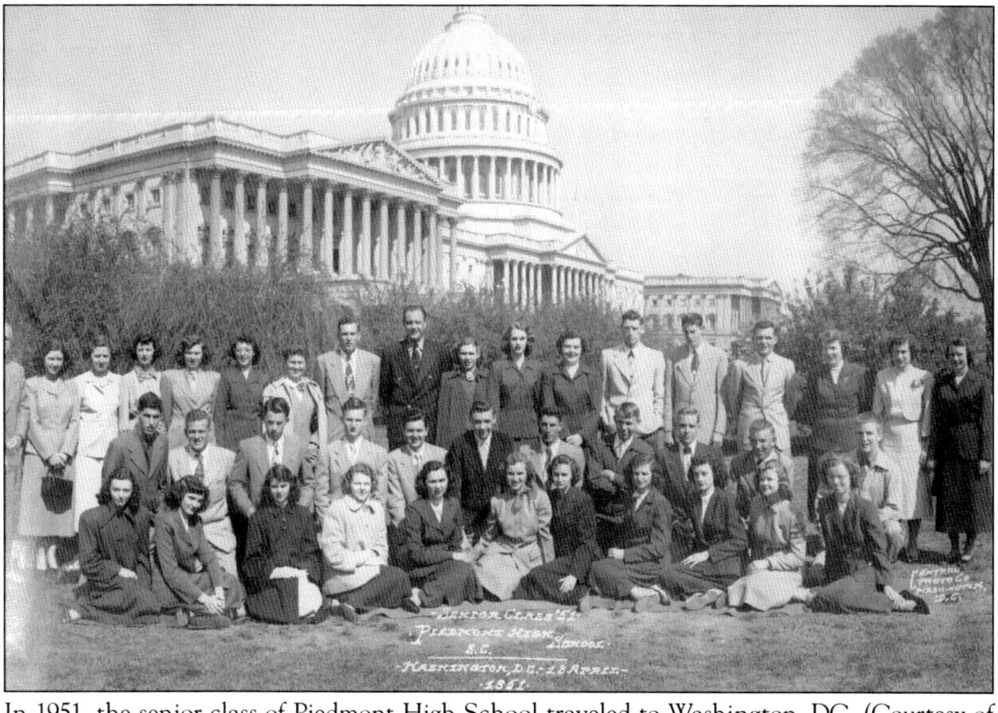

In 1951, the senior class of Piedmont High School traveled to Washington, DC. (Courtesy of Carolyn Reeves.)

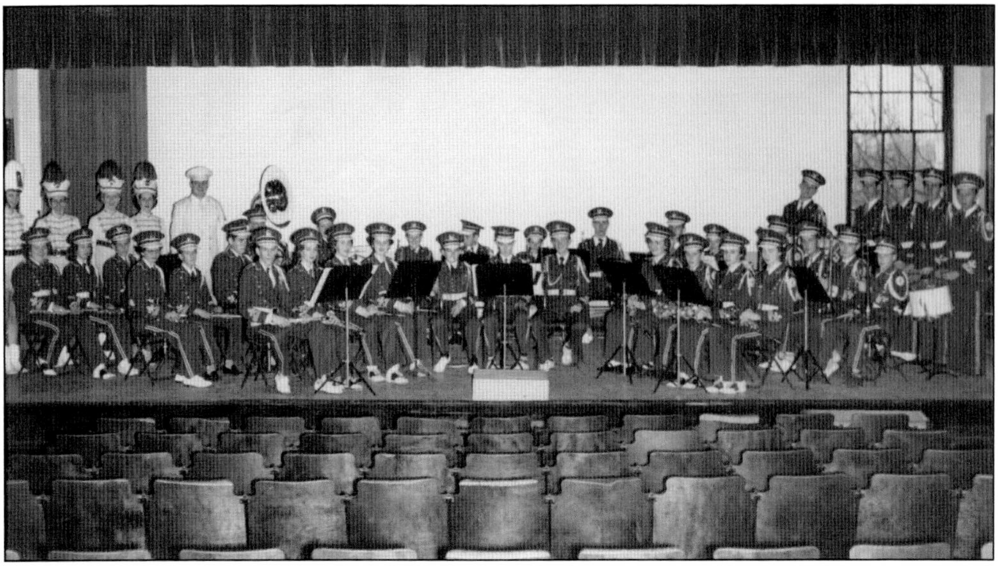

The 1955–1956 Piedmont High School band is ready for a concert. The band director was Carl Smedlund. (Courtesy of Joe Evans.)

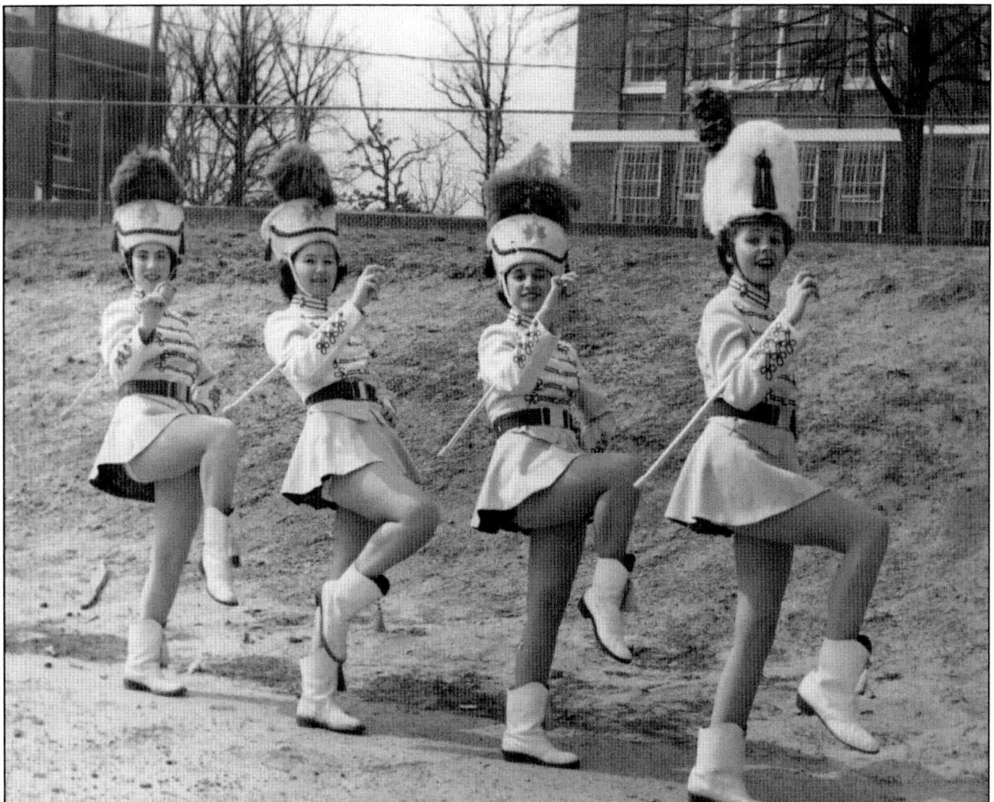

In 1956, the Piedmont High School majorettes were, from left to right, Carole Corbin, Ann Kelley, Joan Davis, and Scarlett Gilreath. (Courtesy of Joe Evans.)

Piedmont High School students enjoy recess in 1957. Seated from left to right are Joe Evans, Lindy Lou Boyce, Nancy Hollingsworth, and David Merritt. Behind them at left are Jessie Lee Anderson and Doris Calvert. (Courtesy of Joe Evans.)

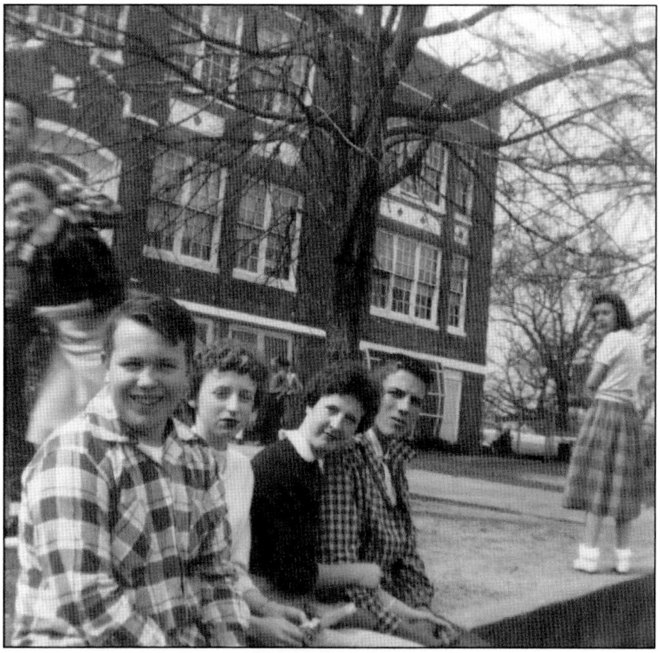

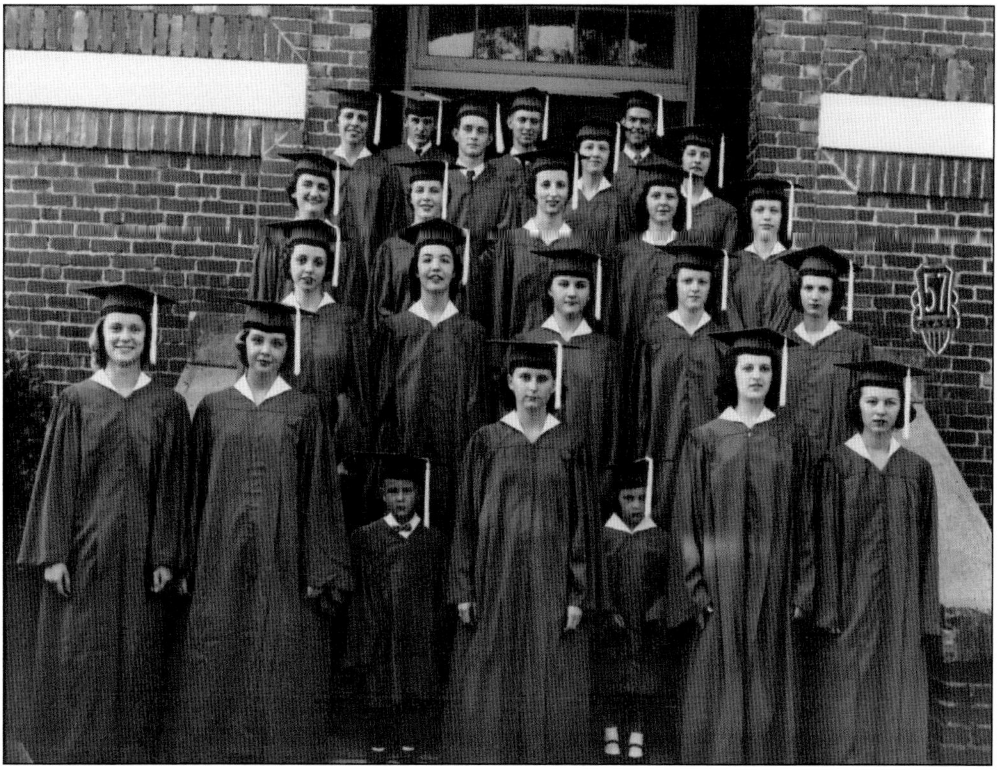

The Piedmont High School graduating class of 1957 poses on the steps. Among the students pictured are Susan Bowie Patterson, Peggy Jenkins Bagwell, Iris Ann Bowen, Margaret Weisner, Pat Tarrant, Fred Jacks, Joyce Pepper, Louise Strickland Wallace, Marie Parks Williamson, and Petie Peden. (Courtesy of Phil and Becky Buckheister.)

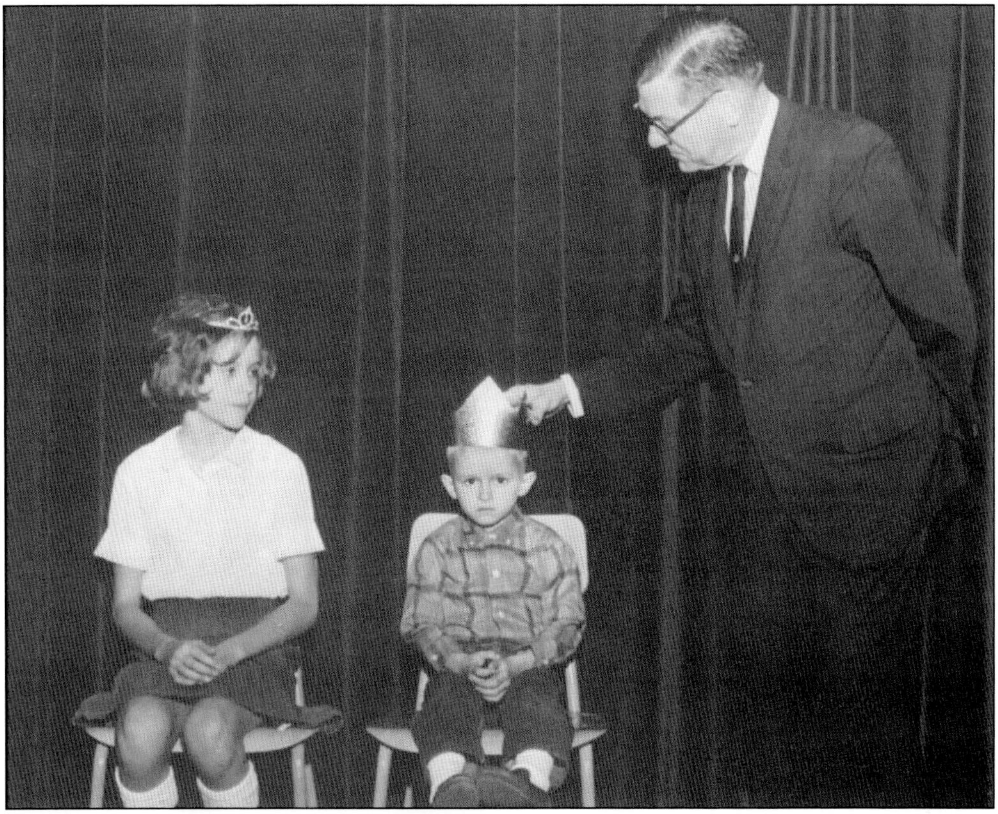

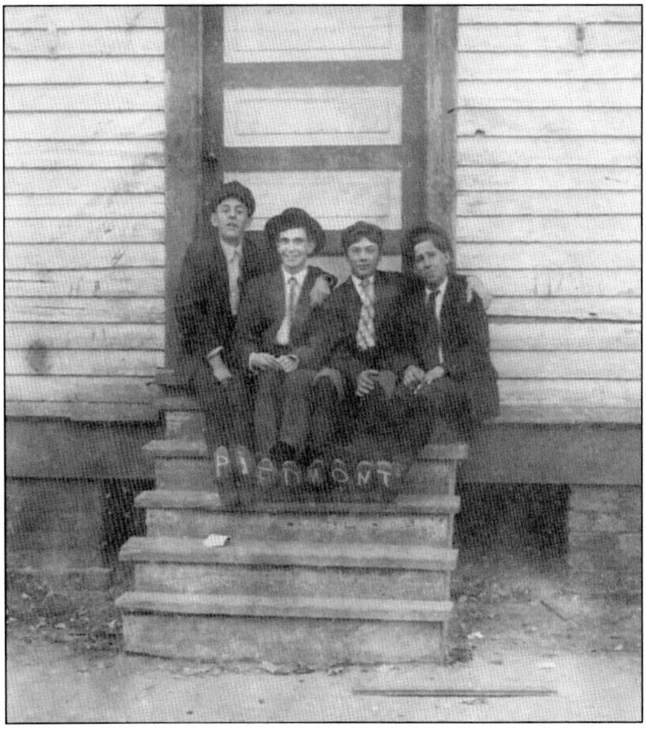

H.A. Loftis, principal of Sue Cleveland Elementary School, crowns the king and queen of the Halloween carnival. (Courtesy of Anne Peden.)

Pictured on the steps of the Piedmont School prior to the turn of the 20th century, these boys make it clear where they go to school. From left to right are Walter Buckhiester, Glenn Davenport, J. Frank Davenport, and an unidentified friend. (Courtesy of Piedmont Historical Collection.)

Six

VILLAGE LIFE

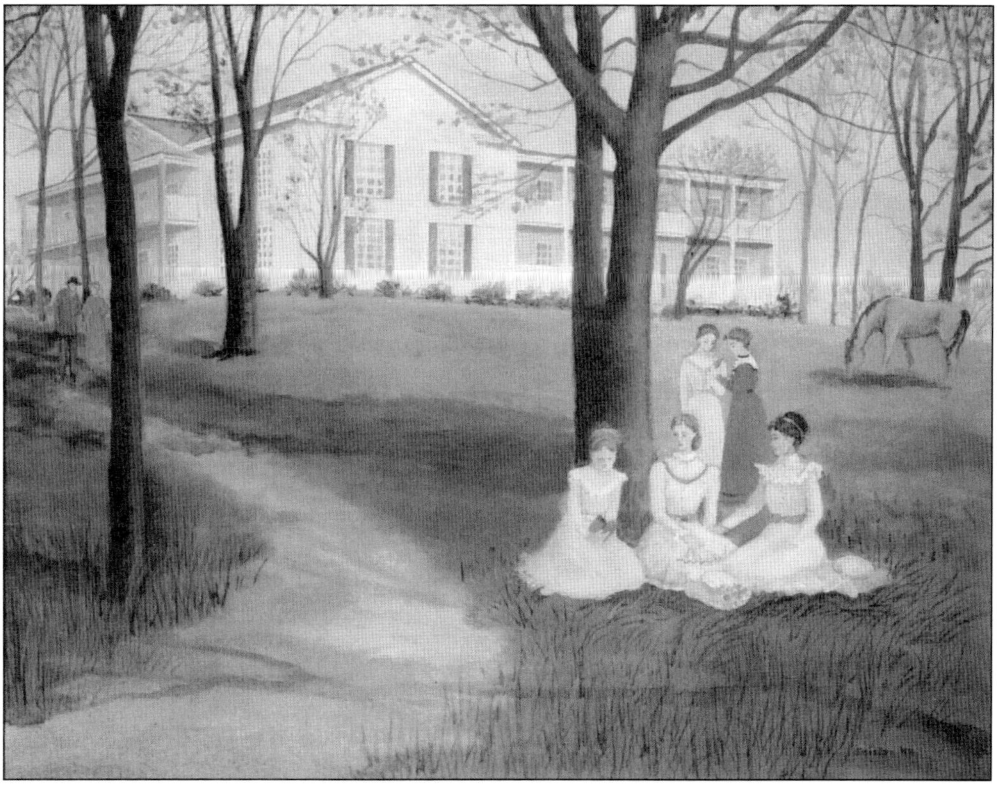

Families have been key to Piedmont life throughout its history. Therefore, village life revolved around all things family. The mill supported a variety of activities for families to participate in and often led in supplying the place for recreation. In this chapter, families and fun are the focus. Since there was a professional photographer in Piedmont, J.L. (Fate) Davenport, there are many early images to share. (Courtesy of the Bonnes Amies Club.)

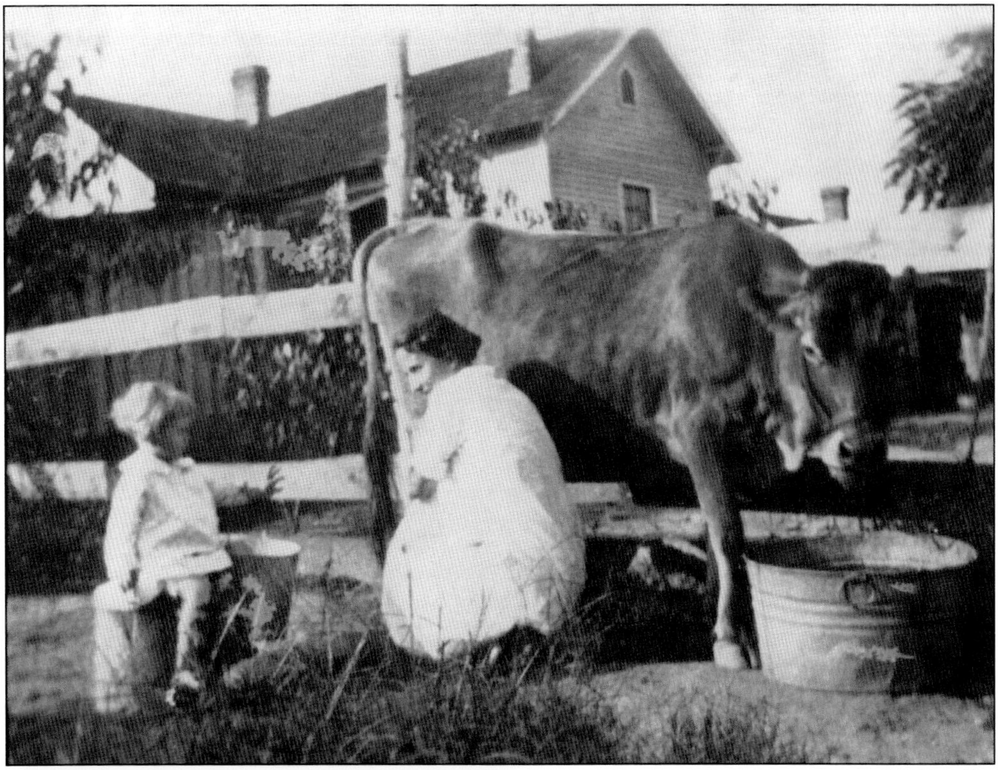

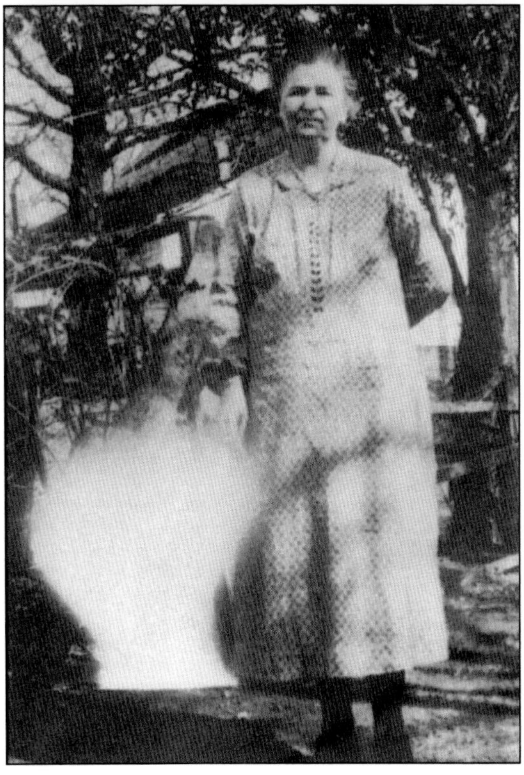

Nannie Mae Thompson sprays fresh milk at her two-year-old daughter, Louise. This would have been a common scene in the early 1900s around Piedmont. The mill owned a bull, and it was loaned out to the villagers as needed. The Thompsons lived at 3 Spring Street. (Courtesy of Betty Thompson White.)

Washday was a true ordeal before running water and the wringer washer. Alice Maude Middleton Thompson boils her clothing in front of her house on Main Street in the early 1900s. (Courtesy of Betty Thompson White.)

James Elliott Peden and Katie Garrison Boiter enjoy a buggy ride in the 1920s. Peden lived on a farm on Old Pelzer Road just east of Piedmont. (Courtesy of Margaret Payne.)

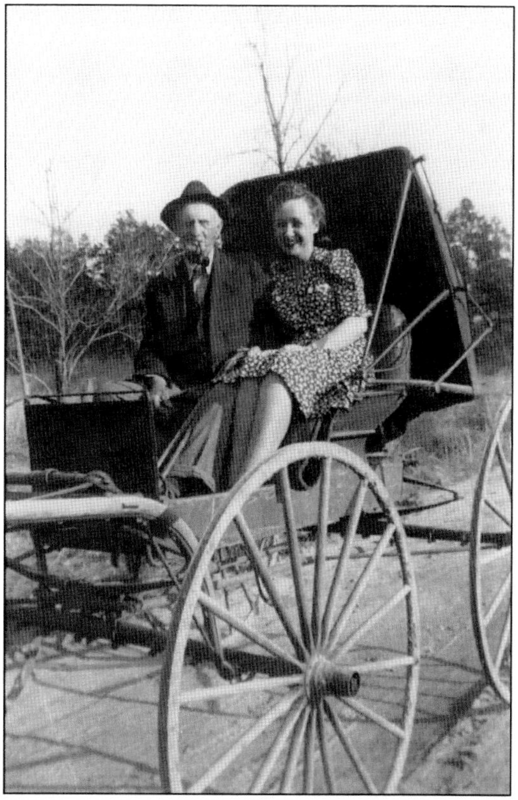

Robert Phillips and his family were photographed on their front porch around the turn of the 20th century. Robert and his wife, Mattie Bishop Phillips, are pictured with their four girls (from left to right), Nannie Mae Taylor Thompson, Marie Trammell, Elsie Trammell, and Winnie Trammell. (Courtesy of Betty Thompson White.)

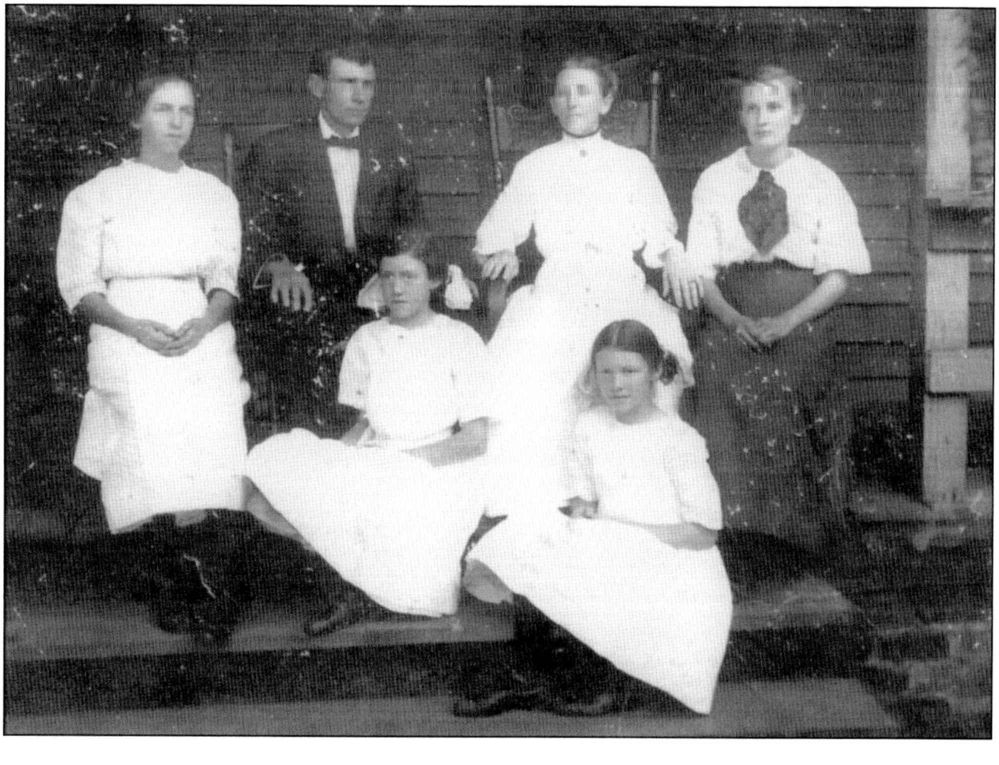

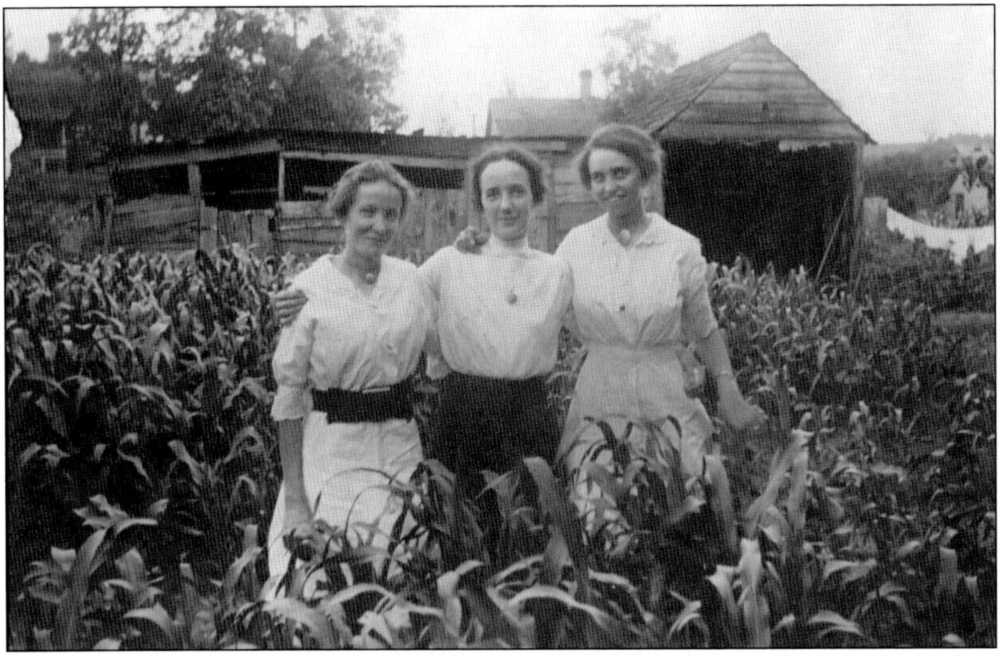

These young ladies are enjoying a day in the corn. Pictured from left to right are Sarah McCoy, Pearl Clardy Smith, and an unidentified friend. (Courtesy of Gayle Payne.)

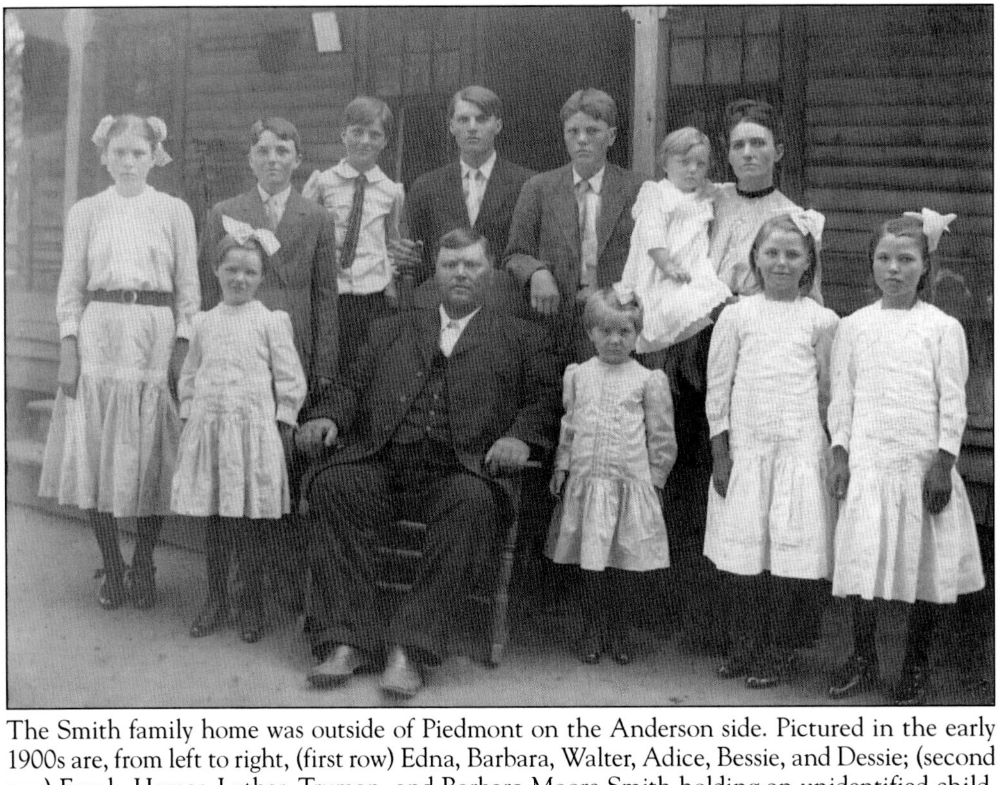

The Smith family home was outside of Piedmont on the Anderson side. Pictured in the early 1900s are, from left to right, (first row) Edna, Barbara, Walter, Adice, Bessie, and Dessie; (second row) Frank, Homer, Luther, Truman, and Barbara Moore Smith holding an unidentified child. This home is still standing on Smith Road. (Courtesy of Gayle Smith Payne.)

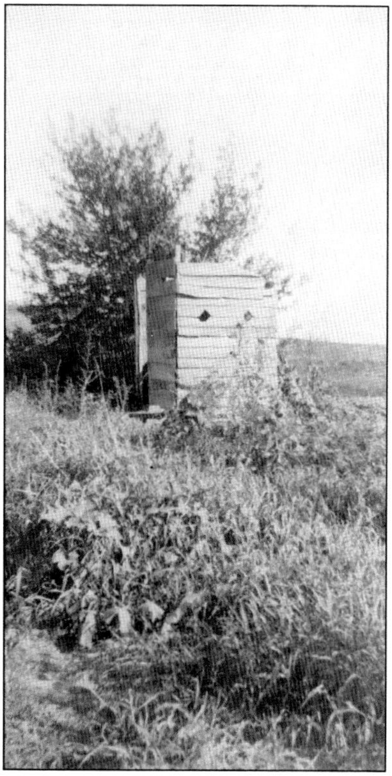

Two common structures seen in the area were the well and the outhouse. Near every house was a dug well, into which a rope on a pulley lowered and raised a bucket for water. With no running water, an outhouse was necessary. They were usually designed to be moved from spot to spot as the hole under them filled. Chamber pots were kept inside and emptied daily. By the time these photographs were taken at the Gillespie Farm, most folks already had indoor plumbing. Ruth Gillespie Cantrell used to kid her family when she returned home from the big city for still having these structures in the yard in the 1940s. (Both, courtesy of Carolyn Reeves.)

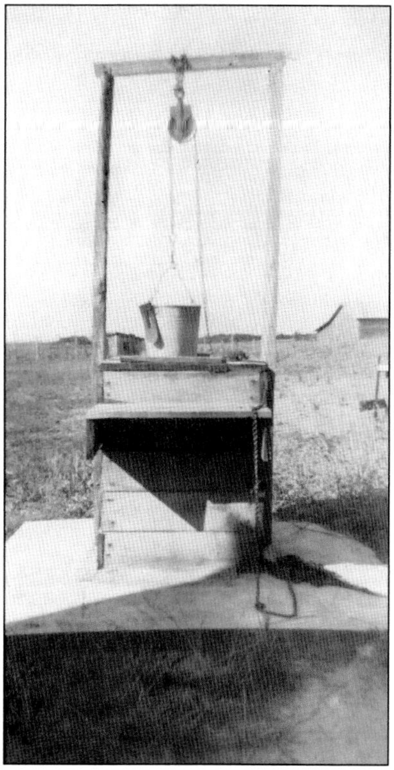

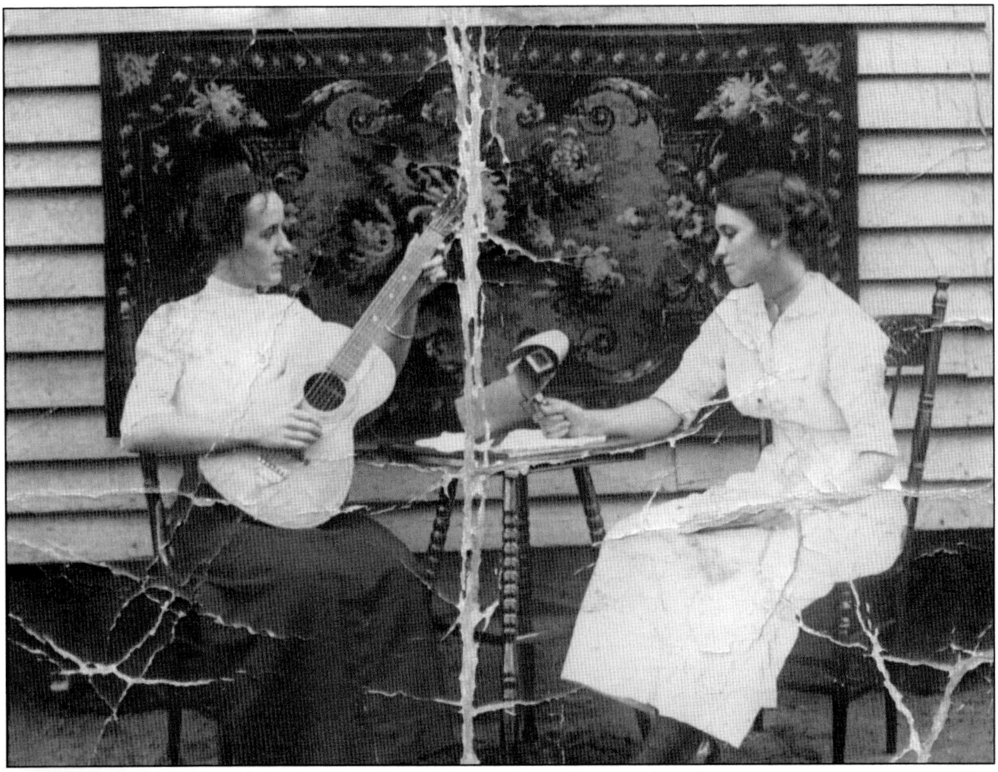

Even though folks worked hard in the mill or on farms, most participated in some sort of cultural affair when available. Here, at the turn of the 20th century, Pearl Clardy Smith (with the stereoscope) and Sarah McCoy (with the guitar) represent the types of activities young ladies spent their leisure time doing. (Courtesy of Gayle Payne.)

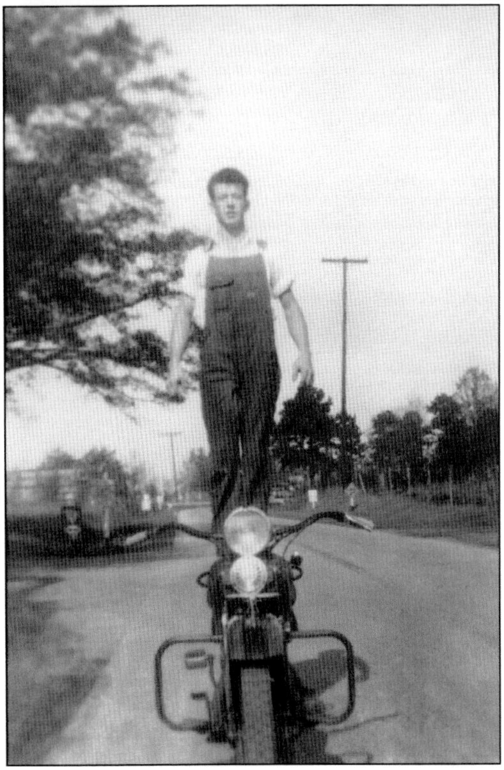

Daredevil Harold Payne stands atop the seat of his Harley motorbike as it rolls along on Main Street in the late 1930s. (Courtesy of Jimmy and Gayle Payne.)

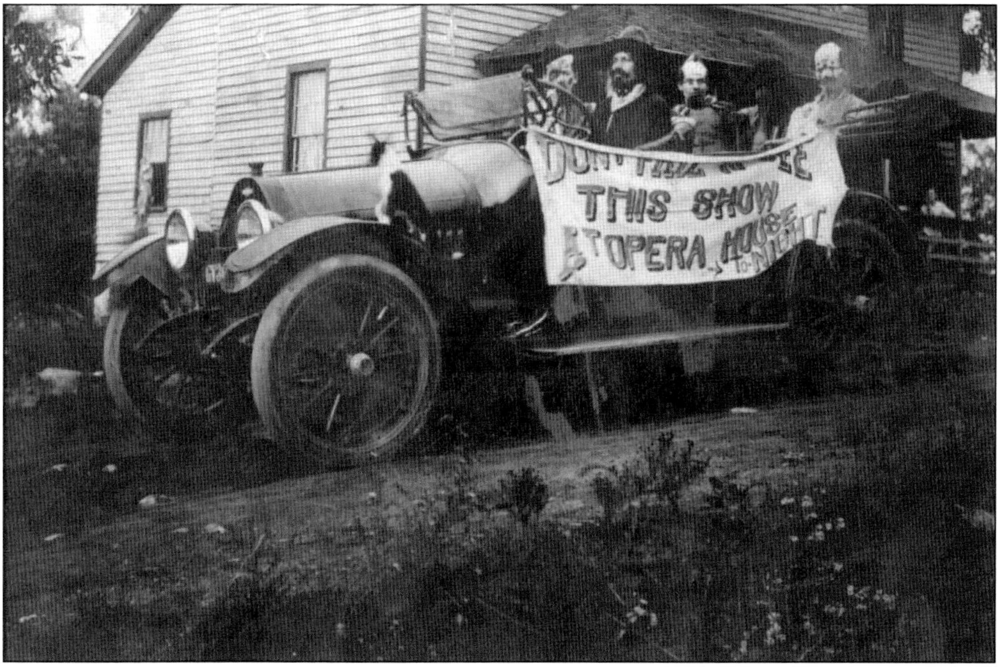

J. Frank Davenport and his friends advertise their minstrel show at the Opera House. They are taking Frank's car and are already dressed for the show. (Courtesy of Betty Davenport.)

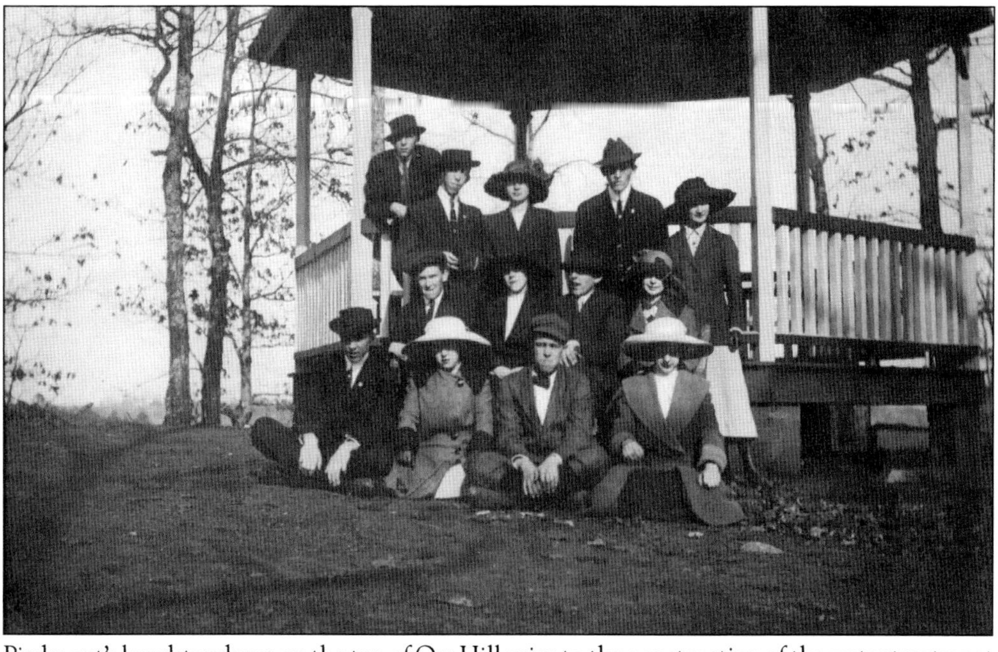

Piedmont's bandstand was on the top of Orr Hill prior to the construction of the water treatment plant in the 1930s. A group of young people pose in front. Notice that men and women continued to wear hats into the 1950s. Picture the hill crowded with listeners enjoying a celebration with the Piedmont Band. (Courtesy of Betty Davenport.)

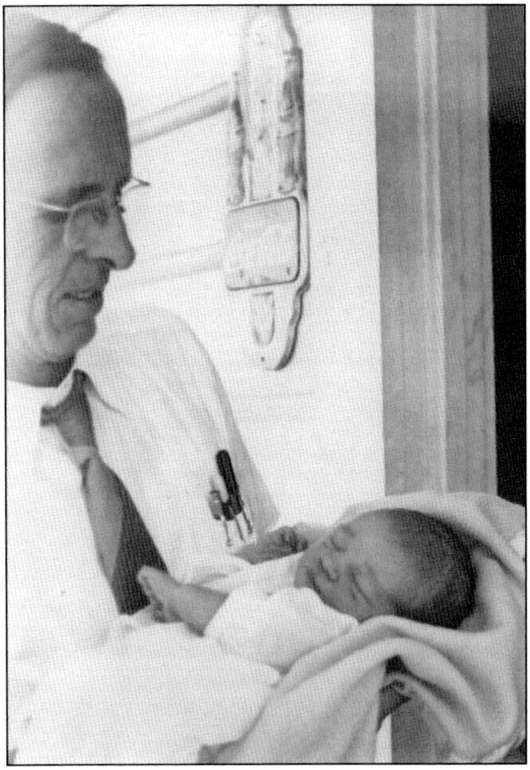

Dr. J.P. Jewell holds one-hour-old Sandra Stewart. She was born at her grandparent's home in Piedmont. Dr. Jewell was the town doctor on the Anderson side in 1915. Folks still remember him dispensing red or green liquids for almost anything. On the Greenville side, Dr. S.D. Campbell served as the mill doctor for decades, birthing many babies. He was the grandfather of Gov. Carroll Campbell. (Courtesy of Sandra Stewart Wood.)

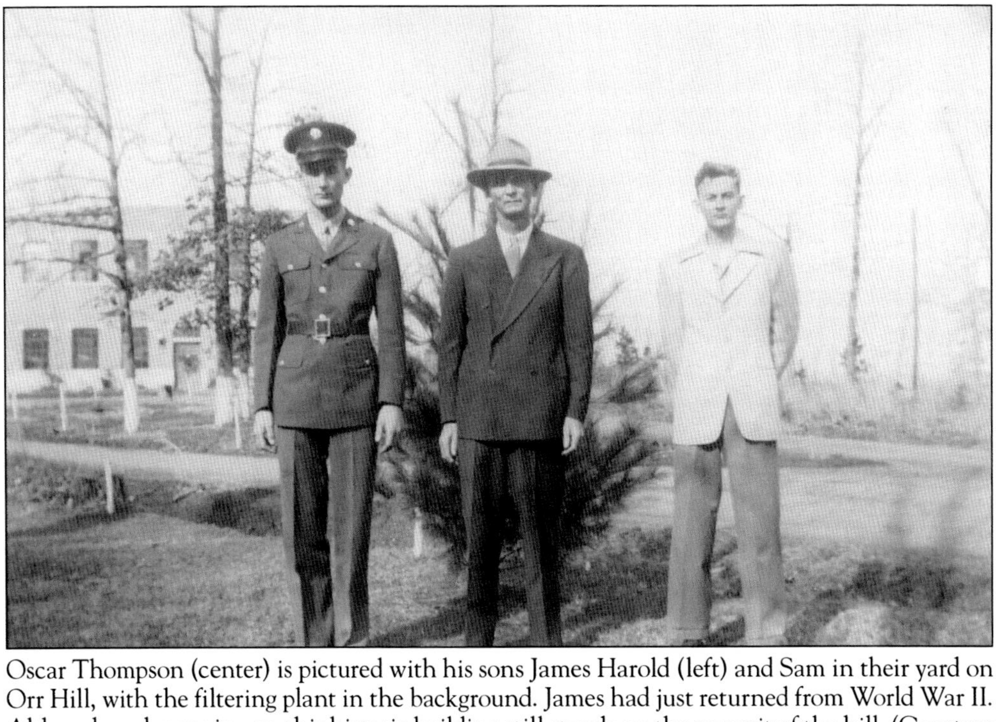

Oscar Thompson (center) is pictured with his sons James Harold (left) and Sam in their yard on Orr Hill, with the filtering plant in the background. James had just returned from World War II. Although no longer in use, this historic building still stands on the summit of the hill. (Courtesy of Betty Thompson White.)

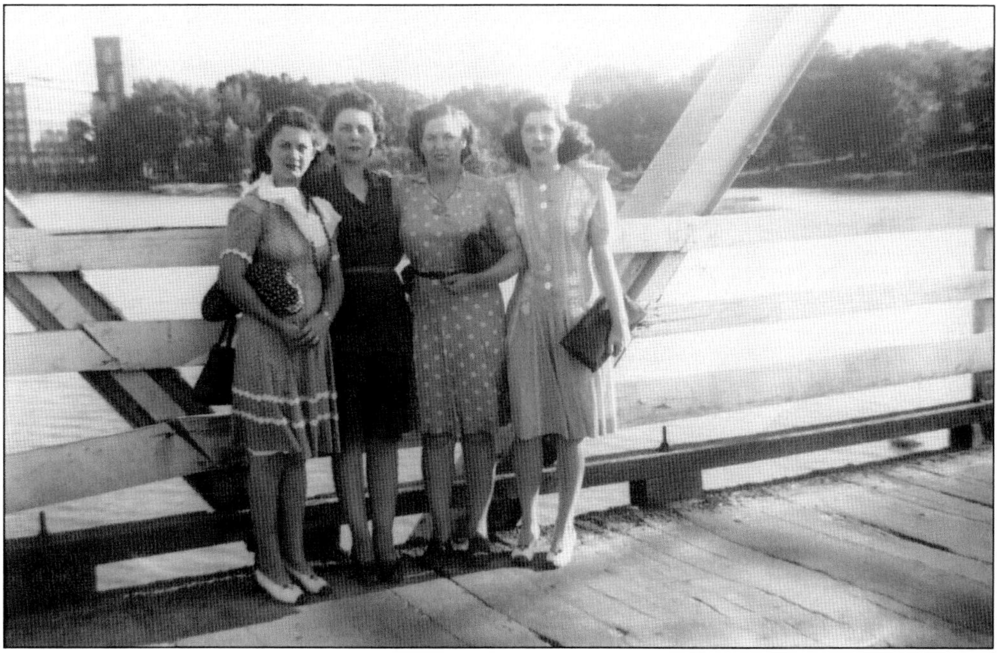

Posing on the wagon bridge are, from left to right, Eunice Gilreath, Reba Hollighsworth, Frances Pack, and Louise Pack Kimbo. This was a popular place to have photos taken. Look at the similar photograph on page 23 from the early 1900s. Guessing by the spectator shoes, this photograph was taken in the 1940s. The current bridge opened in 1948. (Courtesy of Pert Clifford.)

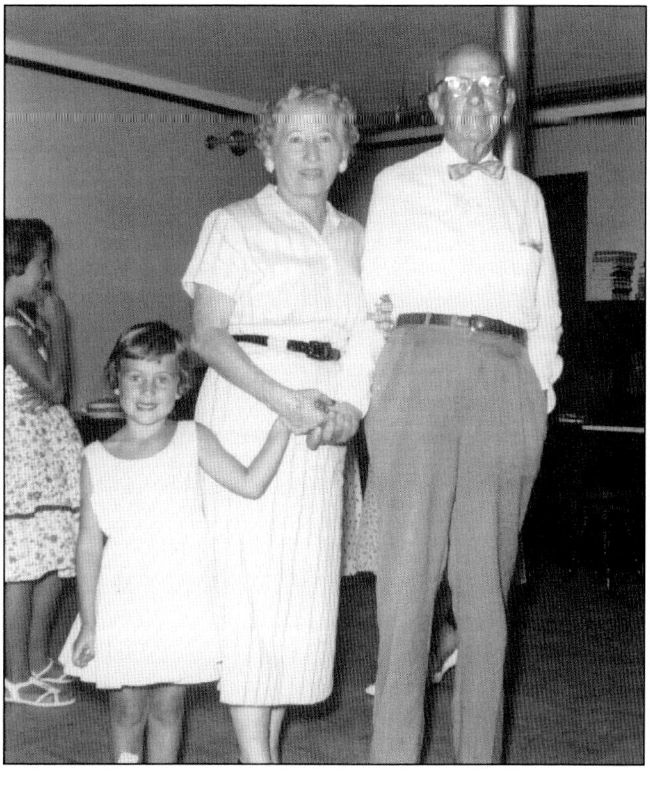

Dr. Frank Suber was an important person in Piedmont. He ran the drugstore downtown for many years. This picture was taken at a celebration honoring him at the Methodist church. He is with his wife, Eva, and a granddaughter. (Courtesy of Shirley Tice Elrod.)

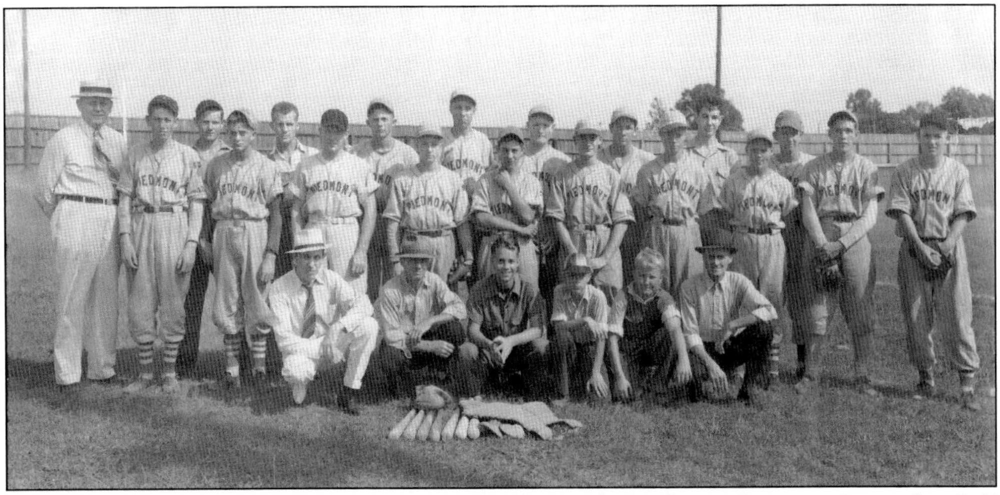

Team sports were vital to life in Piedmont. Pictured here is the Piedmont American Legion baseball team of 1940. Called the "hardest luck team in baseball," the boys are (first row) H.K. Clardy (post adjutant) J.F. Davenport (manager), Charles Garrison, "Batboy" Cox, J.R. Shirley (mascot), and unidentified; (second row) L.B. Templeton (post commander), "Pudding" Stone, Johnny Brock, Eddie Bates, "Shag" Allen, Joe Ed Fleming, Curt Lindley, Ed Fowler, James League, Jack McAdams, Fred Shackelford, Gordon Cooper, Allen Cox, Red Trammell, James Long, Bob White, Robert Rogers, Elwood Fletcher, and Charles Anderson. (Courtesy of Betty Davenport.)

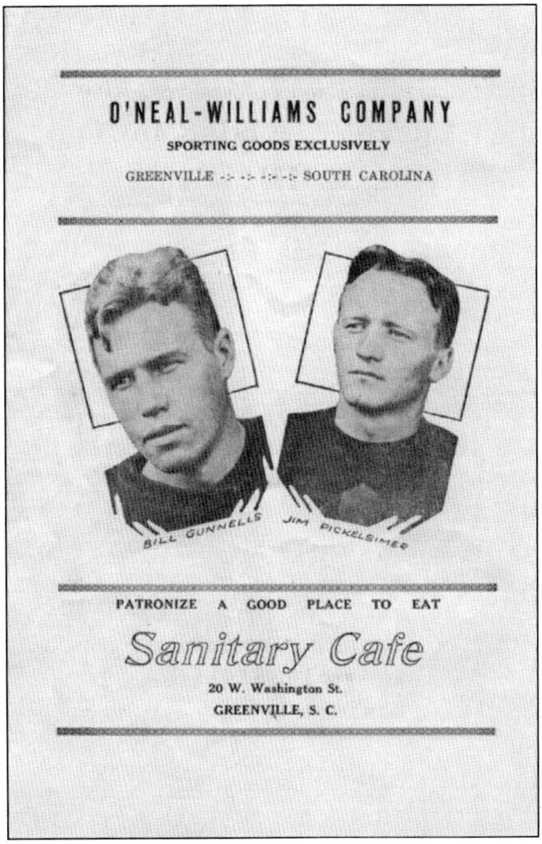

Piedmont native Jim Pickelsimer was an important player at Clemson in the early days of football. This program is from a 1929 Clemson football game. (Courtesy of Elisabeth Pickelsimer.)

Children were important members of the Piedmont village. Here, brother and sister Francis Tice and Shirley Tice Elrod stand at the rose trellis in 1942. Their house was at 5 Spring Street. (Courtesy of Shirley Tice Elrod.)

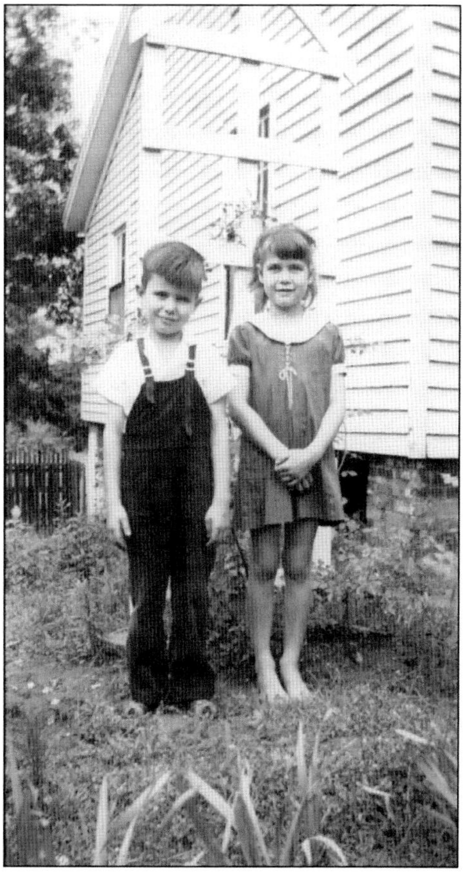

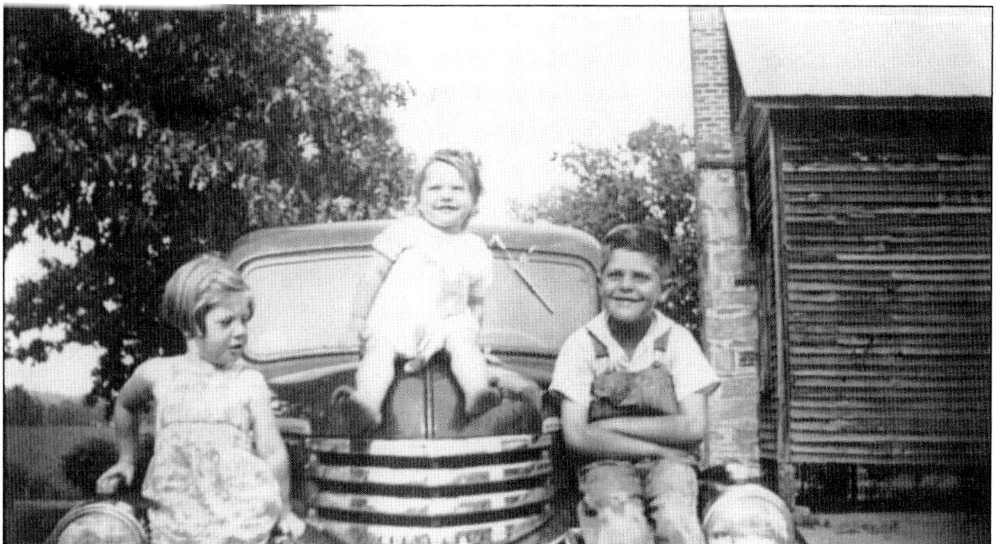

Grandparents are important family members, especially to their grandchildren. From left to right, Joann Wilson Smith, Betty Wilson Burdett, and Jimmy Wilson are pictured visiting their mother's parents in Slabtown in 1942. (Courtesy of Betty Wilson Burdett.)

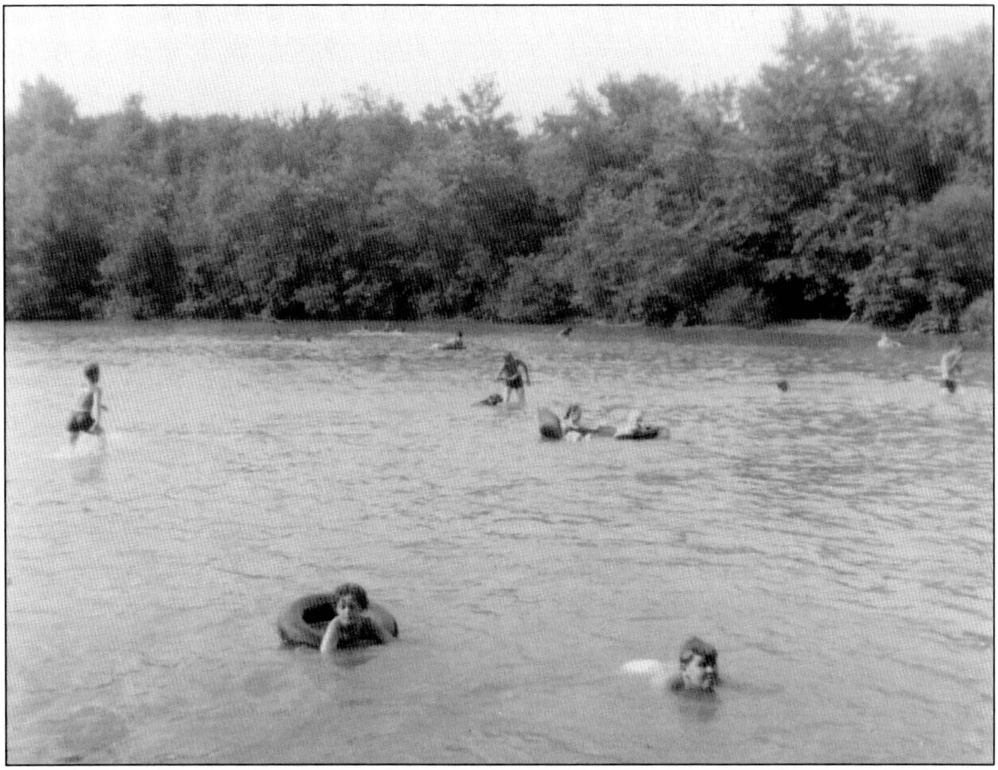

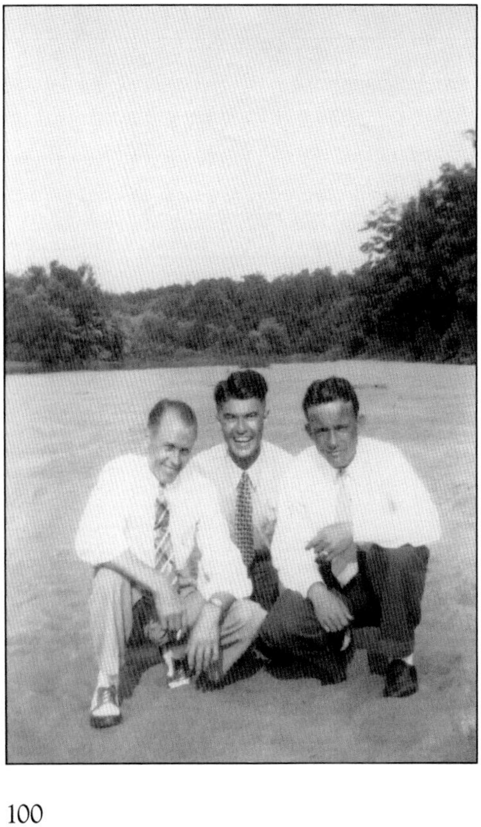

Piedmont Beach, or the "Sand Bar," was a wonderful place to swim and sun in the 1940s. Three handsome guys are pictured at left on the Sand Bar of the Saluda in the 1940s. Frank Grover is in the center, Ham Williams is believed to be the man on the left, and the tan fellow on the right is unidentified. (Above, courtesy of Connie Hunnings; left, courtesy of Betty Thompson White.)

Having one's photograph taken while coming up the steps from the river to the water treatment plant was popular in the 1930s and 1940s. Pictured here are Louise Thompson Evans (left) and Lib Rainey Adkins. (Courtesy of Betty White.)

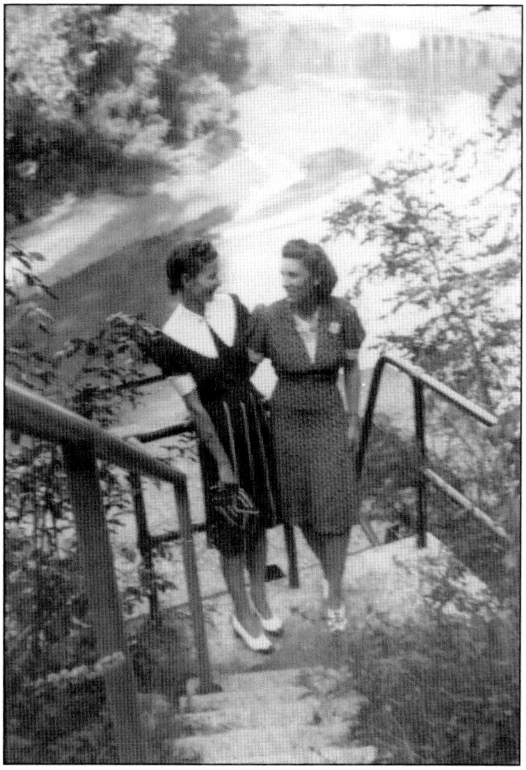

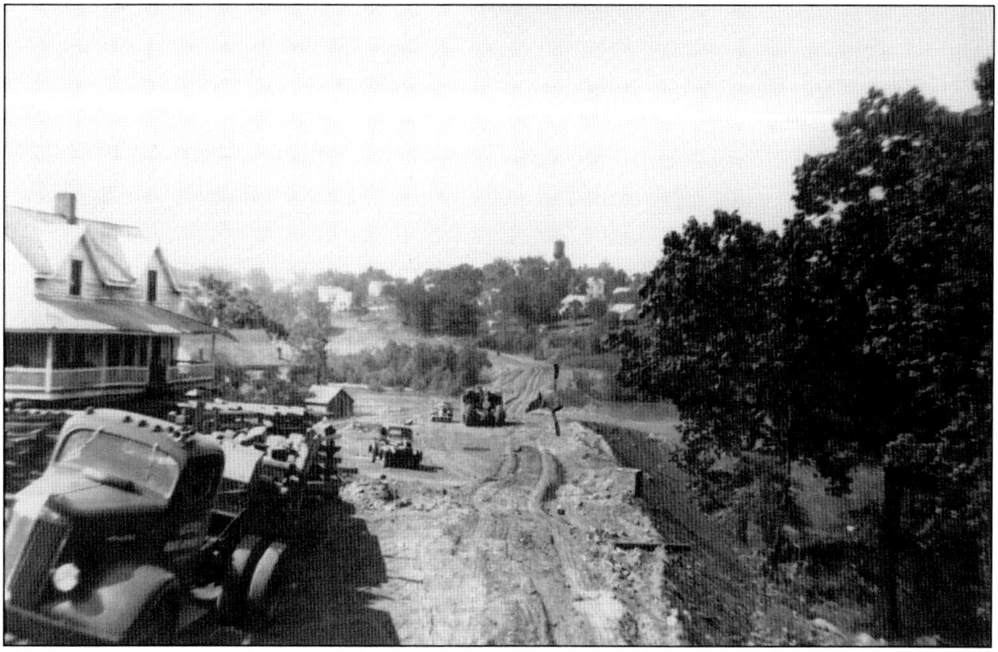

The current bridge was dedicated in 1948, but construction had been going on for a long time. The road from the bridge to the top of the hill at the Methodist church did not exist, and houses filled the area. The YWCA (or Women's Building) and other buildings had to be moved and the street rerouted. (Courtesy of Connie Hunnings.)

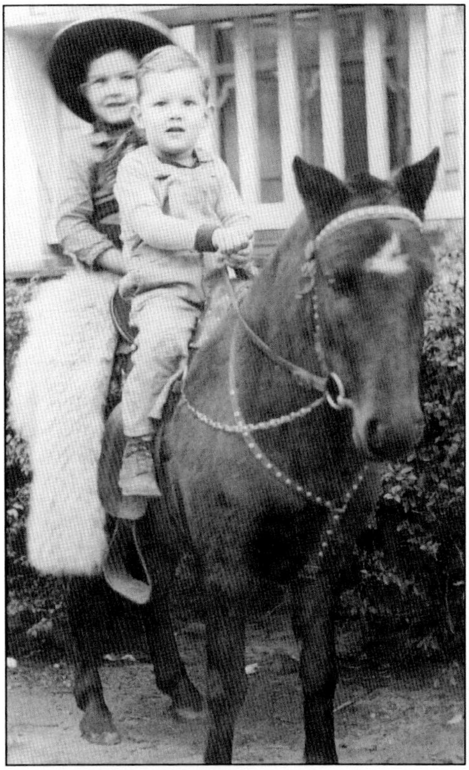

Four-year-old Alton Roper and his two-year-old brother, Donald, enjoy a pony ride on King Street in 1936. Look at those fine chaps Alton is wearing. Don grew up to be Piedmont historian Saluda Sam. (Courtesy of Don Roper.)

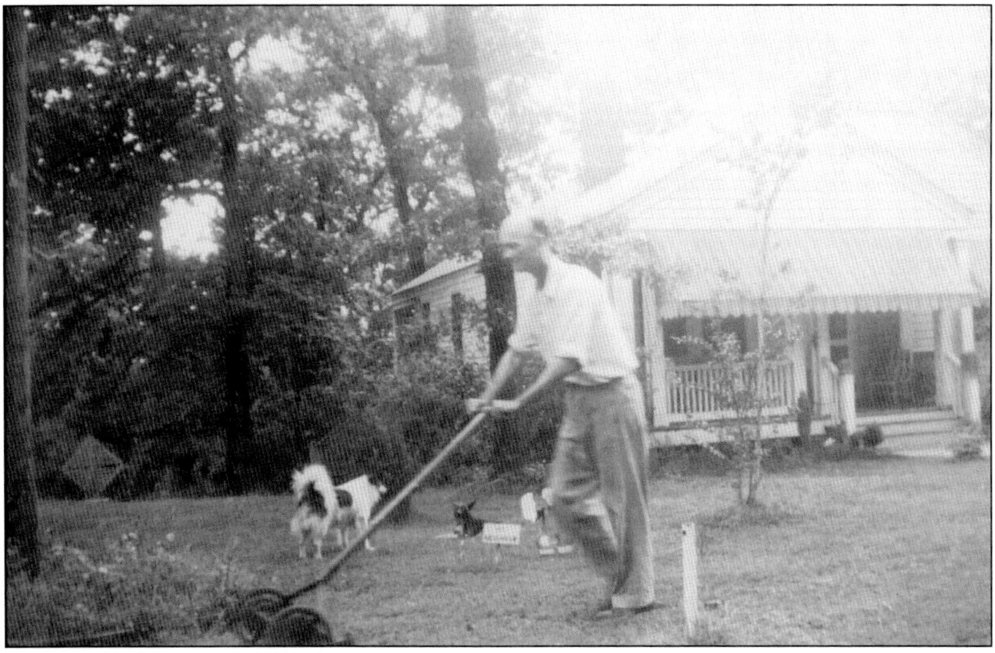

The grass needed to be cut at 6 Orr Hill. Many folks swept their yards before lawn mowers became fashionable. Here, Oscar Ben Tillmon Thompson uses an early model mower. These mowers have become popular again with those who have small yards. Patches the dog is helping all that he can. (Courtesy of Betty Thompson White.)

Herefords were a common site around Piedmont in the 1940s. While cotton was waning as king, cattle farming was becoming popular, and many breeds new to the area were seen among the hills and in the pastures. Here, T.K. Peden gives his son Raymond a ride around 1950. (Courtesy of Billy and Darlene Peden.)

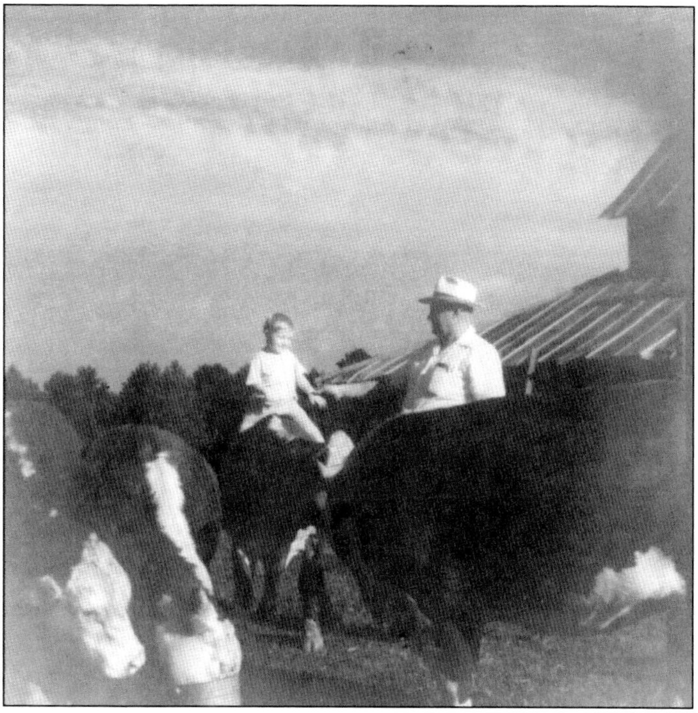

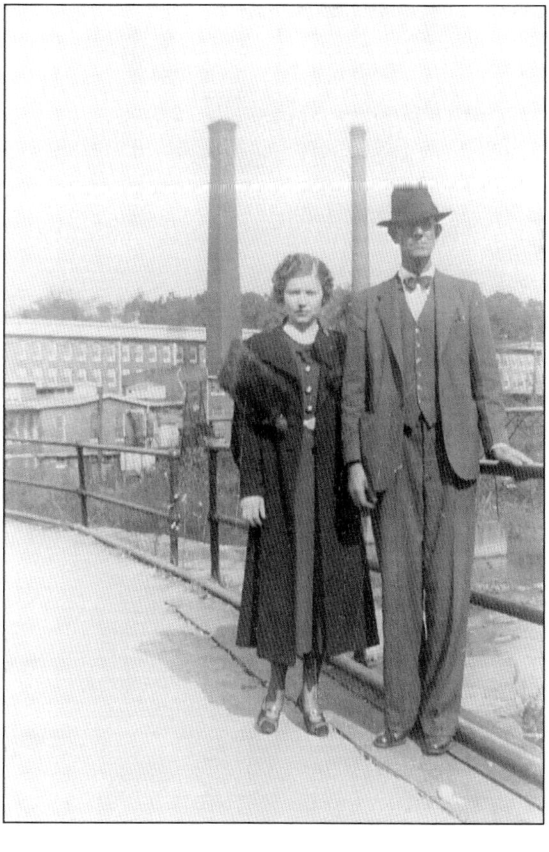

Gracie Capell Ward and her father, Samuel Matthew Capell, pose on the Anderson side of the footbridge. The two mill smokestacks are plainly visible, one square and one round. (Courtesy of Frances Ward.)

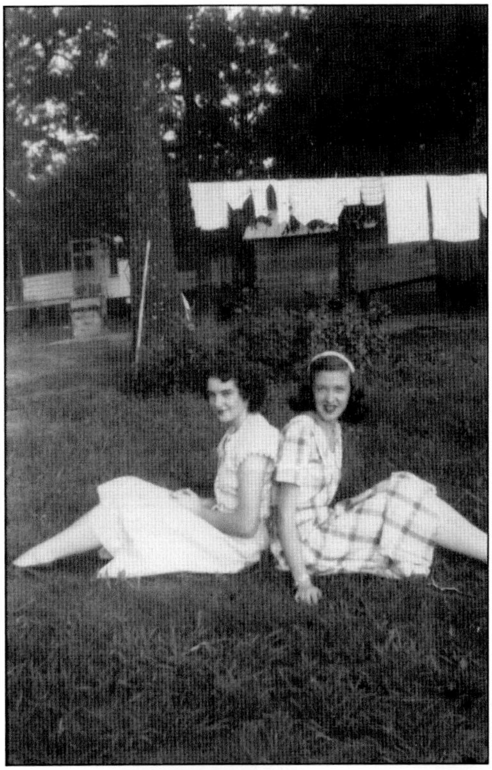

In 1940 as today, clothes needed to be washed and dried. Most people had a clothesline then, and some who like the fresh smell still hang their clothes behind their homes. This was taken in the backyards of the homes of Jennie Jones Lawless and Marie Foster Hiott. (Courtesy of Carolyn Reeves.)

There was nothing like a baseball game at the ballpark. Here, the youngsters and their coaches wait for their turn at bat in the 1960s. Family members watch and cheer in the background. Seated on the bench are, from left to right, two unidentified, Ben Abrams, Milford "Punchy" Howard, John Pearson, Jerry Hooper, "Mo" Howard, and Cary Freeman. Damian McCauley is standing at far left. (Courtesy of Betty Davenport.)

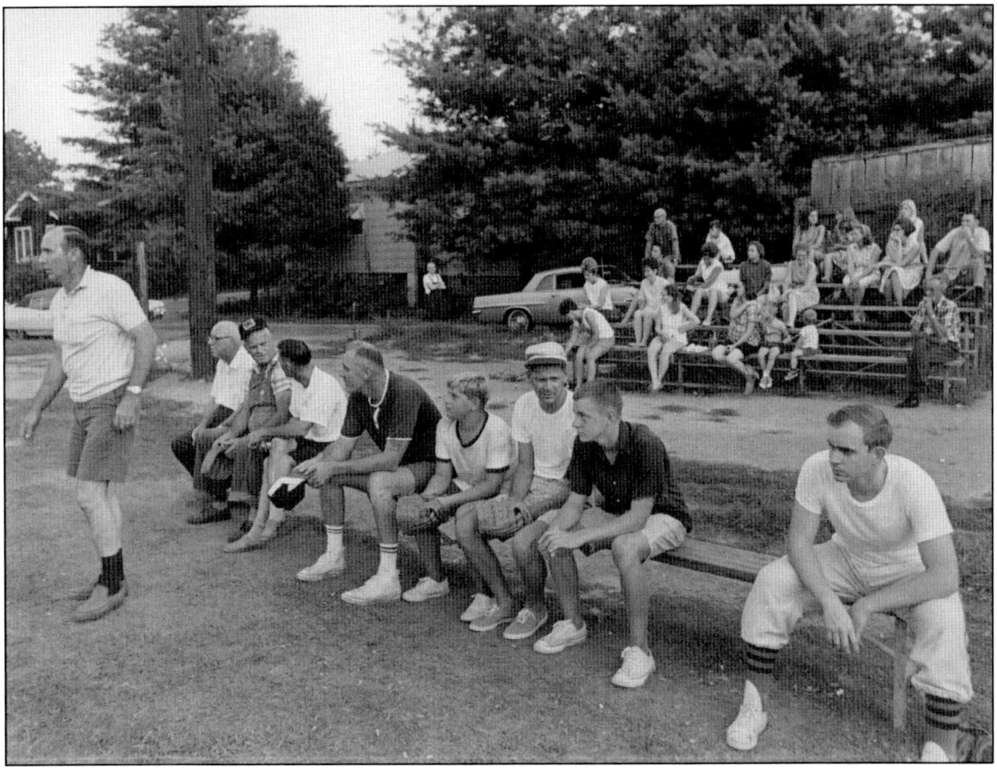

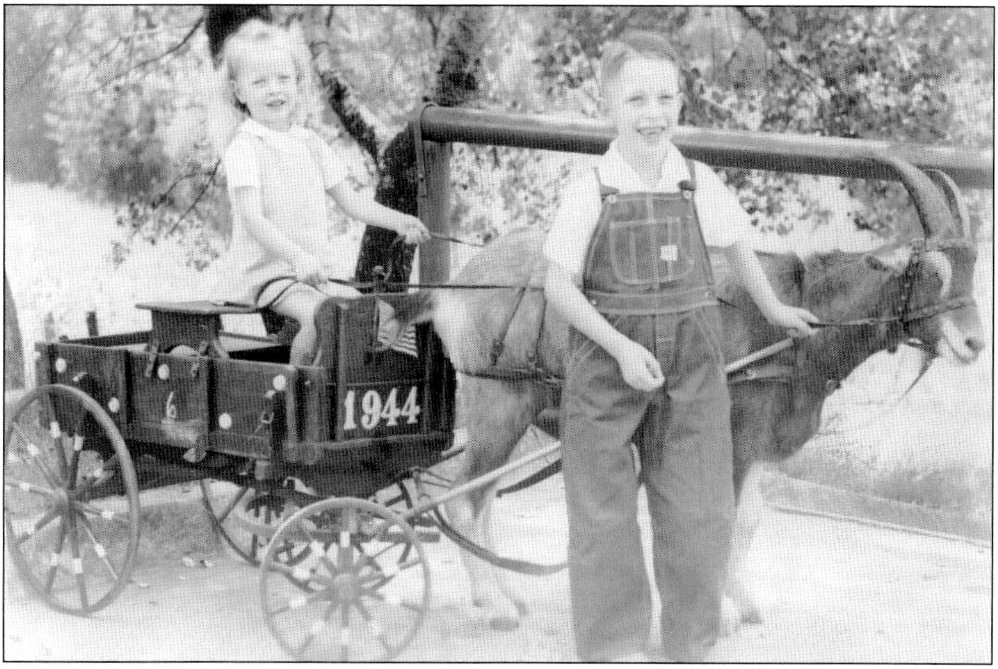

Gwen Vance and her brother pose in a goat cart in 1944. This is probably not the cart of the famous "Goat Man," but he did visit Piedmont from time to time. (Courtesy of Gwen Vance.)

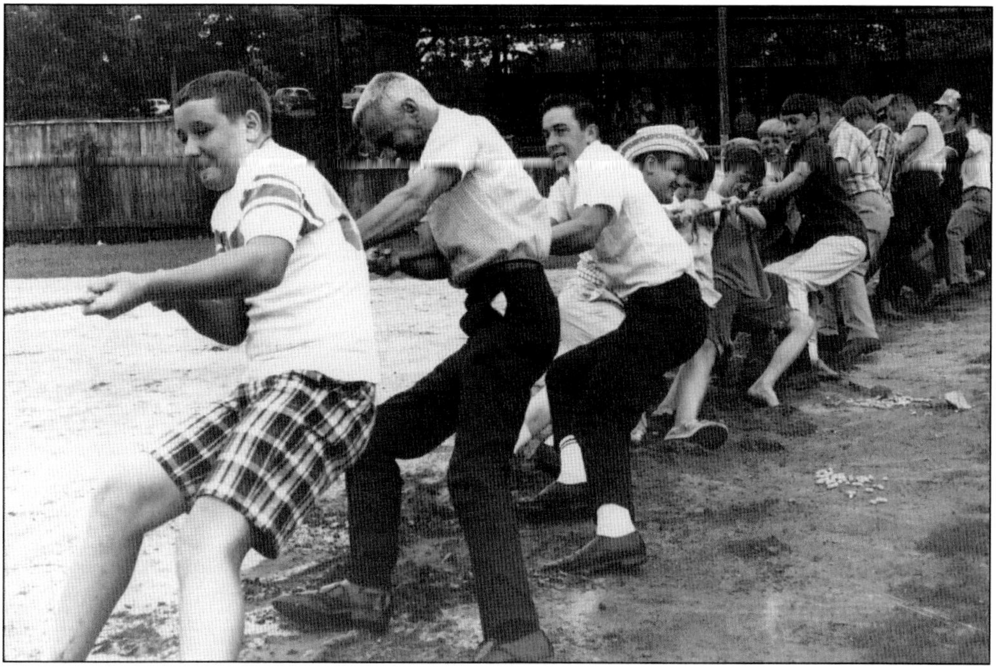

Buchanan Field was across the Saluda in Anderson County, behind the mill houses where the walking park is now. It was a treasured part of Piedmont. Many recreational activities, especially baseball, happened there, and one of the biggest was the annual Fourth of July celebration. Many games and contests were played at this festival. A traditional tug-of-war was always exciting. Notice the stadium in the background. (Courtesy of Piedmont Historical Collection.)

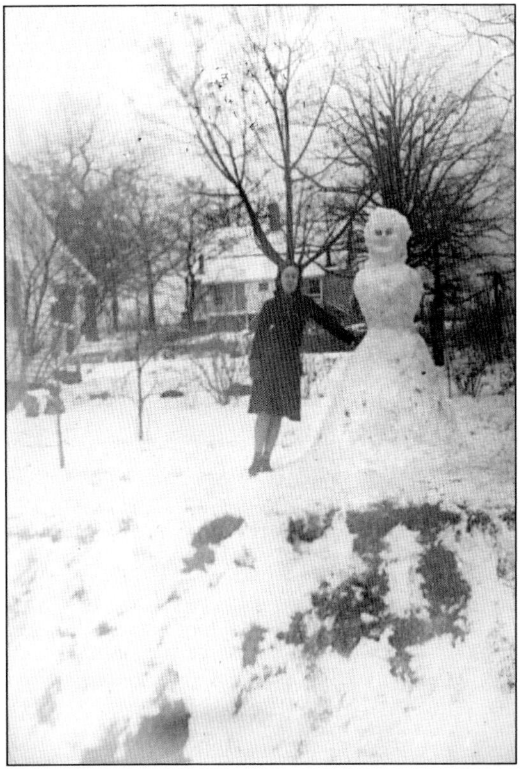

Margaret and George Buckheister built this snow woman in the 1940s. (Courtesy of Phil and Becky Buckheister.)

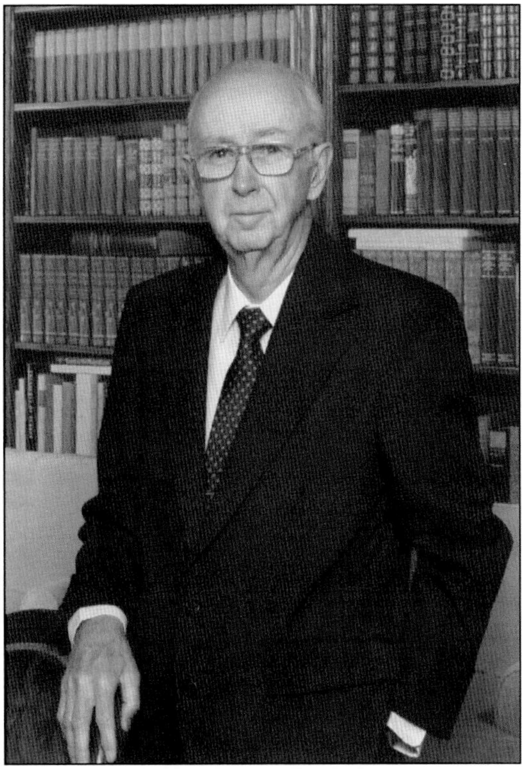

Dr. W.J. Vernon opened his office in 1962 in the Piedmont Community Building. He had previously been a doctor in Pelzer and Georgetown but decided he and his wife would make Piedmont their home. For most of his medical career, Dr. Vernon was the only doctor in Piedmont, and although his services were in high demand, he never required his patients to have an appointment. Patients came into the office, signed their name, and waited patiently for their turn. Most days, the office was packed with patients, but Dr. Vernon managed to treat everyone. Flossie Garner was his nurse and receptionist and was much loved. Dr. Vernon's wife, Martha Dell, later came to work at the office to help out with the many folks who waited to be treated. The doctor also made house calls to those who were too sick to venture out. W.J. Vernon was Piedmont's doctor for 38 years before he retired. He and his wife lived on Highway 86 and raised two children, Jimmy and Alice. (Courtesy of Becky and Alice Vernon.)

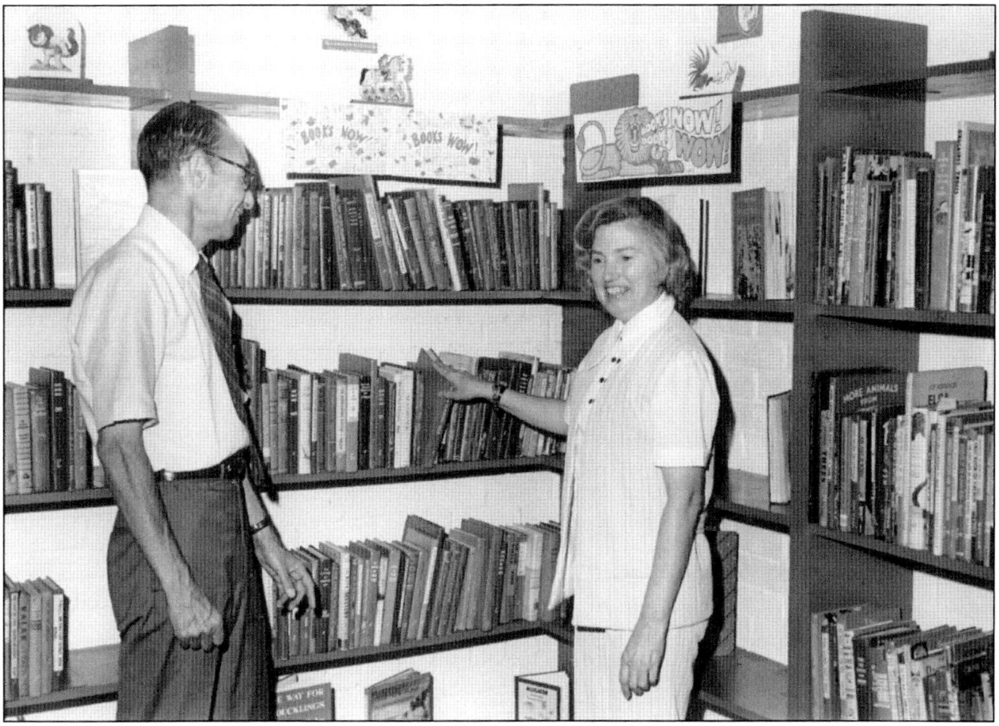

This branch of the Piedmont Library opened in 1972 in the old cement-block jail. Pictured above in the new library are librarian Betty Davenport and Mr. Fineburg from the Anderson County Library. When the building was converted from the jail to the library, the bars had to be removed from the windows. Notice below that Pepsi Cola donated the sign. Harold Gregory of Piedmont worked for Pepsi, which led to many items being donated by that company. Betty Davenport continued as the librarian for over 30 years. The library is now in a new building west of town. (Both, courtesy of Betty Davenport.)

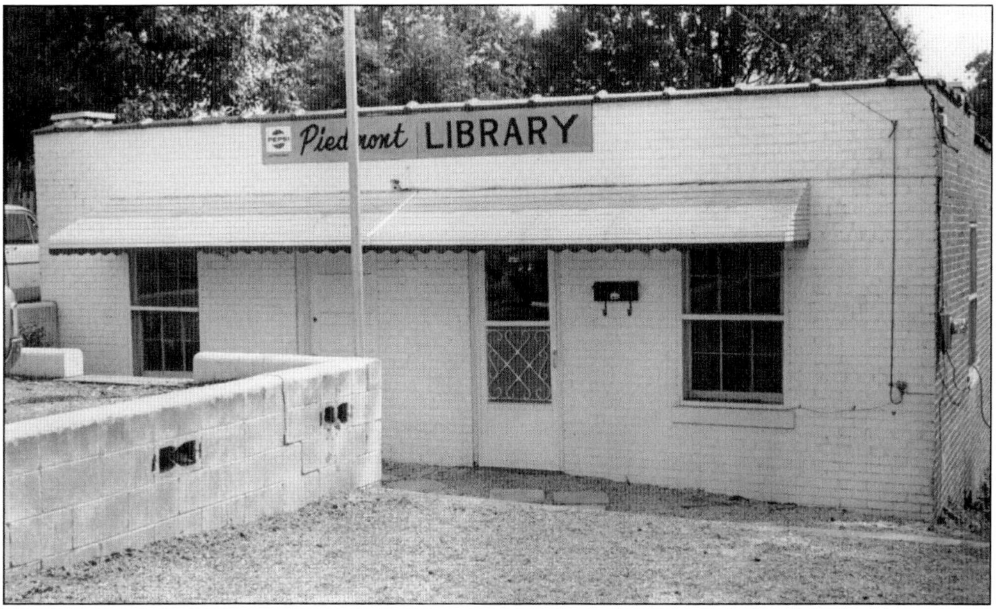

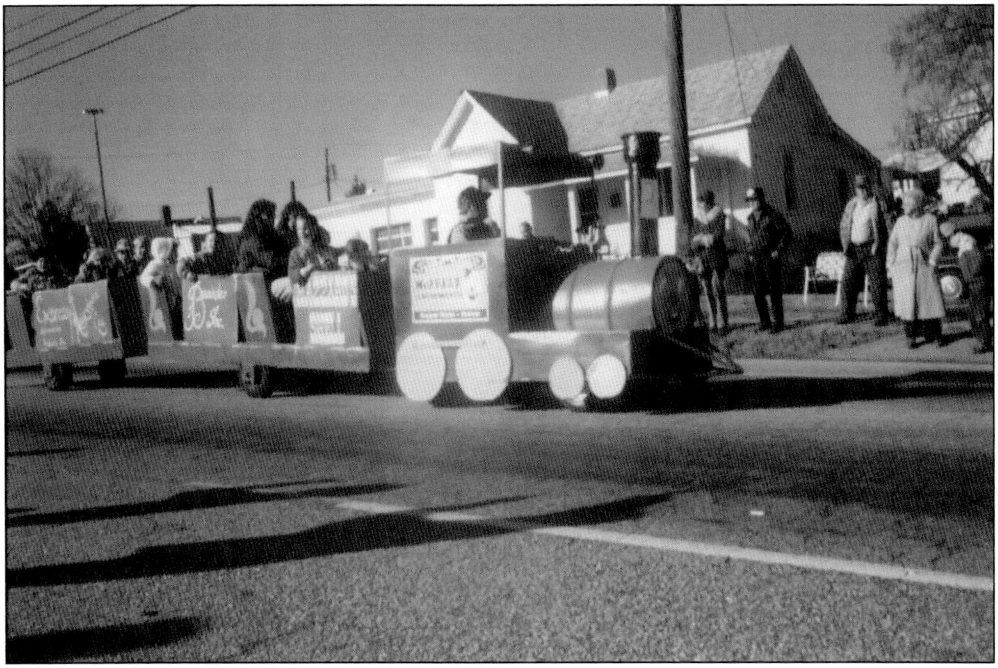

The Bonnes Amies Club sponsors the Piedmont Christmas Parade at the present. These photographs of the parade were taken in 1987. (Both, courtesy of Bonnie Owens.)

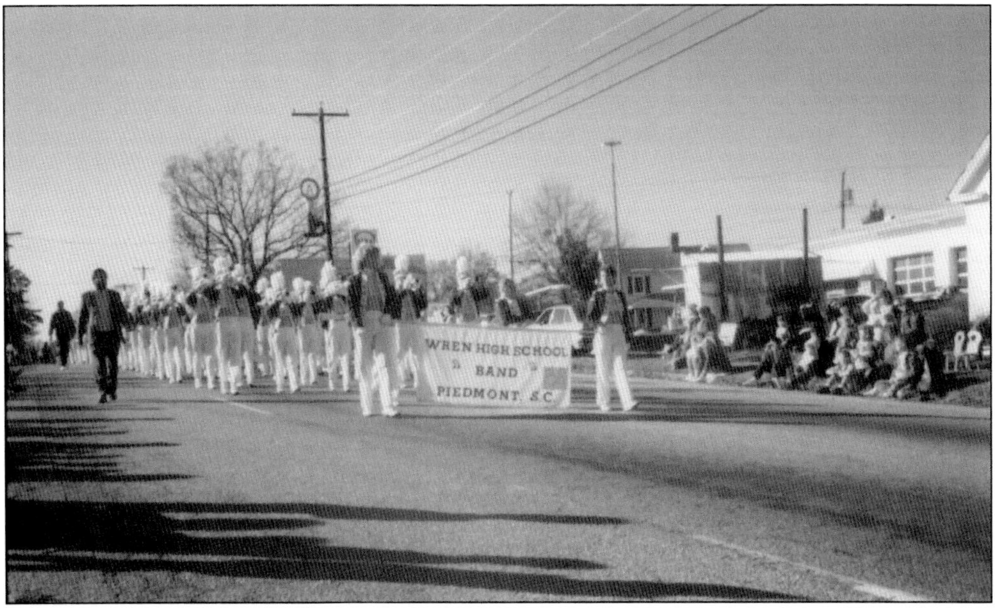

Seven

CHURCHES

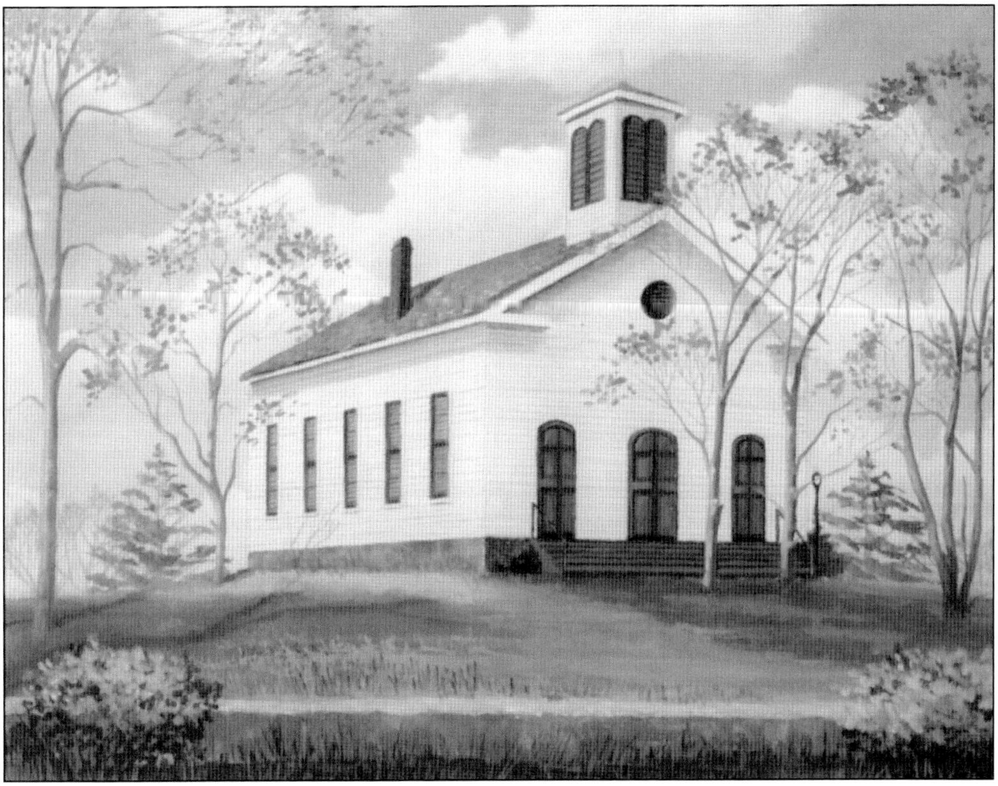

The Union Church was built by Piedmont Manufacturing Company in 1879. It was located on Church Street where Piedmont High School was later built. This church was used by Methodists, Baptists, and Presbyterians, each having their own services with one Sabbath school for all congregations. A.S. Rowell started this Sunday school a couple of times before it became a viable group. These denominations met in the Union Church until they were able to build churches of their own. (Courtesy of the Bonnes Amies Club.)

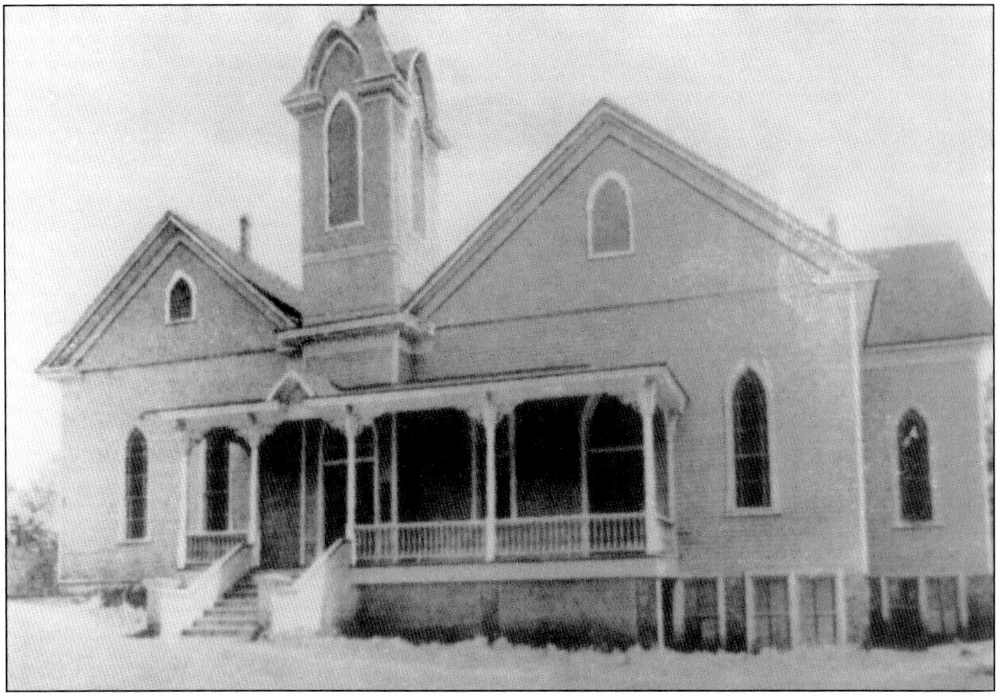

The Piedmont Baptist Church was organized on December 28, 1879. The dedication service for the first cross-shaped church building was held on July 26, 1891. Standing on property donated by the mill, the renovated church is shown here sometime just after 1908 when the Sanborn map still shows it in a cross shape. It was on Hotel Hill near the reservoir. The name was officially changed to Piedmont First Baptist Church in 1947. (Courtesy of Piedmont Historical Collection.)

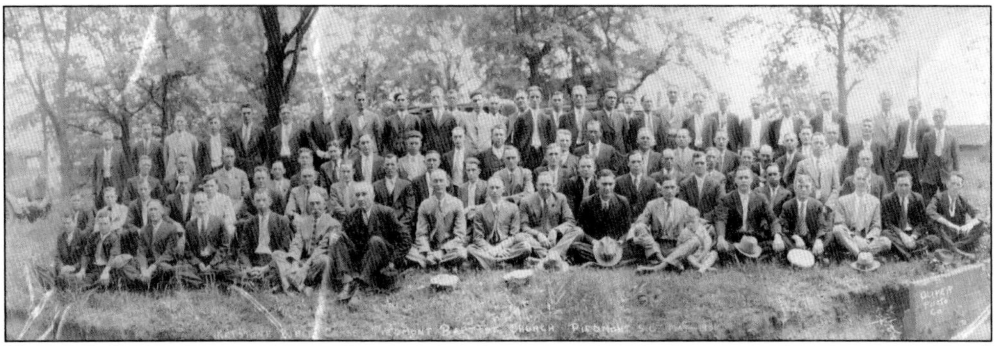

The men's Sunday school class of Piedmont Baptist Church is pictured in the early 1930s on Hotel Hill near the original site of the church. Some of those pictured are Walter Gaillard, Bob Elrod, Wayne Hiott, Joseph Shirley, Tom League, John Brock, Maurice Terry, Robert Creswell, and Harry Waldrop Sr. The child in the front row may be Bill Shirley. (Courtesy of Robert Elrod.)

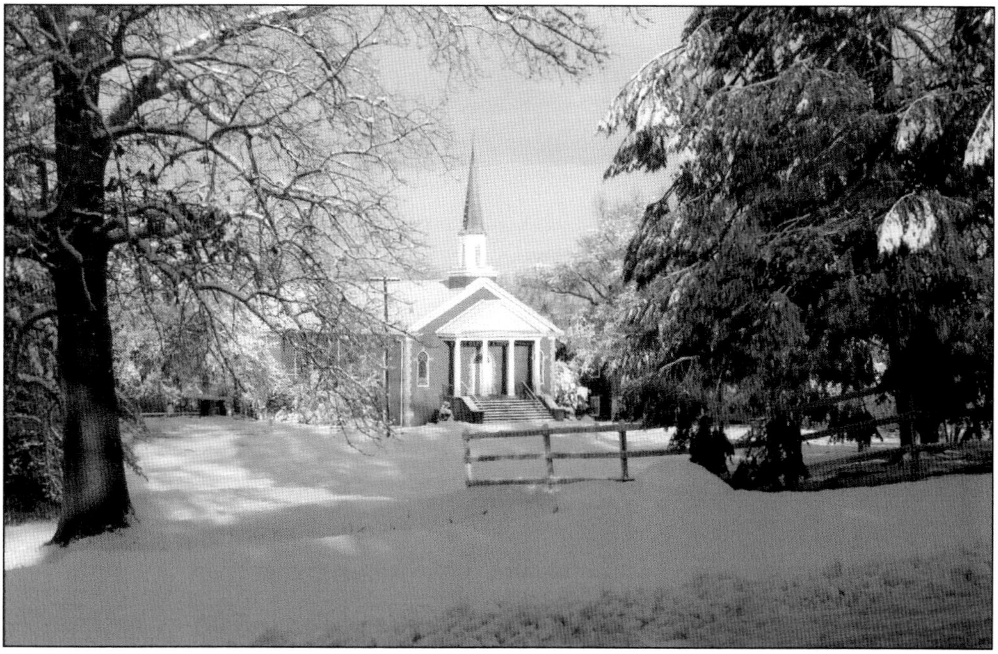

In 1937, Piedmont Baptists made plans to raise money for a new building. The first service was held on December 5, 1941. An educational building was built in 1955 and named in honor of the pastor, Rev. E.S. Morgan. Dr. Thomas DeVenny retired as pastor in 1996 after 35 years of service, the longest pastorate in the church's history. (Courtesy of Betty White.)

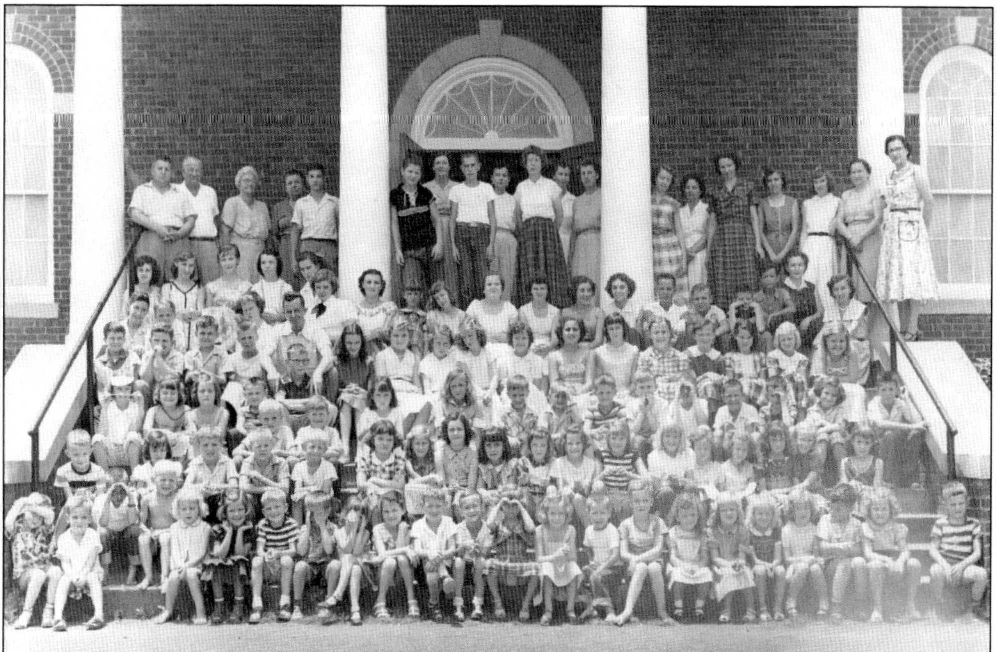

The attendees of Vacation Bible School fill the front steps that lead to the sanctuary of Piedmont First Baptist Church in 1953. There are 117 children and adults pictured. The pastor at this time was Reverend Morgan. (Courtesy of Phil and Becky Buckhiester.)

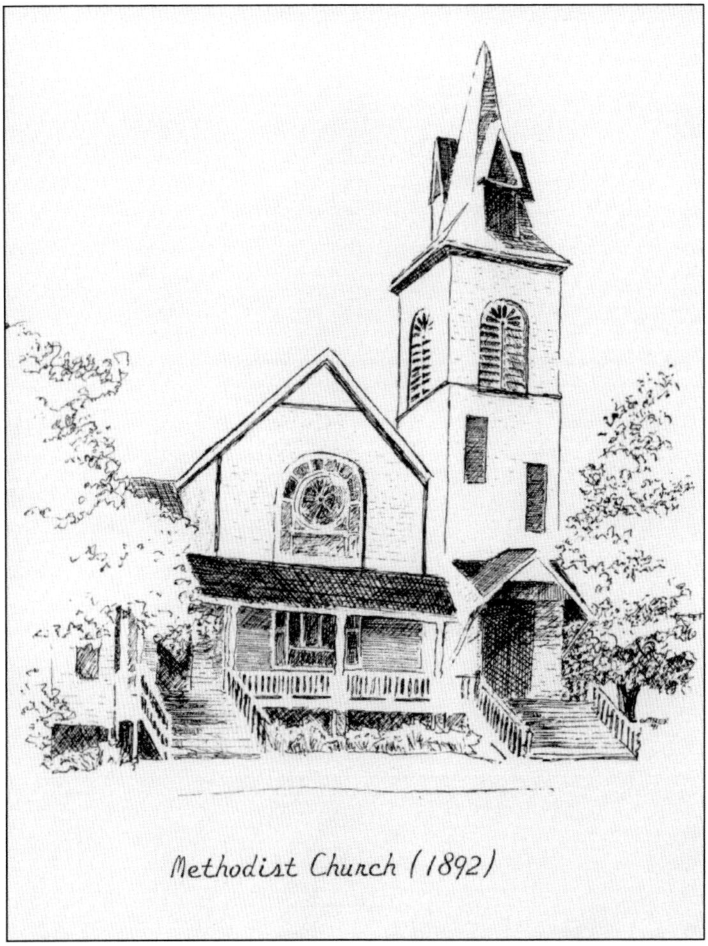

This drawing of the original Methodist church shows its delicate beauty. The first church building was erected in 1892 and was destroyed by fire on January 1, 1933. Rev. S.H. Zimmerman was the first pastor. (Courtesy of Shirley Tice Elrod.)

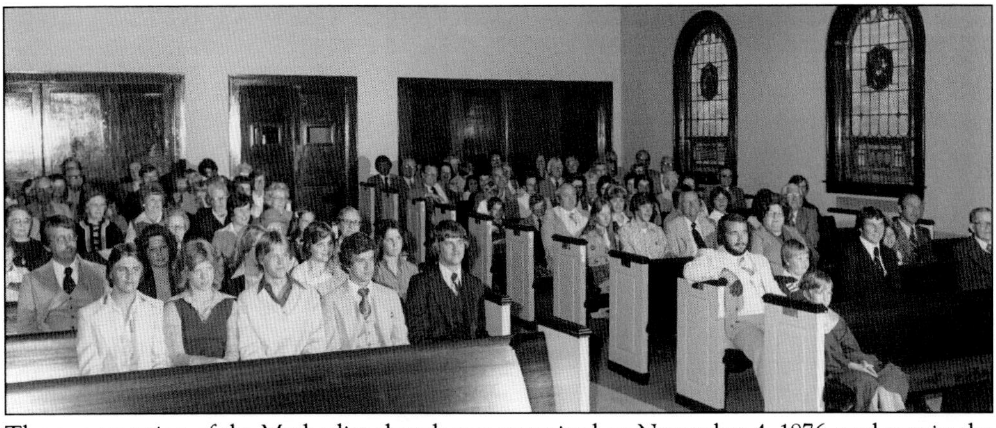

The congregation of the Methodist church was organized on November 4, 1876, and met in the Union Church until their beautiful building was crafted just 16 years later. Church members and members of Golden Grove Methodist Church assisted in placing a new bell in the steeple. On February 15, 1913, it tolled for the first time. When this church burned down in 1933, the bell was given to New Golden Grove Methodist Church. That bell is now on display in front of New Golden Grove on Bessie Road. (Courtesy of Shirley Tice Elrod.)

The current Methodist church sits high atop Hotel Hill and is a replacement for the building that burned. The early parsonage was provided by the mill, and the church provided the furniture. When J.P. Stevens and Company sold the parsonage to the church in 1966, the congregation decided to sell it and build a new parsonage. This home was furnished with the aid of Dr. S.D. Campbell's grandson Carroll Campbell, who later became the governor of South Carolina. Dr. Campbell was the mill doctor for years, and he and his family were active members of Piedmont Methodist Church. (Courtesy of Shirley Tice Elrod.)

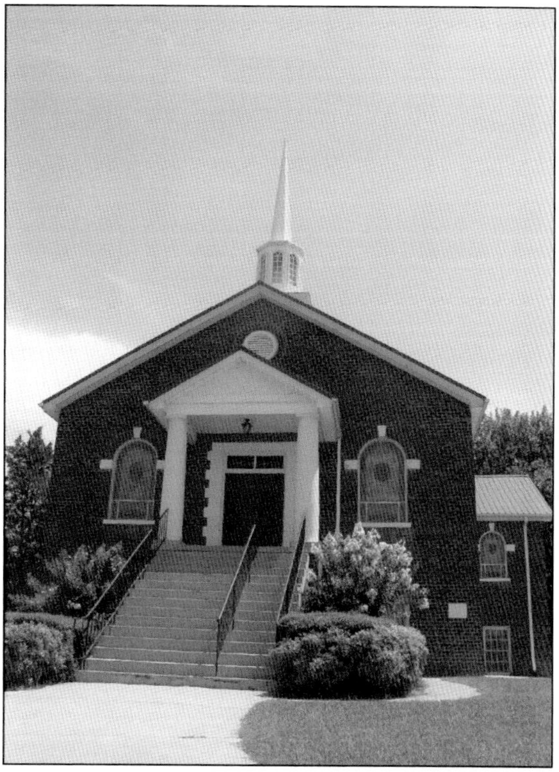

Grouped before the altar, these folks were treasured members of Piedmont Methodist Church. Among them are Fran Gilreath, Francis Buckhiester, and Eva Suber. (Courtesy of Shirley Tice Elrod.)

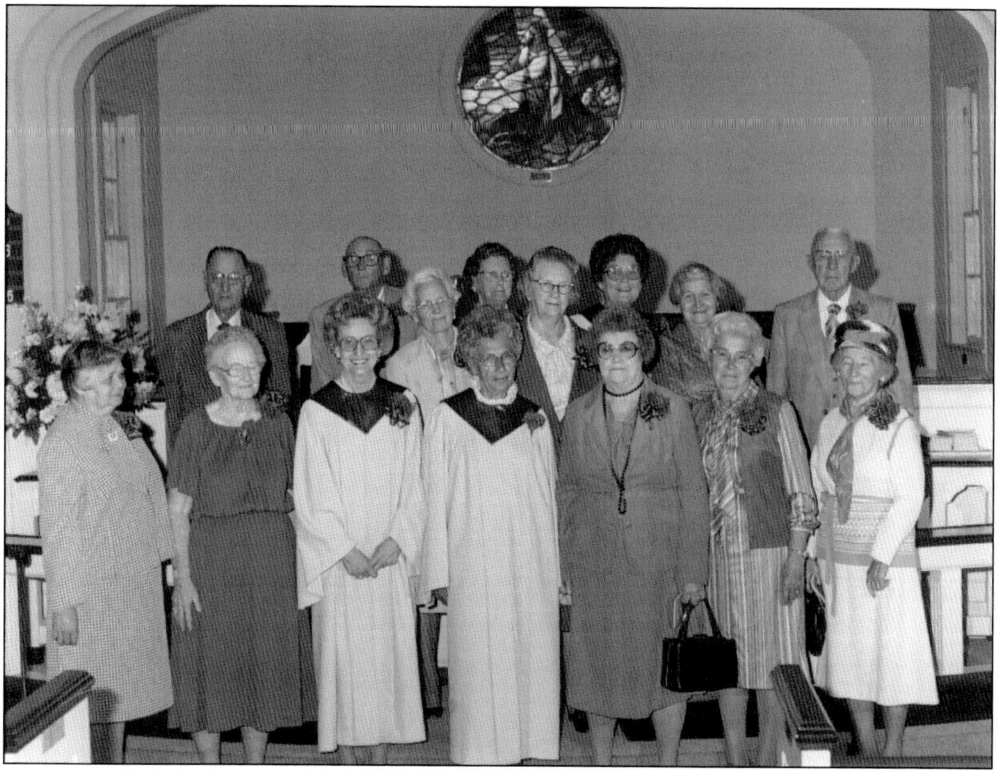

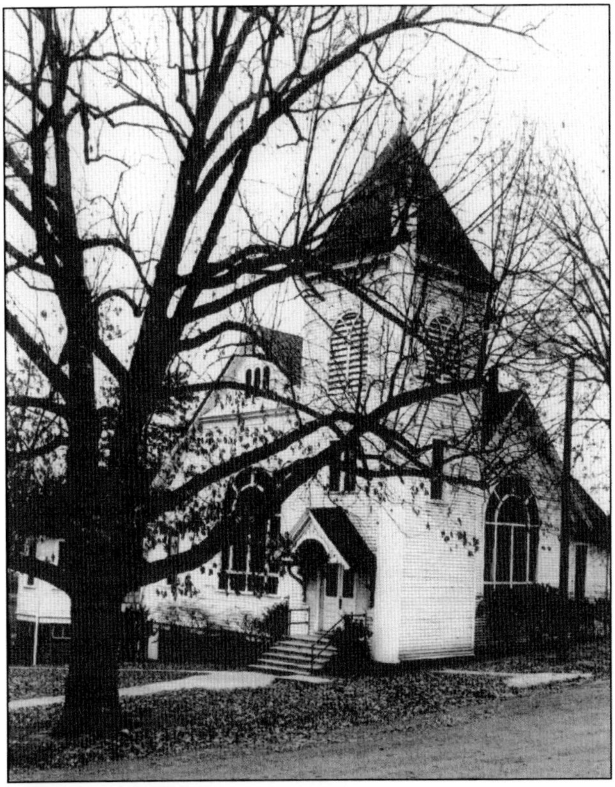

Piedmont Presbyterian Church was organized in 1880 by a commission appointed by Enoree Presbytery. The members met in the Union Church until 1893, when they constructed their own church building. Since Piedmont was growing and expanding into Anderson County, members deemed it expedient to locate their church in the new part of town; therefore, they built near the corner of Iler and Prospect Streets across from the mill. The Presbyterians, being the last to leave the Union Church, fell heir to the old church bell and the organ. The bell hung in the new church until the early 1960s, but in those latter years it was silent due to the fact that the church's wooden structure had weakened with age, and the heavy bell had become a threat. (Courtesy of Pert Clifford.)

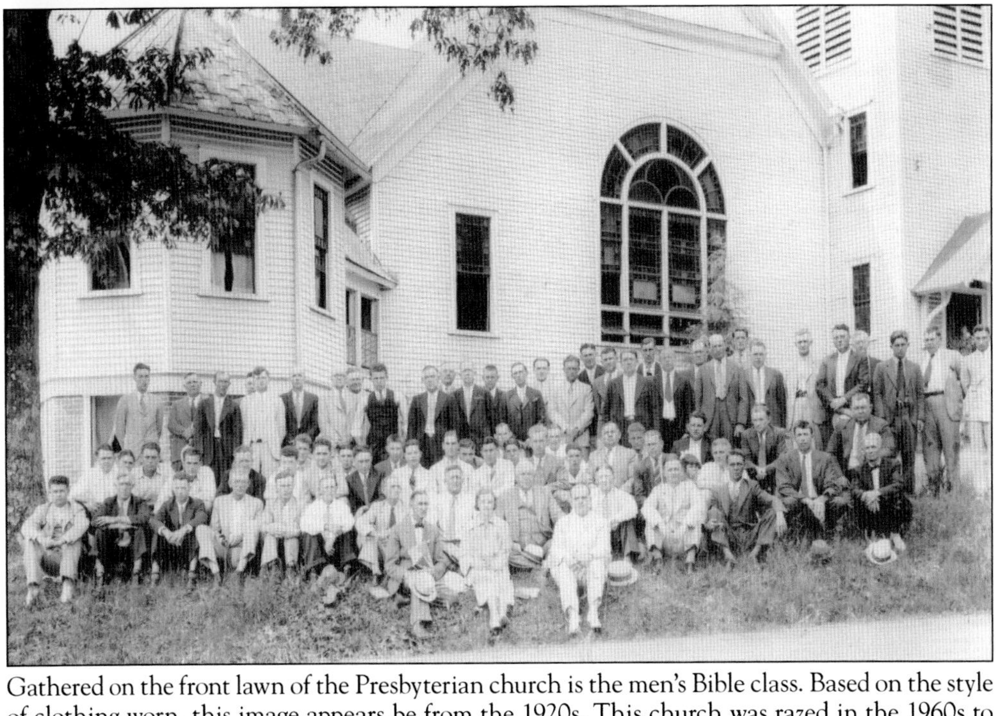

Gathered on the front lawn of the Presbyterian church is the men's Bible class. Based on the style of clothing worn, this image appears be from the 1920s. This church was razed in the 1960s to make room for a parking lot for the mill. (Courtesy of Piedmont Presbyterian Church.)

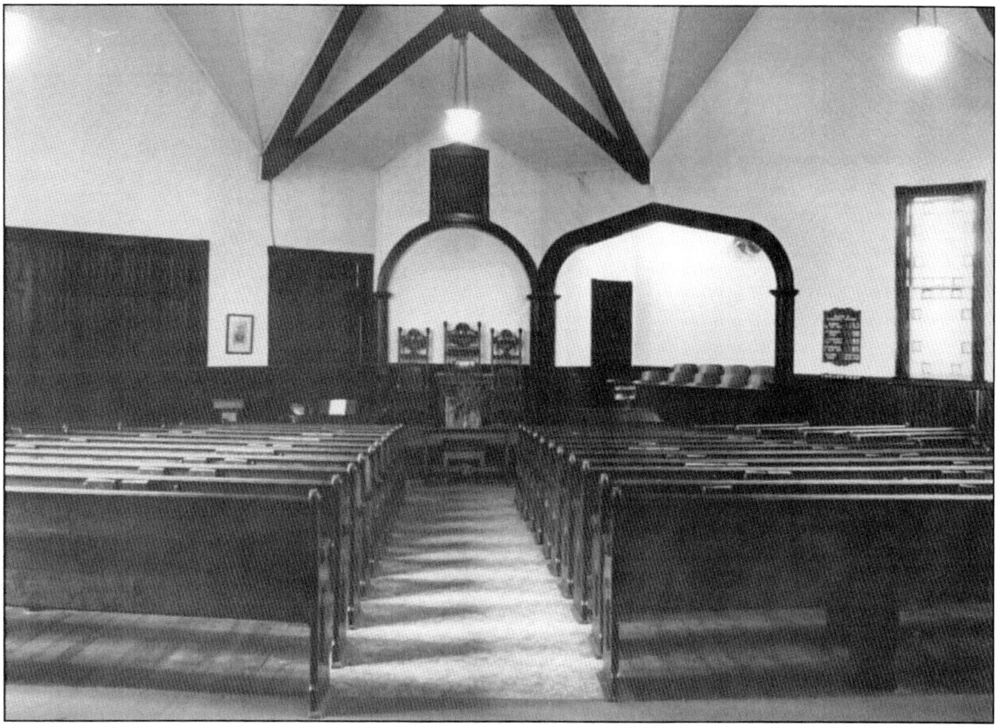

This photograph shows the interior of the sanctuary of the old Presbyterian church. (Courtesy of Betty Davenport.)

Today, Piedmont Presbyterian is located on Academy Street, where Beattie Memorial School once stood. The present church building was constructed in 1964. In 1974, the old bell from the Union Church was placed atop the church in an open framework with a tall cross rising above it. To this day, the bell still rings every Sunday morning. An activities building was added in 1978, and the sanctuary's stained-glass windows were dedicated in October 1984. (Courtesy of Piedmont Presbyterian Church.)

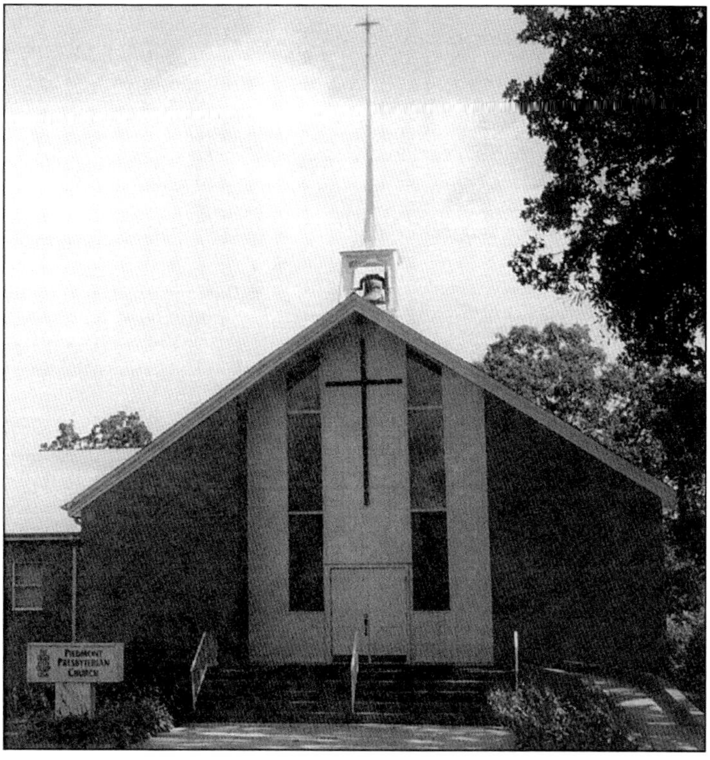

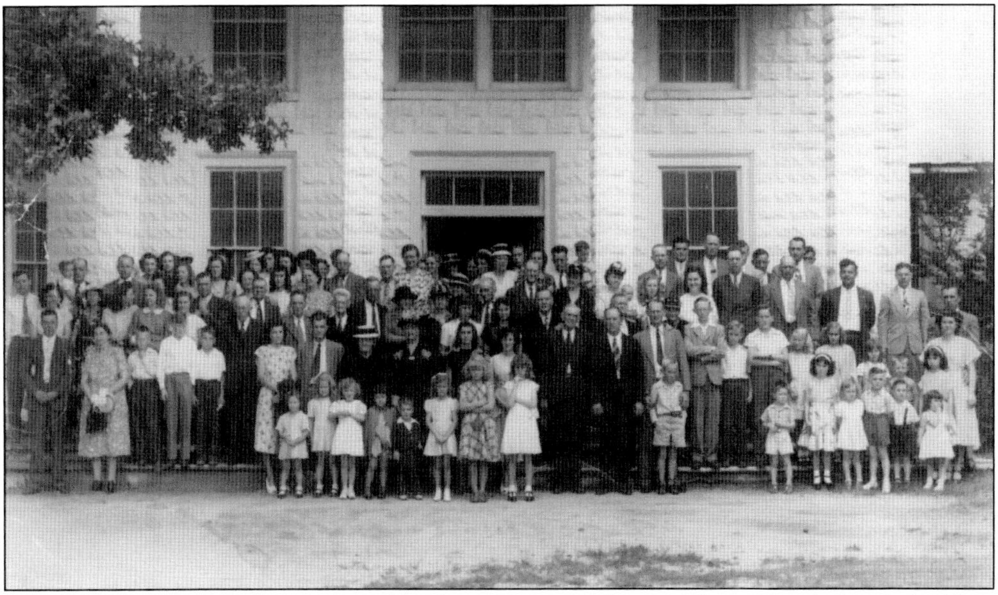

Members of Grove Station Baptist Church are shown in front of their second church building in 1948. The first church was erected around 1857 on these grounds, which were donated by Dr. Howell, the father of the child buried beside Highway 20 just across the road from the church. The first church building was replaced in the 1920s by the beautiful block church shown here. Among those pictured are Rev. Furman Rivers, Nell Dalton, and the families of Alvin Lollis, Jim Richey, Jep Elrod, and James Freeman. (Courtesy of Dot Lollis Evans.)

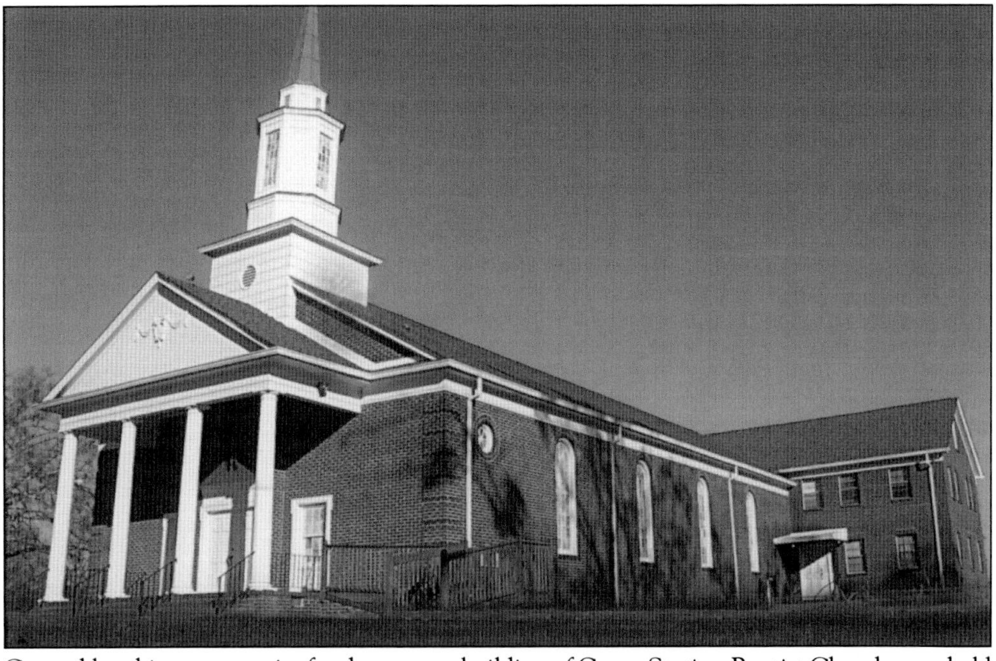

Ground-breaking ceremonies for the current building of Grove Station Baptist Church were held on August 11, 1968. B.T. Barnes, the oldest living male member of the church, had the honor of turning the first shovel of dirt. Opening services were held in the new auditorium on June 8, 1969, with dedication services on August 17, 1969. (Courtesy of Dot Lollis Evans.)

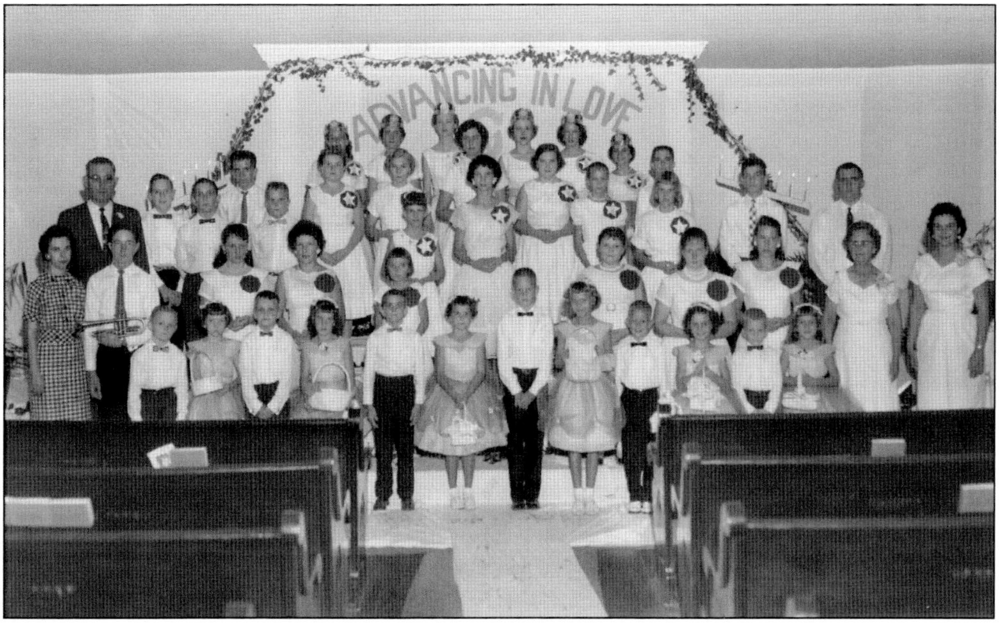

Pictured is the 1959 Girls' Auxiliary coronation of Grove Station Baptist Church. Girls Auxiliary, known today as Girls In Action, is a missions arm of the Southern Baptist Convention's Women on Missions. Among those pictured are Rev. Henry Walker, Elise Timmons, Erwin and Debbie Elrod, Sandra and Nan Moore, Kathy and Sharon White, Faye Anderson, Alvin and Dot Lollis, Elaine Timmons, and Susan, Katie, and June Vinson. (Courtesy of Dot Lollis Evans.)

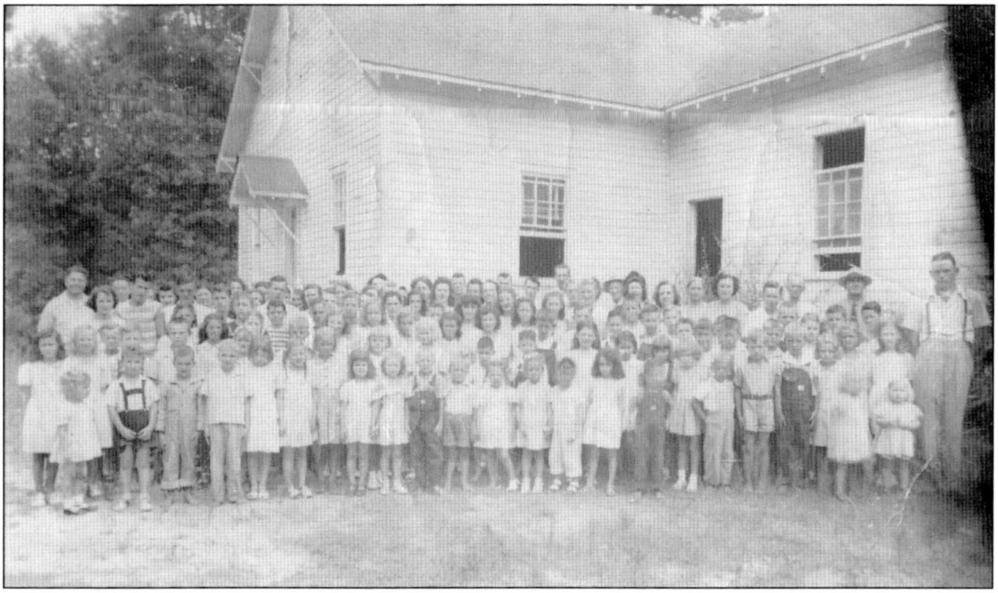

Mountain Springs Baptist Church Vacation Bible School is gathered in 1948. Some of those pictured include Rev. E.C. Neely, Giles Moody, Gayle Smith, JoAnn Moore, Faye Moody, Anne Ayers, Nancy Roper, Joyce Lockaby, George Lockaby, and Julian, Judy, and Margaret Weisner. Reverend Neely was the first full-time preacher at Mountain Springs. This church building was built around 1942 after fire destroyed the original church, which was built in 1860. (Courtesy of Gayle Payne.)

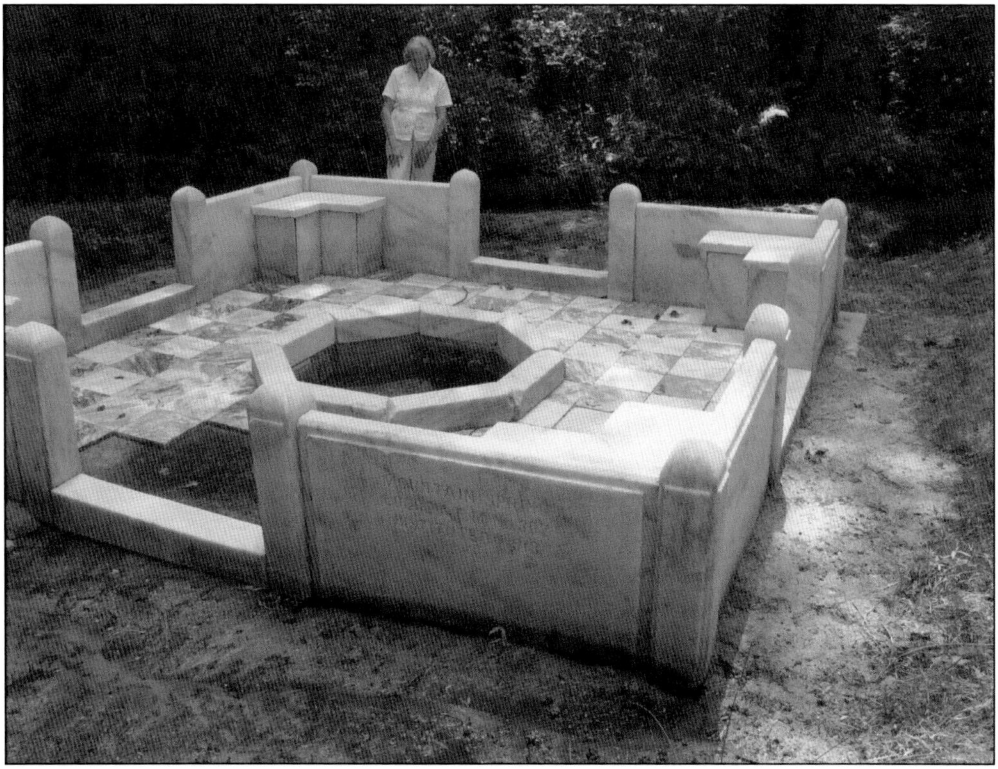

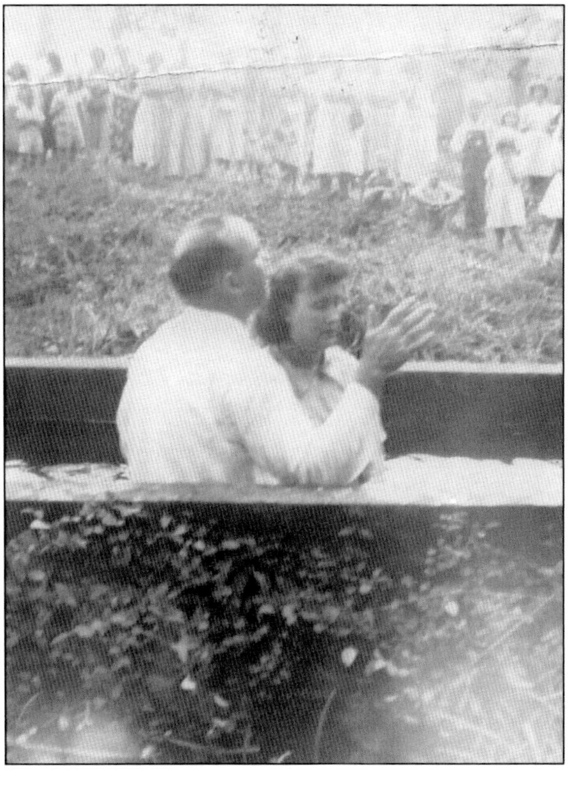

There is an old and repeated story of men who heard a bubbling sound while hunting on Rattlesnake Mountain. Following the sound, they found a spring with water rushing from the ground. In *History of Mountain Springs*, B.F. Wigington repeated the story: "A spring that threw sand and gravel into the air and a mile-long ridge called Rattlesnake Mountain" gave Mountain Springs Baptist Church its name. Some years later around the turn of the twentieth century, the spring was enclosed with marble walls and benches. Above the main spring, the church built an outdoor baptismal pool, which serviced many of the area churches. At left, Faye Capps Phillips is being baptized in the outdoor pool by Rev. Elmer Jones. Reverend Jones also baptized Blease Phillips, Faye's husband, that same day. (Above, courtesy of Fern Durham; left, courtesy of Fred Alexander.)

In 1927, Golden Grove Methodist Episcopal Church (presently named New Golden Grove United Methodist) built a large one-room building to replace the original church constructed in 1894. The original was a two-story structure, shared with the Good Samaritan Lodge No. 32. Prior to 1894, members met in a brush arbor made of mud, sticks, and brush. (Courtesy of Rev. Clara Gary.)

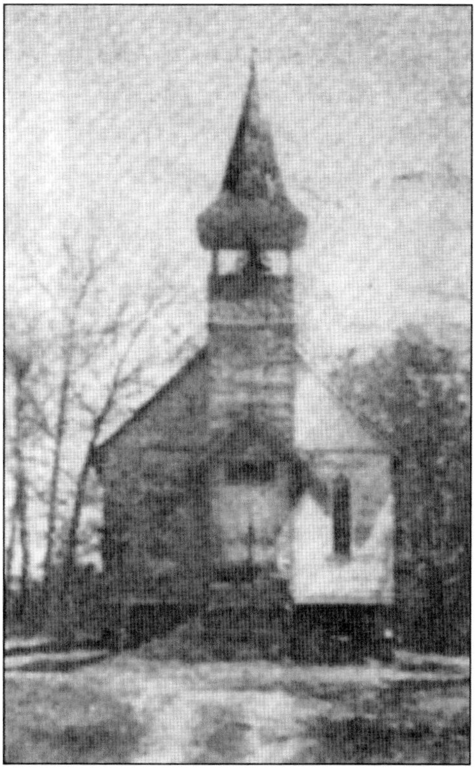

In 1963, Golden Grove changed its name to New Golden Grove. The one-room church on Oil Mill Road built in 1927 was completely destroyed by fire in 1982. On January 1, 1984, the congregation moved into its present brick building on Highway 86 just east of Piedmont. Members of Golden Grove Methodist—including Perry Westfield, Jarrett Johnson, Lawyer Mack, and Jim Dickson—assisted in placing a new bell in the steeple of Piedmont Methodist Church on February 15, 1913. When that church burned in 1933, the bell was given to New Golden Grove Methodist Church. This historic bell is now on display in front of New Golden Grove. (Courtesy of Anne Peden.)

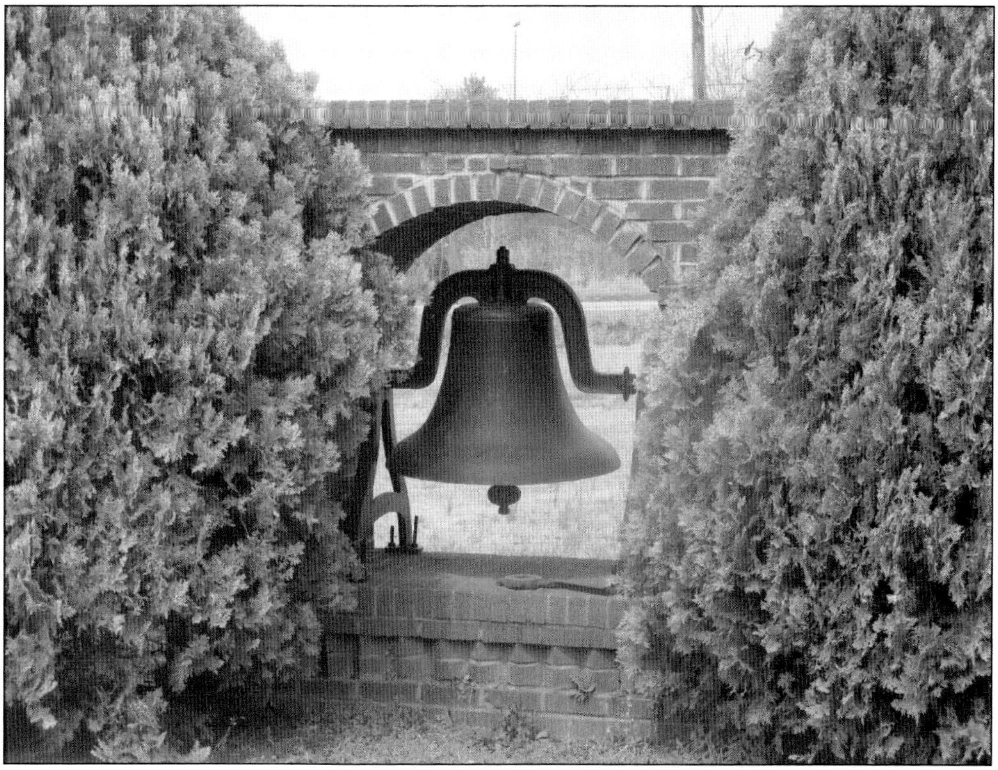

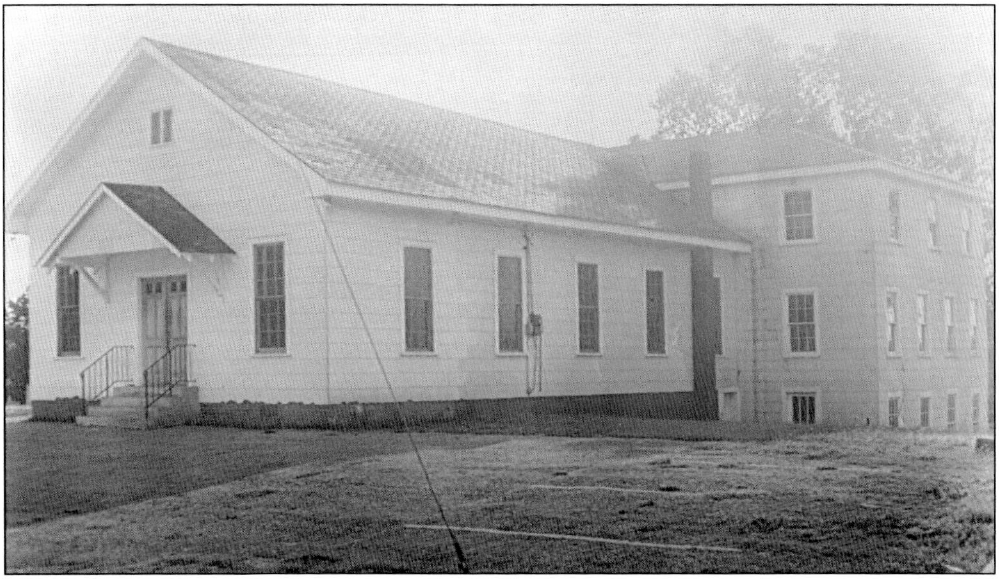

In 1909, nineteen people gathered in the community of Rehoboth on the outskirts of Piedmont in Greenville County, and organized Rehoboth Baptist Church. They purchased the land and a one-room church building (above), which was built in 1832, from the Methodists. The building was remodeled due to its deteriorated condition. Through the years, the church building underwent additions and renovations. A fellowship hall was built, the sanctuary was enlarged, and the Sunday school rooms were remodeled. During the pastorate of Rev. Ralph Bagwell (1967–1972), a new church was constructed (below), including a 400-seat sanctuary and the addition of 22 Sunday school rooms. Since then, the fellowship hall has been remodeled and bricked, a partial gym was added, and the educational building and sanctuary have also been remodeled. In 1996, the church broke ground for its new fellowship building. (Both, courtesy of Rehoboth Baptist Church.)

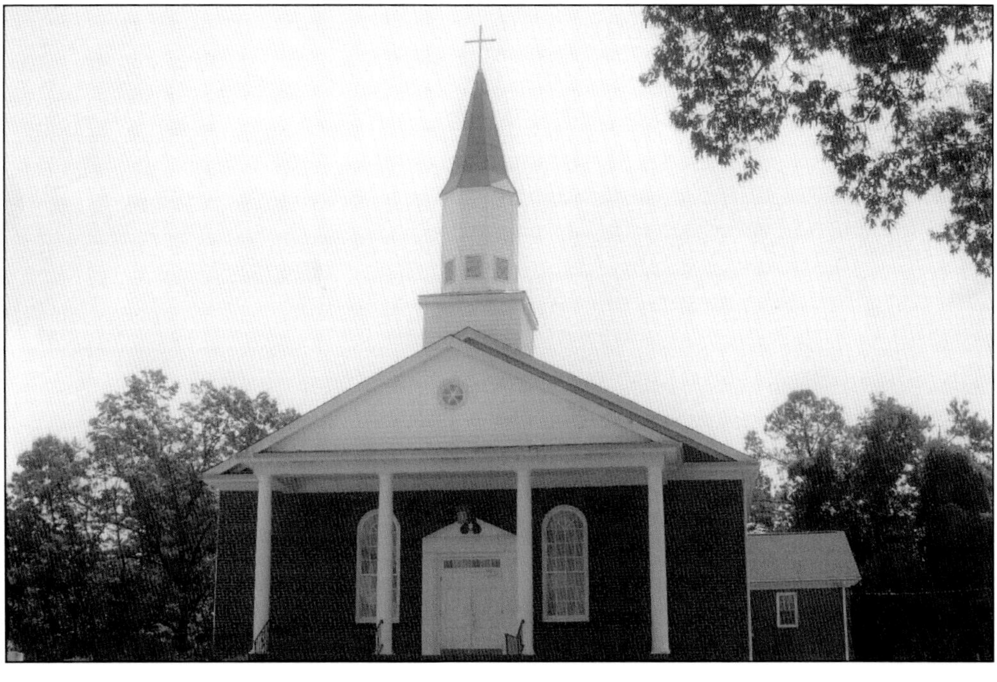

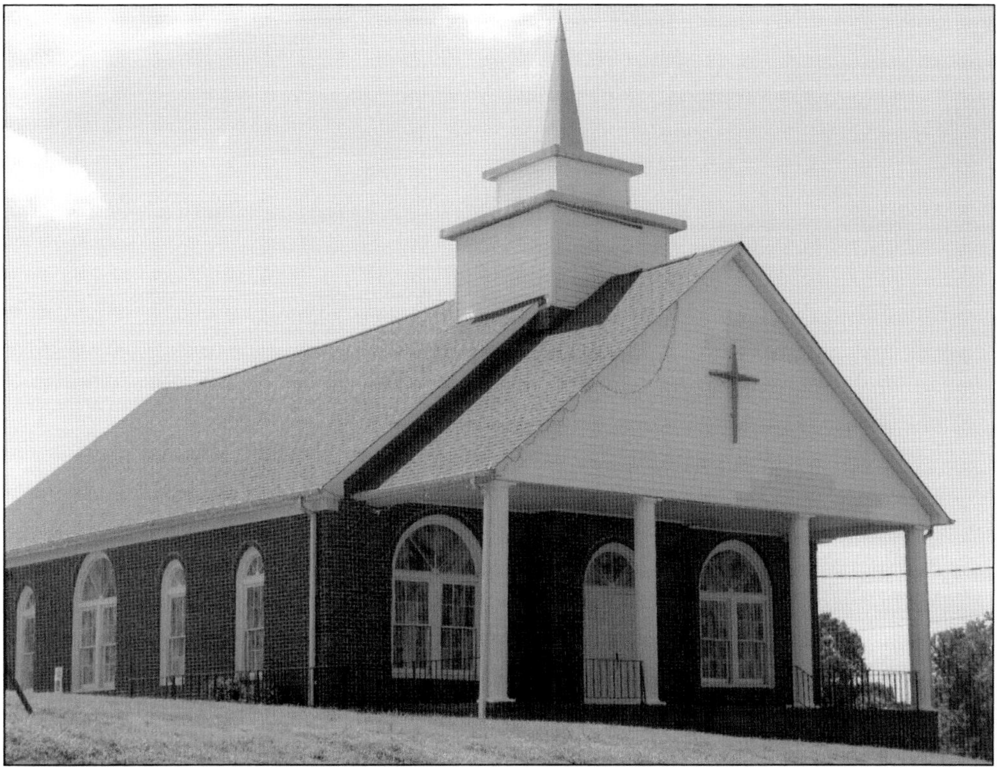

St. Matthew Baptist Church began in 1884 as a brush arbor in Grove Township, east of Piedmont. The original building was constructed in the latter part of the 19th century and was bricked over in the 1940s. Thus, the original structure is still standing underneath the building that one sees today. St. Matthew Baptist built an educational building with a fellowship hall in 1959; in 1975, the church underwent a major renovation that included structural work to strengthen the walls and roof. A new steeple was added, and an indoor baptismal pool was installed in the education building. (Courtesy of St. Matthew Baptist Church.)

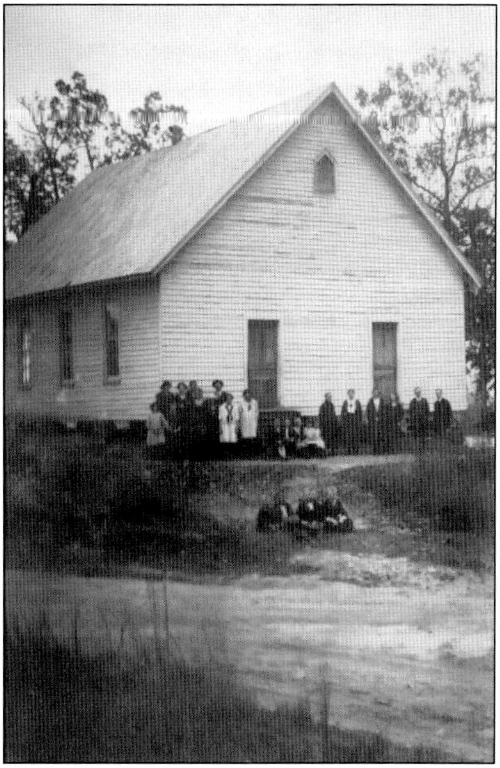

In 1860, Shiloh United Methodist built a frame building to replace the original log and mud structure. This new building was secured with pegs and cut nails. Much of the framing and ceiling planks were hand hewn. Rev. W.L. Mulliken was pastor at Shiloh when this photograph was taken in the 1920s. This building was torn down to make way for a new brick building in 1938. (Courtesy of Carolyn Reeves.)

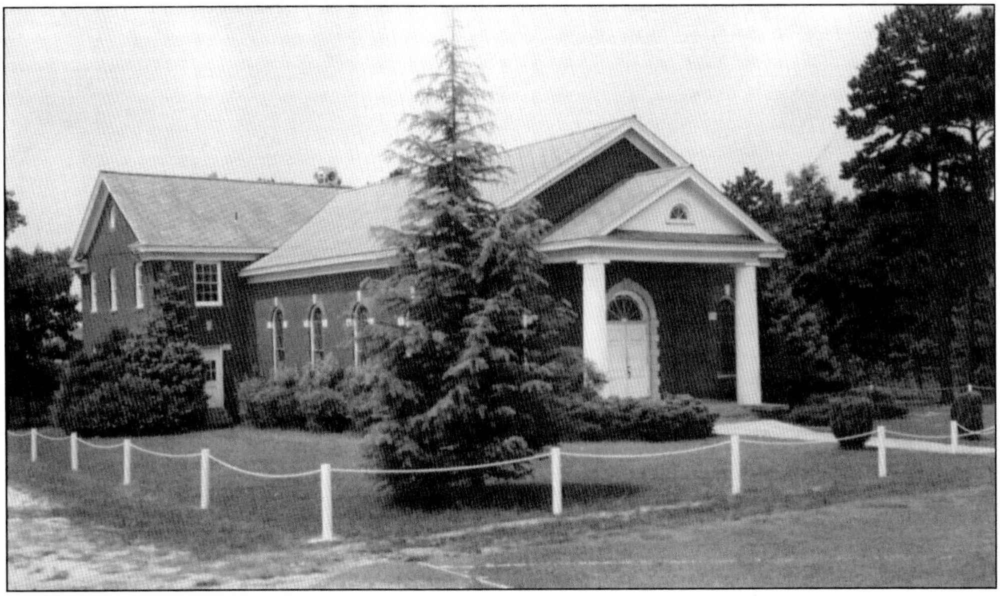

A modern brick and mortar structure was erected to replace Shiloh United Methodist's frame building and was dedicated on Easter Sunday, April 17, 1938; it stood until 1995. The pastor at the time of dedication, S.B. White, said, "If this building fails to last 'til Jesus comes, then let the children of those who built this church rise up and build a better one." (Courtesy of Carolyn Reeves.)

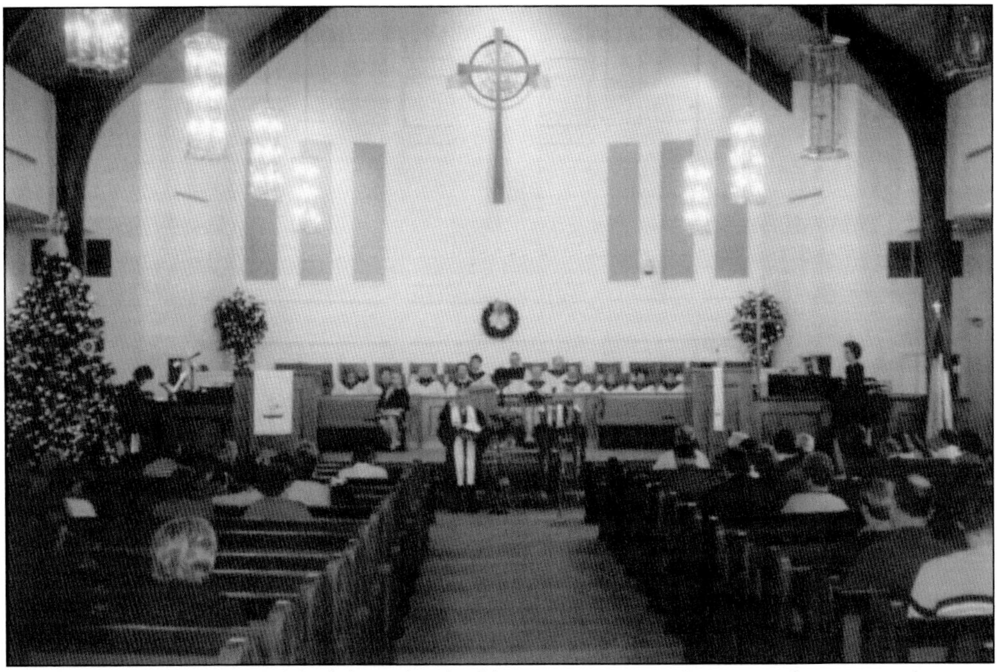

As time would have it, Shiloh did need to build a new sanctuary due to costly structural repairs needed to preserve their building. So, the first service in the present building was held on September 1, 1996. The lovely stained-glass windows from the former Shiloh church were used, and a new prominent feature, a steeple, was added for the first time. Pictured is the current sanctuary. (Courtesy of Charles Adkins.)

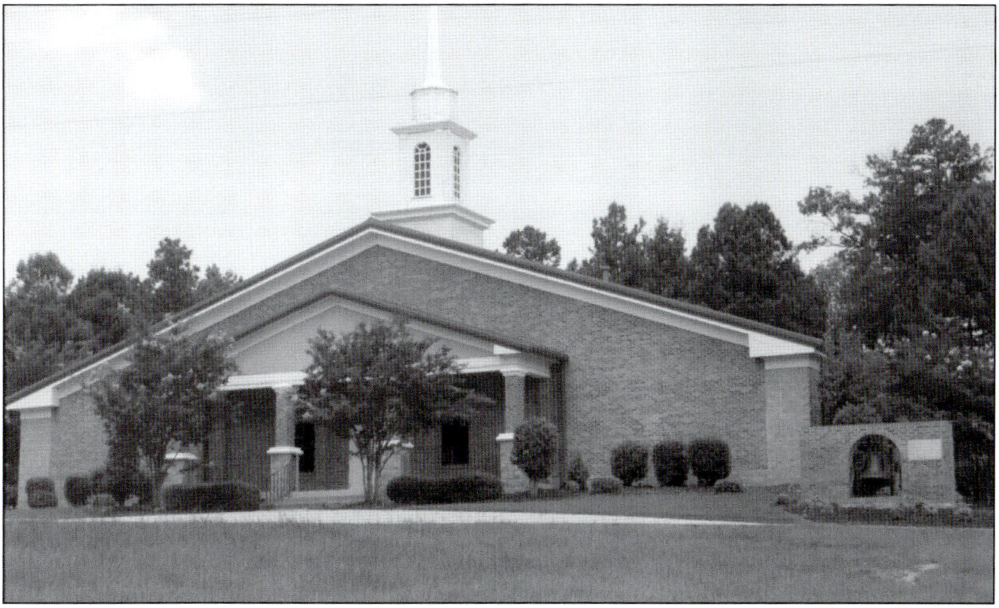

Sweet Canaan Baptist Church was formed in 1877. The founding fathers were offspring of former slaves whose religious services were held under a brush arbor in the woods at night. There was no building at the time of its organization, so members of Sweet Canaan also gathered under a brush arbor, like the one pictured below. Their first church building was located somewhere near Highway 86 and I-85. Around the turn of the 20th century, Sweet Canaan acquired land from Mountain Springs Baptist and relocated their church. They built a wooden structure that stood until 1952. During the early days of the church, services were held on the third Sunday of each month. Other services were added over the years, and in 1985, Sweet Canaan became a "stationed" church with services every Sunday. At some point a baptismal pool was added, which ended the need for the outdoor baptisms in a creek on property owned by the Wigington family. Now, Sweet Canaan Baptist is in its fourth building (above), which was dedicated on June 15, 2003. (Both, courtesy of Mary Bradley.)

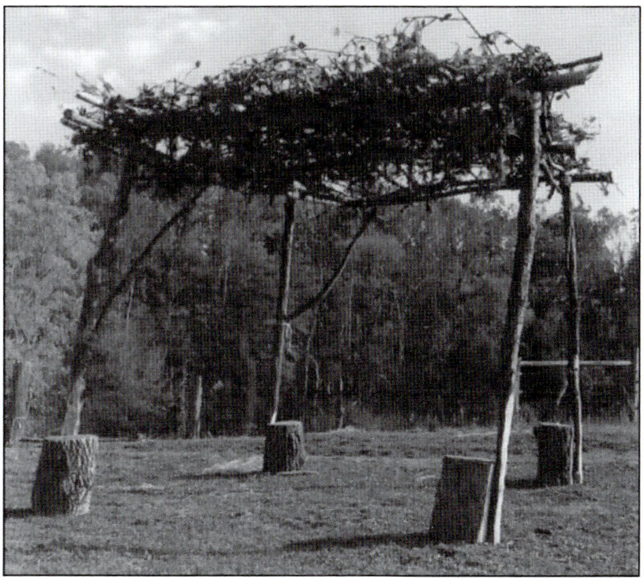

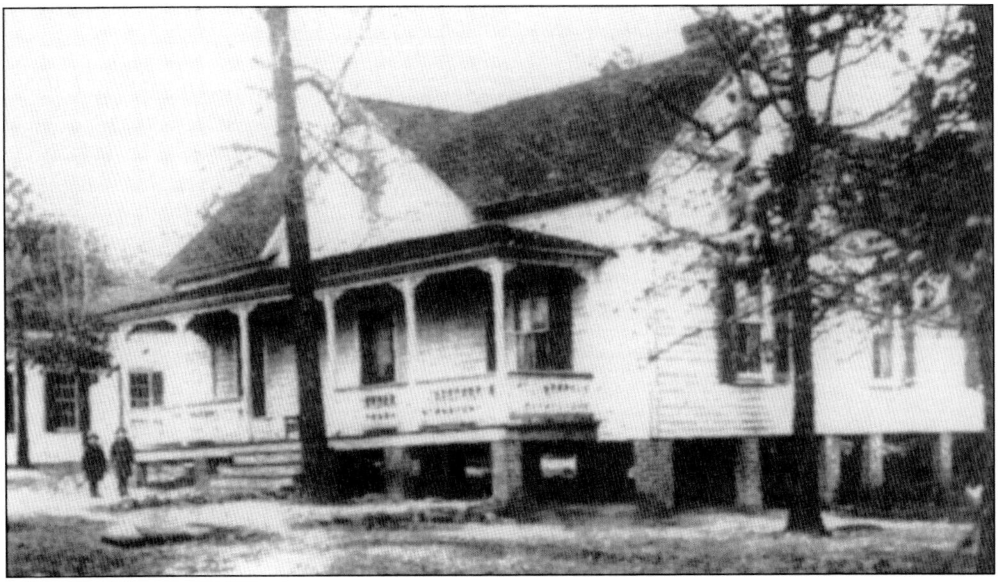

Piedmont Wesleyan Church (formerly Wesleyan Methodist) was organized in 1893 with 20 members. Early services were held as tent meetings until around the turn of the 20th century, when members built a parsonage. Services were held there until a white, wood-framed sanctuary was built around 1911. This structure has never been torn down; instead, it has been built around and added on to throughout the years. In 1948, a two-story Sunday school wing and front vestibule were added and everything was finished in brick. The most recent remodel in 1980 was the enlargement of the front entryway. A steeple was added to the structure at some point. (Both, courtesy of Connie Hunnings.)

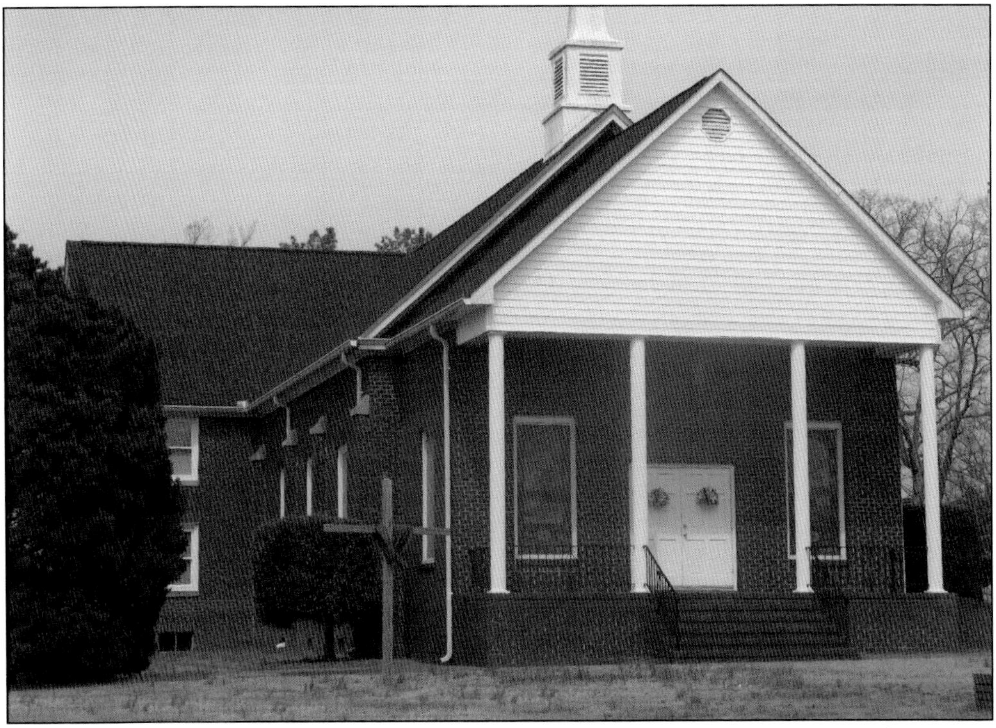

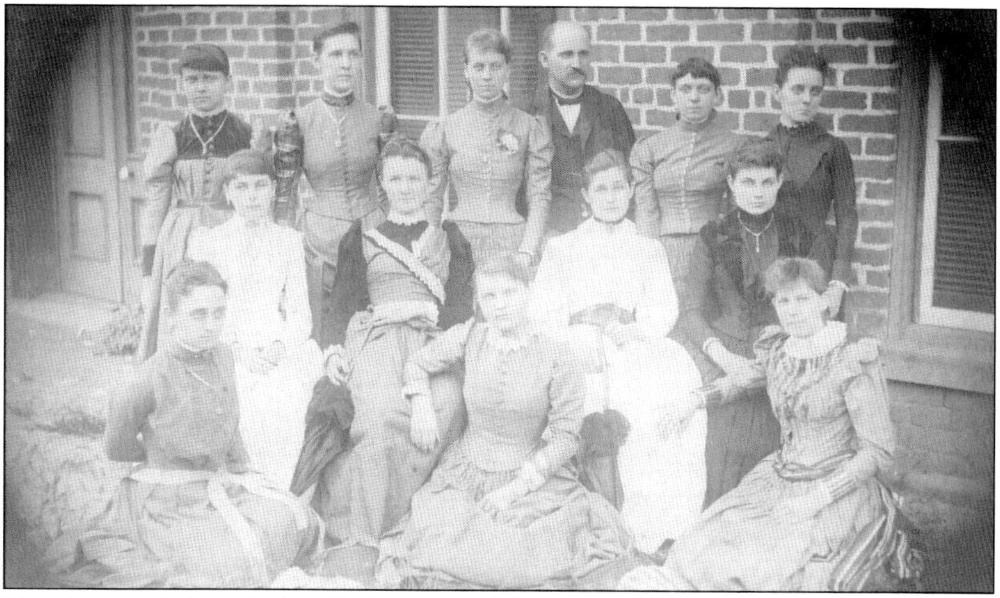

This photograph from the late 1800s captures A.S. Rowell and his first Sunday school members at Union Church. Rowell was dedicated to establishing a school for Bible study, and although the first attempt failed, his persistence established a tradition. Most of these ladies were the wives and daughters of mill supervisors. From left to right are (first row) Hattie Rambo, Hattie Carroll, and Andrella Buchanan; (second row) Corrie S. Osteen, Minnie Rogers, Sue Buchanan, and Laura Rogers; (third row) Alice Cobb, unidentified, Lillie Poole, A.S. Rowell, Hettie Ashmore, and C. Rambo. (Courtesy of the South Caroliniana Room, Greenville County Library.)

This structure is seen on the cover towering over the mill from Hotel Hill sometime after 1888. Is it a church or a school? Folks have identified it as possibly being Golden Grove Church, the Union School, or the original Baptist church. Although the bell towers are completely different, other architectural details are consistent with the later Baptist church, including the arched windows, shape on the map, and foundation pillar elevations. Major renovations must have taken place after 1908, including changing the position of the tower, adding a front room, and crafting an ornate porch. (Courtesy of Piedmont Historical Collection.)

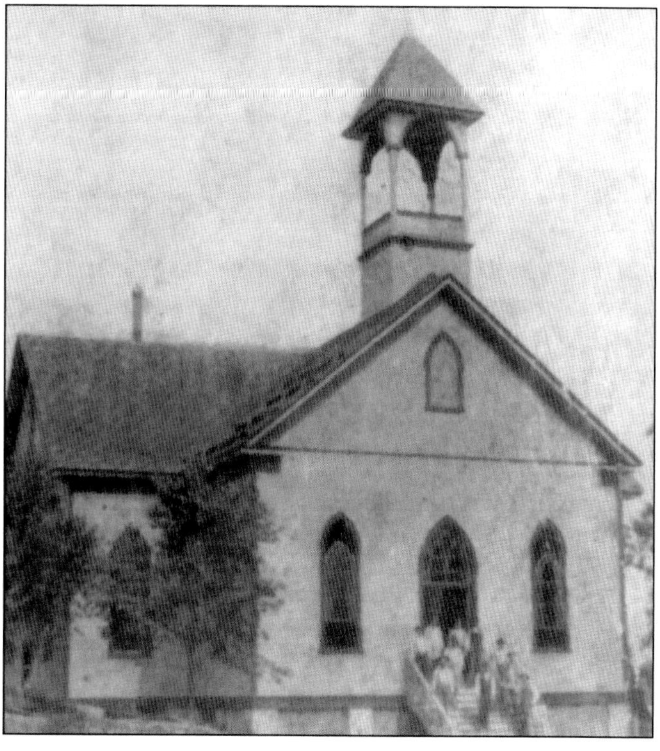

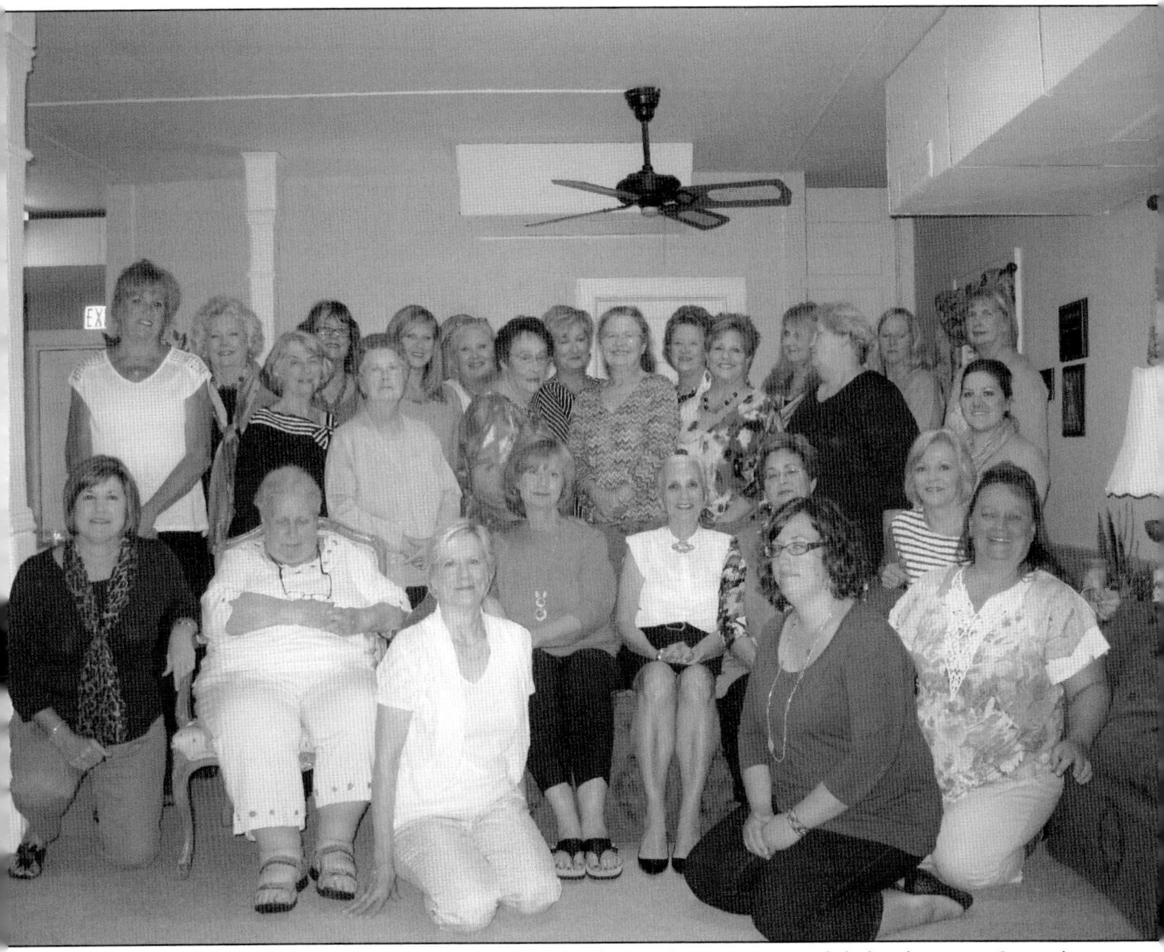

The Bonnes Amies Club of Piedmont was formed in 1954 as a service club for the area. Over the years, this club has raised funds to improve Piedmont in many ways and provided entertainment as well. For many years, they put on the Footbridge Festival, the Piedmont Christmas Parade, and the Southern Traditions Luncheon. This group of women supports Piedmont by choosing to spend their funds to benefit all. They have provided a play area for the walking park, painted a historical mural on the side of the old mill warehouse (which is now the Saluda River Grill), commissioned an artist to paint historic pictures of Piedmont, redecorated the Community Building, hung greenery on the bridge at Christmas, and regularly collected trash along Highway 86. This group of dedicated women is planning much for the coming years. Please consider supporting their upcoming causes. Let it be said that Piedmont is a better place to live because of the work they have done.

Club members pictured here in 2014 are Jane Bayne, Angela Boggs, Lisa Brashier, Jane Carpenter, Joy Clark, Paige Crawford, Janna Doughty, Judy Elrod, Shirley Elrod, Maxie Freeman, Sandie Garrison, Katie Gillespie, Lisa Greer, Kathy Hand, Lynn Helms, Bettie Lown, Lorri Lundgren, Gloria McAbee, Jane McClain, Debbie Merritt, Sandy Miller, Gayle Payne, Anne Peden, Carolyn Reeves, Lynn Camp, Gwen Vance, Lori Vance, Jessalene Watson, Betty White, and Miranda White. (Courtesy of the Bonnes Amies Club.)

Let us as Piedmonters, whether natives or transplants, cause the future to outshine the past.

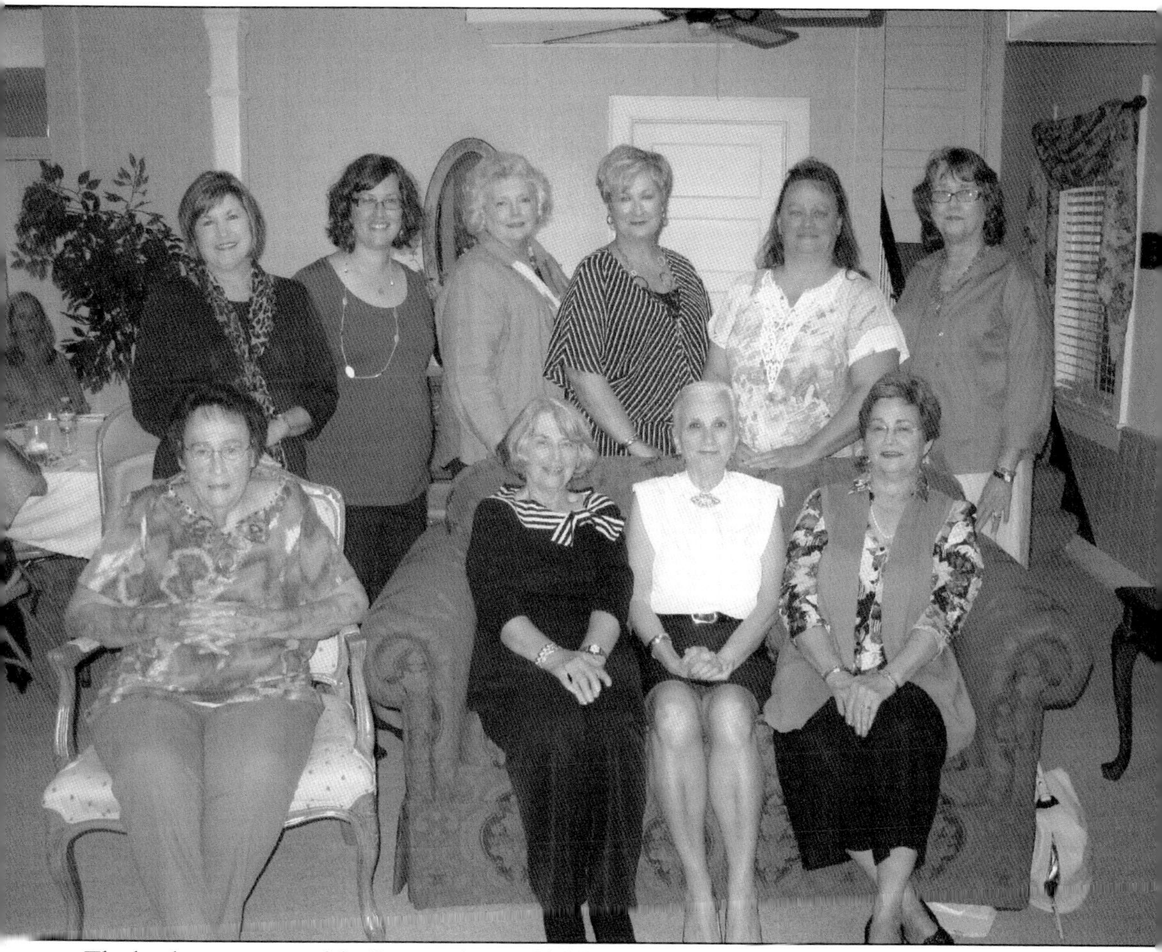

The book committee of the Bonnes Amies Club has spent many hours putting this book together for the benefit of Piedmont. We hope you will enjoy reading and rereading about Piedmont like we have delighted in crafting this pictorial history. If you find errors, please let us know, and if you have photographs that you think we would benefit from preserving, please share them with us, for we want to continue to collect our stories.

Pictured from left to right are (first row) Maxie Freeman, Jane Carpenter, Carolyn Reeves, and Gayle Payne; (second row) Jane McClain, Miranda White, Jessalene Watson, Betty White, Paige Crawford, and Anne Peden. (Courtesy of the Bonnes Amies Club.)

Chapter 1. Early History: Anne Peden
Chapter 2. Clubs and Organizations: Jane Carpenter
Chapter 3. The Mill: Gayle Payne, Carolyn Reeves, and Jessalene Watson
Chapter 4. Businesses: Betty and Miranda White
Chapter 5. Schools: Jane McClain
Chapter 6. Village Life: Anne Peden
Chapter 7. Churches: Paige Crawford and Maxie Freeman